HAKE'S GUIDE TO PRESIDENTIAL CAMPAIGN COLLECTIBLES

AN ILLUSTRATED PRICE GUIDE TO ARTIFACTS FROM 1789-1988

TED HAKE

WALLACE-HOMESTEAD BOOK COMPANY
RADNOR, PENNSYLVANIA

NOTICE

Values for items pictured in this book are based on the author's experience as well as actual prices realized for specific items sold through the catalogues of Hake's Americana & Collectibles Mail & Phone Bid Auctions. The prices are offered in this book for information purposes only. Many factors, including condition and rarity of the item, geographic location, and the knowledge and opinions of both buyers and sellers, influence prices asked and prices paid. As the prices in this book are approximations, neither the author nor the publisher shall be held responsible for any losses that may occur through the use of this book in the purchase or sale of items.

ACKNOWLEDGMENTS

This book was prepared with assistance from my staff at Hake's Americana: Deak Stagemyer, Joan Carbaugh, Alex Winter and Vonnie Burkins. Special thanks are due Russ King and Jeff Robison for photography and research. Ellen Ehlenbeck provided the typesetting and recommendations on design. My appreciation also goes to my wife Jonell and son Ted for their support, along with my thanks to the Wallace-Homestead staff for their contributions.

Ted Hake
September, 1991

Published in Radnor, Pennsylvania 19089, by Wallace-Homestead,
a division of Chilton Book Company

Color photography by Jim Conroy
Cover photos (actual size):
Front: Taft/Sherman litho tin plate, 1908, $250; Roosevelt button, circa 1936, $400.
Back: T. Roosevelt brass shell pin with movable jaw that has a campaign slogan on a paper label, 1904, $400; Harding button, 1920, $200; Harding brass nose-thumber, 1920, $200; T. Roosevelt button, circa 1900, $225; McKinley/Hobart ribbon badge, 1896, $175.

Library of Congress Cataloging-in-Publication Data
Hake, Theodore L.
(Guide to presidential campaign collectibles)
Hake's guide to presidential campaign collectibles: an illustrated price guide to artifacts from 1789-1988 / Ted Hake.
p. cm.
Includes bibliographical references and index.
ISBN 0-87069-644-0
1. Political collectibles – United States – Catalogs. 2. Campaign paraphernalia – United States – Catalogs. 3. Presidents – United States – Election – Miscellanea – Catalogs. 4. United States – Politics and government – Miscellanea – Catalogs. I. Title. II. Title: Guide to presidential campaign collectibles.
E183.3.H35 1992
324.923'0075 – dc20 91-32796
CIP

Manufactured in the United States of America

1 2 3 4 5 6 7 8 9 0 1 0 9 8 7 6 5 4 3 2

CONTENTS

INTRODUCTION

The election of an American president every four years is a unique process. Combining the elements of serious purpose with the atmosphere of a country carnival, the major candidates traverse the country attempting to excite enthusiasm and win the hearts, minds and votes of the electorate.

Campaign collectibles are the graphic and tangible symbols of voter involvement. The use of these objects arose from necessity. Our earliest presidents did not actively seek votes; the office was supposed to seek the man. The rules changed in the 1820s and 1830s as the two-party system emerged and voting rights were granted to a larger percentage of the male populace. Candidates were forced to find support among individual voters. Any object that would get the candidate's name, portrait, and ideas before the voters was a welcome tool of persuasion. By 1840, circumstances combined to produce an abundance of campaign material, some for Democratic candidate Martin Van Buren, but much more for Whig candidate William Henry Harrison, the victor. This campaign laid the groundwork for an incredible variety of devices designed to influence voters. Although much was discarded, a remarkable number of artifacts were preserved by the original owners for reasons of utility or sentiment or appreciation of their beauty and historical significance. The actions of these people allow today's collectors to experience the excitement these objects were intended to create.

USING THIS BOOK

Campaign collectibles spanning 200 years are pictured, described and evaluated in this book. While my earlier three books show and evaluate 12,000 presidential campaign artifacts, those books are organized chronologically by candidate. This book takes a different and unique approach as a pictorial price guide by grouping similar items together into 50 different categories. While many collectors specialize in a particular candidate, probably an equal number specialize in a particular kind of item, be it an immensely broad group like buttons or a form more limited such as paperweights. For the beginning or established collector, the following pages offer a fascinating cross-section of presidential Americana that is largely available, rather than already cloistered in museums or private collections formed long ago.

CATEGORIES: The vast world of presidential campaign collectibles is divided here into 50 categories. Most categories are arranged alphabetically, but the 19 devoted to lapel devices are arranged alphabetically as their own unit because the objects are so closely related in purpose and usage.

COLLECTIBLES PICTURED: Nearly all collectibles shown in this book appeared in the mail and phone bid auction catalogues of Hake's Americana & Collectibles from 1977 to 1991. While many rarities are included, the primary goal is to picture, describe, and evaluate campaign collectibles likely to be encountered in the marketplace.

NUMBERING SYSTEM: Each category and each item is numbered. Therefore, any item in this book can be referenced by combining these two numbers, separated by a dash, for example 31-12. It must be noted that "Hake numbers" are already widely used in the hobby. These numbers derive from the Encyclopedia of Political Buttons, three books published in 1974 and 1977. The Hake number is a combination of the candidate's initials and the numbered photo in one of the three books. Numbers below 1000 are from Book I, covering 1896-1972 items; numbers in the 2000 series are from Book II, covering 1920-1976 items; and numbers in the 3000 series are from Book III, covering 1789-1916 items. Thus an auction catalogue description of a McKinley item may say "Hake 3016" or "Hake MAC 3016" meaning the item is pictured as item 3016 in the McKinley section of Book III. Since the numbering system for this book employs a dash between the category and item number, this system is compatible with the earlier system. Collectors or dealers are welcome to use this new set of "Hake" numbers provided that advertisements, sales lists or auction catalogues acknowledge the title of this book, author, and publisher.

QUOTATION MARKS: Any text within item descriptions set off by quotation marks actually appears on that item.

DATES: When items are dated or when the specific election campaign date can be deduced with certainty, the date is specified in the description. Some candidates ran for president a number of times and many items are not marked with a date. In these cases, a date designated c. for circa is provided as an estimate.

ABBREVIATIONS: A lithographed tin button is known in the hobby as a litho. This short form is used in the descriptions. If the word *litho* does not appear, then the button is a celluloid. The following abbreviations for colors are sometimes used:

bw = black and white	br = black and red
bwr = black, white and red	rw = red and white
bwbl = black, white and blue	rwb = red, white and blue

PRICES: While most collectibles shown in this book were offered in Hake's Americana & Collectibles mail and phone bid auction catalogues, the prices indicated are not auction "prices realized" for several reasons. Some items in every auction go unsold while some are subject to intense bidding by two or three bidders. In addition, auction prices for many of the items are outdated since they apply to items sold as long as 14 years ago. The price estimates in this book are based on a combination of factors, including the author's experience, auction prices realized, sales lists and typical prices at collectibles shows. Prices assume the item is in excellent, complete condition without damage or significant wear. If an item is illustrated with a box or other packaging, the price reflects this fact. The same item, even in excellent condition, may have a value 25%-50% less if the box or packaging is missing. IMPORTANT: Prices specified are retail prices. Dealers will pay a percentage of these prices based on the quality of the material and their individual business practices.

CONDITION

Campaign items in perfect condition command premium prices. But few items with any age qualify as perfect, since nearly all were meant to be used or at least displayed in some fashion. Collectors, being realists, will accept normal minor wear on an item if it is otherwise in complete condition. Obviously heavy wear, defacement, permanent soiling or missing parts all severely reduce an item's value. Repairs or cleaning may increase value but lack of expertise can easily result in additional damage. Caution, and perhaps advice, are recommended before irreversible actions are taken. On buttons, a moist cotton swab will remove dirt. Foxing on buttons cannot be removed.

The following terms and definitions are used to describe items in Hake's Americana & Collectibles auctions. These definitions are fairly standard throughout the collectibles hobby:

Mint: Flawless condition. Usually applied to items made of metal or items that are boxed or otherwise packaged. MIB stands for Mint in box.

Near Mint (NM): Just the slightest detectable wear but appearance is still like new.

Excellent (Exc.): Only the slightest detectable wear, if any at all. Usually applied to buttons, paper and other non-metallic items. Also used for metallic items that just miss the near mint or mint level.

Very Fine (VF): Bright clean condition. An item that has seen little use and was well cared for with only very minor wear or aging.

Fine: An item in nice condition with some general wear but no serious defects.

Very Good (VG): Shows use but no serious defect and still nice for display. Metal items may have detail or paint wear. Paper items may have some small tears or creases.

Good: May have some obvious overall wear and/or some specific defect but still with some collectible value.

Fair: Obvious damage to some extent.

Poor: Extensive damage or wear.

At Hake's we grade our items conservatively; less than 1% of the 20,000 items we sell annually are returned due to an error in describing the item's condition. However, in the collectibles business much wishful thinking occurs regarding condition, particularly by less experienced dealers and among the general public attempting to sell items found around the house. When purchasing items through the mail, it is best to have a clear understanding with the seller that the item can be returned for a refund if the item has more wear than the seller specified.

Buttons in particular are frequently overgraded. On a 3'x4' poster a $\frac{1}{4}$" edge tear is easily ignored. On a 1$\frac{1}{4}$" diameter button, a $\frac{1}{4}$" celluloid crack or brown age spot can be very noticeable and may reduce the item's potential value by as much as 50 to 75 percent. Celluloid buttons can suffer any combination of the following defects: scratches, foxing (brown stain or spots), dents, age cracks, rim splits, and bumps or air pockets on or under the celluloid covering. A button may have a number of these problems and still look "fine" to the eye of a person not acquainted with the condition standards applied to buttons. On buttons, "small" problems can mean big differences in value. In the field, use a magnifying glass. Through the mail, patronize dealers whose descriptions are accurate and don't hesitate to return an item with a significant flaw that was not specified.

PRICES

Campaign collectibles are available in all price ranges. Regardless of financial resources, collectors interested in American political history can find an area of specialization to match their budget. Since items range from free hand-outs for a current campaign to a select few from past elections that exceed $10,000, the financial state of the hobby must be assessed as a whole rather than on the basis of a few items.

The best vehicle for such an examination are the 12,000 presidential campaign items pictured in Hake's three-volume Encyclopedia of Political Buttons. Book I was published in 1974 and largely covers buttons and other lapel devices used between 1896 and 1972. In 1977, two additional volumes were published. Book II covers all types of items from 1920 through 1976 that were not already in Book I. Book III covers the years 1789 through 1916. All types of items are included, again without duplication of any in Book I.

Each book pictures and prices approximately 4000 presidential campaign collectibles. Because the books are self-published in limited press runs, it has never been feasible to reset type to update prices. The solution was to print a small supplement with updated prices to go along with each book. This was done in 1984 and again in 1991. To arrive at the prices for individual items, a small group of experienced collectors, dealers, and mail bid auctioneers submitted their evaluations to Hake's. Over 100,000 evaluations were averaged with the aid of a computer. The following table demonstrates the remarkable growth in interest and consequent increases in values over the last five-year period.

BOOK #	*1991 Total $*	*1984 Total $*	*Percentage Increase*
1	709,131	199,559	255.34
2	502,724	143,654	249.95
3	1,522,448	633,257	140.42
Totals for all 3 books	2,734,303	976,470	180.02

The greatest price increases come in the area of golden age celluloid buttons (1896-1916) and for other rare celluloids from later campaigns. However, there have been significant increases across all time periods and for all types of items, except the most common examples.

With values for these 12,000 items all but tripling within five years, one might wonder if further appreciation is possible and if reasonably priced items remain available. The answer is "yes" to both questions. The fact is, presidential campaign item collecting was for many years a well-kept secret. The hobby's single organization has never made publicity and recruitment a high priority. During this time, large numbers of items were under-valued in relation to their degree of scarcity. The graphic appeal of campaign collectibles and their historical significance will continue to attract collectors who appreciate the artifacts of our democratic process.

REPRODUCTIONS & FANTASY ITEMS

Probably 90 percent of the presidential campaign item reproductions are buttons. The remaining small percentage is comprised of George Washington inaugural buttons, a few medalets and posters, some 19th century glassware, and a scattering of miscellaneous objects.

Reproductions are close or exact copies of authentic campaign artifacts. Fantasy items are newly created objects in a design that never existed before but depicting some older collectible subject. The American Political Items Collectors (APIC) organization uses the archaic British word *brummagem* to denote both reproductions and fantasy items. The word means a "showy but inferior and worthless thing." While reproductions make campaign button collecting treacherous for the uninformed, with basic information reproductions and fantasy items are easily avoided. Fortunately, the APIC has prepared a booklet that not only pictures most brummagem objects but also offers specifics for discerning the differences between originals and reproductions. Access to this guide alone is well worth the price of membership in the APIC (see Appendix V).

The majority of reproduced political buttons come from sets produced for advertising and promotional purposes in the late 1960s and early 1970s by companies such as Abbott Laboratories, American Oil, Borax, Kleenex, Exxon, and Proctor & Gamble. Many of the reproductions are made in sizes larger than the original, many are lithographed tin reproductions of buttons issued originally as celluloids, and many are actually dated and marked "Repro" or "Reproduction," although these markings can be scratched off or painted over.

Collectors have some protection from unmarked reproduction campaign items thanks to the Hobby Protection Act, signed into law November 29, 1973, by Richard Nixon. The legislation requires any reproduction political item to be plainly and permanently marked with the date of manufacture. Failure to mark items is a violation under The Federal Trade Commission Act. While this legislation has been beneficial, unmarked reproductions remain in the marketplace. The best defense is to study the APIC's Brummagem Handbook, become familiar with the material, and avoid any dealer who does not unconditionally guarantee his campaign collectibles as authentic artifacts.

COLLECTING TIPS

FINDING A DIRECTION: Buying whatever items one crosses paths with is one way to build a collection. However, it will be a collection without any unity or theme. The world of presidential campaign collectibles spans 200 years and many thousands of different objects are available. This book includes the main types of campaign collectibles that exist in quantities sufficient to form a collection of at least 100 pieces. Many categories present the opportunity to build a collection with 1000 or more objects.

While this book is organized into categories of similar items, this is only one approach to the hobby. There are many other options open to the collector and it is recommended that some collecting strategy be developed, rather than haphazardly purchasing whatever item is available or appealing at the moment. On the broadest level, one might consider twentieth century vs. nineteenth century items or mass produced vs. hand-made, perhaps unique, items. Other large scale options include specializing in the candidates of a single major party or one, or all, of the third parties. Hopeful candidates, convention items, inauguration souvenirs, and mourning artifacts are other broad areas. Political issues provide added choices. Collections can be built around the themes of temperance/prohibition, slavery/civil rights, or conservative/liberal. Political symbols or recurring graphic elements can provide the focus for collecting. Donkeys, elephants, eagles, Uncle Sam, and Miss Liberty appear on numerous items. One of the most popular forms of specialization is to select a particular candidate. The most frequently chosen are Lincoln, Theodore and Franklin Roosevelt, Truman, Kennedy and, from the third parties, Eugene V. Debs. Selecting one of the foregoing specializations or creating a different one, will give a collector a sense of purpose in the hunt and the resulting collection a sense of cohesion.

FINDING CAMPAIGN COLLECTIBLES: Many sources exist for campaign collectibles. Places to look include garage sales, although it's likely a lot of other people's junk will have to be viewed before a treasure turns up. With more potential are flea markets, individual antique shops, cooperative antique stores, and antiques or collectible shows. While all these sources hold promise, they are also the places where the greatest percentage of reproductions are offered for sale. Coin shops sometimes offer political items and estate auctions present another source.

Relatives and friends should not be overlooked and some collectors try classified ads in local newspapers.

If a campaign is in progress, other sources materialize, especially for buttons and paper. Candidates open headquarters in larger cities and political parties may have offices at the city, county or state level. Items are usually available prior to national conventions in those states that hold primaries. The national conventions are a great source for current buttons but attendance requires expense and logistical planning. Back on the local level, items are frequently available at fairs, political rallies, and, occasionally, at fund raising events. Local labor unions should be checked out, usually for Democratic Party items.

The best way to find political collectibles is to join the organized hobby group known as American Political Items Collectors (APIC). Details about this group are provided in Appendix V. In brief, members receive a roster so people sharing the same interests can communicate, the club sponsors regional shows throughout the country, and dealers will send new members sales lists and auction catalogues. Much of the best material available is sold by auction with the bidding conducted by mail and telephone. There are also two monthly newspaper-style publications devoted to the political hobby (see Appendix V). Campaign items can be collected without joining the APIC, but only by joining this group can a collector be fully informed about events and trends in the hobby.

CARING FOR A COLLECTION: Once a collection starts to grow, care and storage become important considerations. An essential aspect of collecting is preservation. Campaign collectibles are tangible artifacts of our history and, hopefully, every collector wishes to pass on his collected objects without having them damaged while he is the caretaker. This seems so basic, and yet there are people who will use pencil or even ink to write a price or other notes on a paper item. Adhesive stickers are often applied to fragile fabric items such as ribbons. Finally, there are those devoted to repairing tears with copious amounts of tape. These are not proper conservation methods. Prices or notes can be made on separate papers, stickers placed on mylar sleeves rather than on the item and non-staining archival paper tape can be used on damaged paper.

Other perils to collections include dust, smoke, moisture and sunlight. Glass cases for three-dimensional items can overcome the dangers of soiling and yellowing from dust and smoke. Drapes can block bright sunlight. In most environments, housing a collection in the living area will be enough to avoid the dangers of excessive heat, cold, moisture, and silverfish found in attics and basements.

Glass frames, known as Riker mounts, work well for the flat storage of celluloid button collections; but, if the lining in the bottom tray is cotton, in high humidity areas the cotton will attract moisture that will extensively damage the backs of buttons before any signs appear on the front. Litho buttons may adhere to the glass and lose paint when removed. Many button collectors also use plastic sheets with pockets designed to hold coins. This works provided litho buttons are not placed in the sheets. At least some sheets contain chemicals that react with the inks on the buttons to virtually melt the ink after a period of time. If these sheets are used at all, they should be stored vertically rather than flat to keep the accumulated weight off the bottom sheets.

The best method for storing both celluloid and litho buttons and other small items is in a cabinet with stacks of shallow drawers. Such cabinets are available because they are also favored by coin collectors. The cabinet provides darkness, protection from dust and smoke, there is no pressure on the objects and the doors can be locked for security.

SEEING WHAT IS AVAILABLE: Viewing and, if possible, handling campaign collectibles is the best way to learn about them. Large amounts of material are accessible at APIC shows, in private collections, and in institutional collections.

APIC regional shows or the national convention are ideal for the hands-on approach. Thousands of items are on the floor representing virtually every type of collecting option.

Visiting other collectors can be an educational adventure. Most collectors enjoy sharing their collections with interested people. The conversation is frequently filled with gems of knowledge it may have taken them years to acquire.

Many local historical societies, museums, and colleges hold campaign artifacts among their collections. A prior appointment may be necessary if objects are not on permanent display. Two places appointments are not necessary and great items abound are the Smithsonian Institution Museum of American History and the University of Hartford's Museum of American Political Life. The Hartford, Connecticut museum is recently opened and offers comprehensive exhibits expanded from the major collection of J. Doyle DeWitt, an early APIC member and former president of The Travelers Insurance Company.

CAMPAIGN COLLECTIBLES HISTORY

The earliest political collectibles available are metal clothing buttons from 1789 issued to commemorate George Washington's inauguration. Because the two-party system had not yet developed, the rare surviving artifacts related to our Founding Fathers commemorate their selection as president and are not objects from a campaign to achieve the office. China pitchers, mugs, and similar objects, known as Liverpoolware because of their English origin, were produced over a number of years and examples exist for John Adams, Jefferson, Madison, and Monroe. Some fabric and paper items are also available for the earliest presidents but opportunities to acquire these items will be limited at best.

Andrew Jackson's 1824 campaign produced the first widely circulated items actually used prior to election day. These were three different brass medalets with his portrait and an inscription recalling his victory in the Battle of New Orleans or the Congressional Medal executed to honor him. During the next several elections, the variety of campaign objects continued to increase and includes medalets, clothing buttons, sewing boxes, snuff boxes, flasks, ribbons, sulfide brooches, and paper items.

William Henry Harrison's 1840 "log cabin and hard cider" campaign generated considerable excitement and a greatly increased quantity of campaign material. A multitude of campaign medalets, ribbons, and china objects was produced. Campaign flags with Harrison's portrait and/or a slogan were popular as were bandannas. The use of these objects continued throughout most of the nineteenth century. Innovations along the way include Currier and Ives jugate prints of the candidates beginning in 1844, canes, tobacco-related accessories, razors, posters, the introduction of ferrotype portrait badges in 1860 and cardboard portrait badges in 1864, parade torches and lanterns, lapel studs, stickpins, mechanical lapel devices and a myriad of other objects for grabbing the attention of voters.

The development of various types of campaign items mirrors the history of invention and the creation of technologies that produced these items. Beginning in 1839, events got underway that would revolutionize the production of political campaign materials.

Celluloid was the revolutionary material and its creation began in 1839 when Anselme Payeu, a French chemist, discovered cellulose, the chief substance composing the cell walls or fibers of all plant tissue. Additional research by other scientists eventually led to the vast plastics industry of today.

The perfection of celluloid is attributed to John Wesley Hyatt who was searching for an ivory substitute. His creations included, in 1863, a "collodion" billiard ball, considered a failure since it detonated during play due to its highly flammable composition. Improvements led to an 1870 patent for "celluloid," the nation's first commercially profitable synthetic material.

Celluloid was rapidly utilized for many products including campaign objects. In 1888 celluloid was used for the first time as part of a lapel device to be worn in support of a candidate. Ink was printed directly on a flat celluloid sheet and the picture was then made into a lapel stud. The sole manufacturer using the process appears to have been Baldwin & Gleason Co., Ltd., 61

B'way (Broadway) N.Y. Lapel studs exist for Republican Benjamin Harrison, Democratic candidates Cleveland and Thurman, and Prohibition candidate Clinton Fisk. In 1888 and 1892 somewhat larger celluloid sheets were also being used as bookmarks picturing the candidates or as added embellishments on ribbons, thus creating the first ribbon badges.

By 1896, technologies were in place to revolutionize campaign lapel devices. Celluloid could now be made as a very thin and flexible transparent sheet. Campaign pinback buttons, as we know them today, were first patented by the Whitehead & Hoag Company of Newark, N.J. in 1896, with related patents acquired earlier in 1893 and 1895.

Amazing quantities of buttons in a staggering variety of designs highlight the 1896 election. Their appealing size, imaginative designs, and beautiful colors immediately prompted many people to save them. Quickly surpassed, and largely replaced, was the practice of collecting advertisers' trade cards so advertisers jumped on the button bandwagon with their own custom designed advertising give-away buttons. The period from 1896 through 1916 is now considered the "golden age" for political and other types of buttons.

Whitehead & Hoag were soon joined by other manufacturers and one of these, the J. E. Lynch Company of Chicago, developed a less expensive alternate to the celluloid-covered button. During World War I, the company introduced lithographed tin buttons. The inks were printed directly on metal sheets and then the images were stamped out into a button shape. Gone was the need for printed papers, celluloid coverings and collets to hold the materials together. The economies of this process did not replace the celluloid button but they did drastically reduce the variety of celluloids. For celluloids to stay reasonably price competitive, the expenses of full color art were often sacrificed in favor of sepia, two color process, or red, white and blue combinations.

From the 1920s through the 1960s, there were no major changes in button design or technology, except that larger buttons were produced more frequently after World War II. Beginning in 1972, trends from the art world like pop art and cultural influences like the psychedelic movement made an impression on button design and resulted in more color with less adherence to the standardized design formats, a favorable trend that continues today.

While the button became the dominant lapel device in 1896, other campaign objects came into favor as the twentieth century progressed. Lithographed tin trays, paperweights, ribbon badges, and watch fobs enjoyed their primary popularity until 1920. After that, license plates, tabs, pennants, and increasing amounts of campaign jewelry joined the wide array of artifacts already on the scene. The Reagan years brought buttons that light up and play music. What's next must be left to the imagination.

1. Advertising Cards

Advertising cards, also called trade cards, were issued by many manufacturers or product distributors with portraits of the current president or, during election years, the presidential candidates. Frequently, the cards also pictured a vice-presidential candidate or spouse. Although use of the portraits was unauthorized, the cards explicitly stated or clearly implied that the person pictured endorsed the product being advertised. During election campaigns, the wise advertiser issued separate cards picturing the candidates of both major parties so as not to offend a large group of potential consumers. The products with tie-ins to political personalities number in the hundreds and range from sewing thread to threshing machines. Advertising cards were most popular from 1880-1900 and were issued as single cards or sometimes in small sets that might include all previous presidents or all the major and third party candidates for the current election year. Cards with a moving part (known as metamorphic cards), clever fold design or optical effect have added desirability to collectors. Unlike postcards with a blank reverse for a message and address, advertising cards usually have promotional copy or a chart showing each state's electoral vote on the reverse. The majority of cards are still priced under $25 each and offer much to collectors interested in political and advertising history, as well as graphic design.

1

2

3

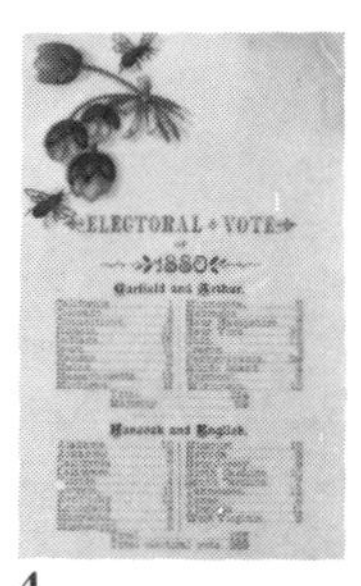

4

5

6

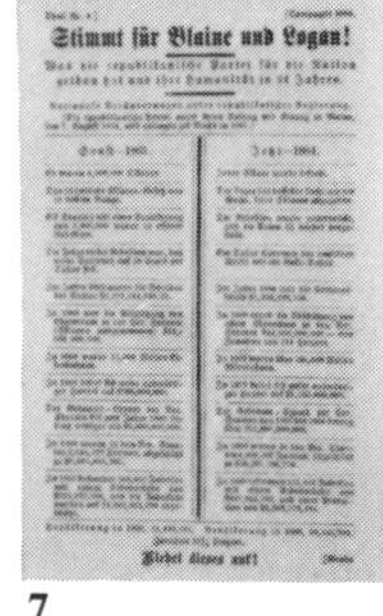

7

8

9

1
"LET US HAVE PEACE AND A U.S. GRANT CHARTER OAK STOVE IN EVERY HOUSEHOLD." 2.5x4" stiff card w/1.5x1.75" sepia paper photo of Grant in military uniform. 1872. $60.

2
"WHAT I KNOW ABOUT CHARTER OAK STOVE IS, THAT THEY ARE ALWAYS THE CHEAPEST TO BUY! BEST TO USE!" Card depicts Horace Greeley and is a mate to #1 although the sepia paper photo is larger. 1872. $75.

3
TILDEN/GRANT "BLACKWELL'S DURHAM" TOBACCO METAMORPHIC CARD. 3x4" closed. 1876. $30.

4
"ELECTORAL VOTE OF 1880-GARFIELD AND ARTHUR/ HANCOCK AND ENGLISH." 3x5.5" advertising "Morse's Yellow Dock" blood purifier. 1880. $12.

5
GARFIELD/HANCOCK METAMORPHIC. 3.5x5" bw/pink with cover that swivels so portrait of one candidate shows in oval opening. Issued by Springfield, Mass. shoe dealer. 1880. $70.

6
"HOOD'S SARSAPARILLA PRESIDENTIAL CAMPAIGN CARD" has brown/white portrait of Blaine along with 1880 electoral results. Apportionments for 1884 are on the back. $10.

7
"VOTE FOR BLAINE & LOGAN" Republican Party card listing achievements on one side in English and on the opposite side in German. 3.5x6". 1884. $10.

8
CLEVELAND/HENDRICKS "CAPADURA" CIGAR card with bw/ beige cartoon depicting them extolling the cigar. 3.25x5.25". 1884. $20.

9
CLEVELAND 3x4.5" bw card with reverse advertising for "Neutraline-A Deoderizer And Detergent." 1888. $12.

10
LARKIN SOAP PRESIDENTIAL CARDS. Set of 3x4.5" bw/gray cards picturing presidents Washington through Cleveland. Circa 1884. $30.

11
CLEVELAND AND STEVENSON. 3x4" sepia card advertising "The Ale And Beef Company" 1892. $25.

12
"MRS. PRESIDENT CLEVELAND" 4x6" black/gray/brown card with caption above "Use Sulphur Bitters." Circa 1892. $15.

13
"THE REPUBLICAN BANDANNA" 6x10" large card with portraits of Harrison and Morton set within a bright rwb flag design with lettering in yellow. Reverse advertises "Dr. W. W. Watson's Quick Cure Linement." 1888. $30.

14
"WE ADVOCATE IRON-CLAD CLOTHING FOR WORKING MEN/ BENJAMIN HARRISON" 3.5x5" bw card issued by "Quincy Shirt And Overall Co. Quincy, Ill." Circa 1888. $20.

15
HARRISON/MORTON 3x5" card with flag in rwb and endorsements of the candidates by two Irish publications. 1888. $10.

16
McKINLEY/BRYAN 3.5x5.5" card from a Maine clothing store pictures 1896 candidates with 1892 vote totals on the reverse. $60.

17
"THE AFRICAN SERIES-NATIONAL CANDY CO. BUFFALO N.Y." set of 15 different colorful cardboard stand-ups picturing Teddy Roosevelt, Africans and animals. 1910. $250.

18
TAFT CAMPAIGN NOVELTY CARD. Small bw card picturing a metal puzzle inscribed "The Nation Builder William H. Taft-God Bless Him." Circa 1908. $30.

19
"IKE LIGHTS YOUR WAY" 3.5x6.5" bw stiff card picturing an Eisenhower cigarette lighter available from Zippo. Circa 1956. $30.

10

11

12

13

14

15

16

17

18

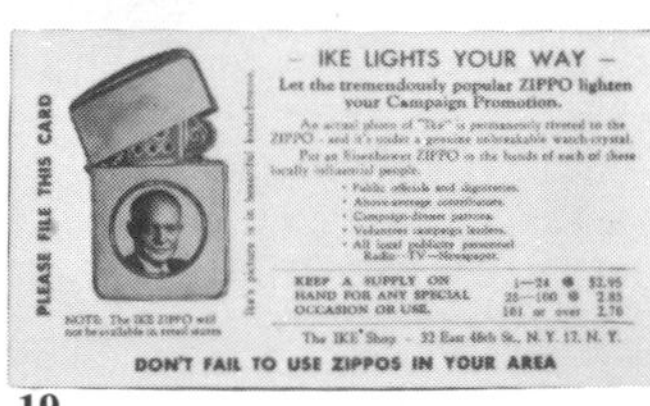

19

2. Ballots & Electoral Tickets

Before the advent of voting machines, voting was done with paper ballots. Although ballots were printed in many sizes, during the 1920s and 1930s they were often as large as a newspaper sheet. While not graphically very exciting, some do include pictorial symbols of the various parties and they can be helpful in researching items since they include the names of local candidates. Electoral tickets are paper sheets, usually 3x8" or smaller, listing a party's candidates for national office, usually in combination with state and local candidates. Some tickets just list the presidential candidates and the electors pledged to vote for those candidates. Electoral tickets date back to at least 1824 and were distributed to remind voters of the names of party candidates. Nineteenth century tickets often feature candidate's portraits or attractive patriotic motifs. Campaign newspapers sometimes included a list of candidates' names that visually resemble an electoral ticket; but such a list, clipped from a newspaper, would normally have unrelated text on the reverse. Most actual nineteenth century tickets have blank reverses but some from California c. 1860s are known with illustrated reverses and printing in several colors. Electoral tickets picturing candidates or those for third parties are generally the most valuable.

1

2

3

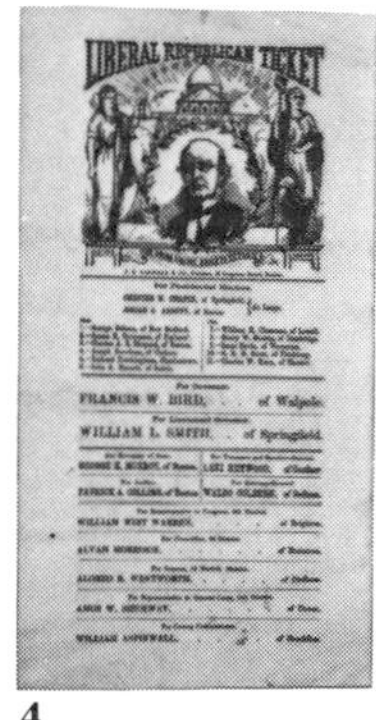

4

5

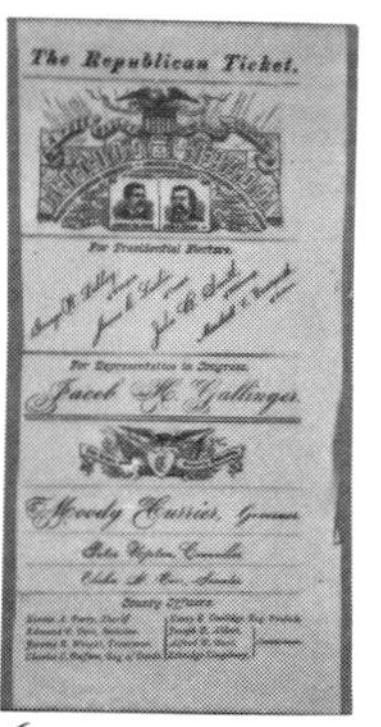

6

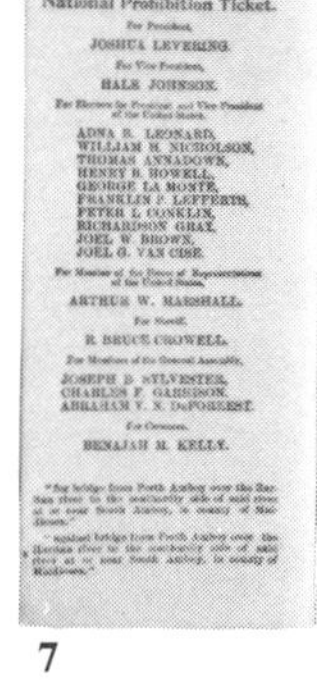

7

8

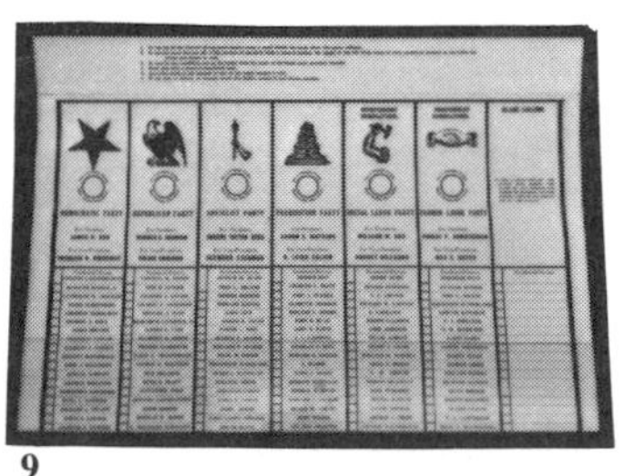
9

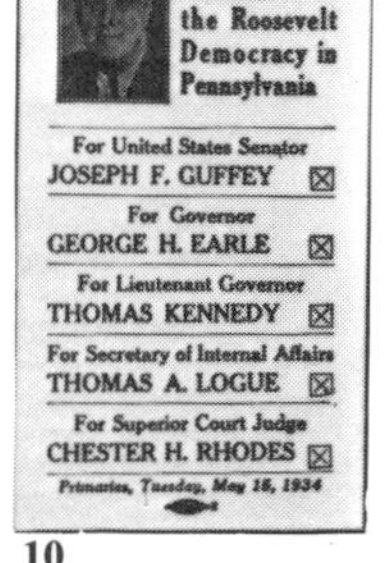

10

1
LINCOLN/JOHNSON 1864 "OHIO-UNION PRESIDENTIAL TICKET." 3x8.5" in rwb. $150.

2
"ABRAHAM LINCOLN/ANDREW JOHNSON UNION TICKET" 3x7.5" showing the ship "Kearsarge" sinking the ship "Alabama." 1864. $150.

3
"GRANT AND COLFAX/REPUBLICAN TICKET" 6x12.5" bw paper ticket from Massachusetts. 1868. $40.

4
GREELEY "LIBERAL REPUBLICAN TICKET" 6x12". 1872. $70.

5
"TILDEN-HENDRICKS" 4x7" bw paper ticket inscribed at top "Democratic Republican Ticket." 1876. $35.

6
"FOR PRESIDENT...BLAINE/ FOR VICE PRESIDENT...LOGAN/ THE REPUBLICAN TICKET" 6x13" listing New Hampshire electors and state candidates. 1884. $40.

7
"NATIONAL PROHIBITION TICKET" 3x7" ticket for Joshua Levering and Hale Johnson. 1896. $60.

8
"THOU SHALT NOT STEAL" 5x15" small poster listing Progressive Party local candidates with jugate pictures of Roosevelt and Johnson. 1912. $400.

9
1920 PRESIDENTIAL BALLOT on 18x21" bw paper. The ballot lists the names of presidential electors for the major parties. $75.

10
F. D. R. CARD 3x4" bw listing Pennsylvania candidates. 1934. $8.

3. *Bandannas & Kerchiefs*

Bandannas and kerchiefs were campaign mainstays throughout the last 75 years of the 1800s but with greatest popularity from the 1840s onward. The fabric of either was usually cotton, linen or sometimes silk. Bandannas have a larger size, typically about 20x22" with red background and pictorial or text elements in black and white or red, white and blue, although other color combinations are occasionally used. Smaller fabrics are generally handkerchief size, normally about 12x13" or larger. Bandanna use waned in the early 1900s but still emerges with known examples from the Eisenhower through Reagan years. The primary reference for political textiles is Herbert Collins' *Threads of History* (see bibliography) which pictures and describes hundreds of examples from the earliest period through 1976.

1
GARFIELD/ARTHUR BANDANNA. 20x21". Bw/red 1880. $275.

2
BLAINE/LOGAN BANDANNA. 17.5x19". Bw. 1884. $200.

3
CLEVELAND/THURMAN BANDANNA. 19.5x19.5". Bw. 1888. $200.

4
HARRISON/MORTON BANDANNA. 20x20". Bw/blue. 1888. $225.

5
HARRISON/MORTON KERCHIEF. 18x18". Blue/white. 1888. $75.

6
HARRISON/MORTON KERCHIEF. 16x17". Bw. 1888. $150.

7
HARRISON BANDANNA. 22x23". Bw/red. 1888. $350.

8
HARRISON/MORTON BANDANNA. 19x19". Rwb. 1888. $175.

9
HARRISON BANDANNA. 20x20". Blue/white. 1888. $80.

10
HARRISON AND REID BANDANNA. 19x19". Bw. 1892. $125.

11
ROOSEVELT BANDANNA. 20x20". Bw with blue stripe. 1904. $150.

12
ALTON B. PARKER BANDANNA. A mate to #11. 1904. $150.

13
PARKER/DAVIS BANDANNA. 22x25". Rwb. 1904. $350.

14
ROOSEVELT BANDANNA. 21x24". Red/white/brown. 1912. $150.

15
THEODORE ROOSEVELT BANDANNA. 19x20". Red, white, and brown. 1912. $125.

1 2 3 4 5 6 7 8 9 10 11 12 13 14 15

16 17 18 19 20 21 22 23

24

25

26

27

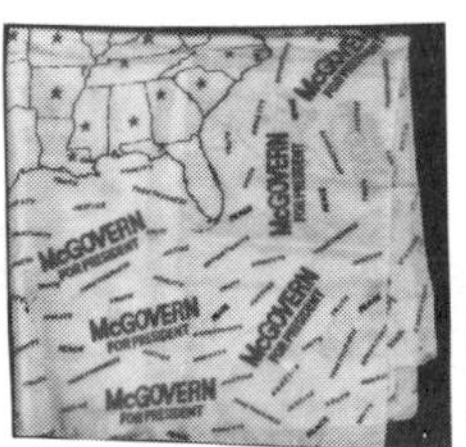

28

29

16
THEODORE ROOSEVELT BANDANNA. 22x22". Red/white. 1912. $125.

17
WILLIAM TAFT KERCHIEF. 18x18". Bw. Our photos show the bandanna and a detail of the illustration in the lower right corner. 1908. $250.

18
TAFT/SHERMAN BANDANNA. 16x16". Multicolor. 1908. $300.

19
HERBERT HOOVER BROADSIDE. 14x18". Sepia photo with rwb border on silk crepe. 1928. $60.

20
HOOVER BANDANNA. 17x18". Rwb. 1932. $50.

21
HOOVER AND SMITH HANDKERCHIEFS. 11x11" w/2.5" oval bw photo. 1928. *Each* $40.

22
"WE WANT WILLKIE" KERCHIEF. 12x12". Rwb. 1940. $50.

23
"WIN WITH IKE FOR PRESIDENT" BANDANNA. 26x26". Rwb. 1956. $60.

24
"I LIKE IKE" BANDANNA. 29x29". Rwb. 1952. $25.

25
"DEMOCRATIC PARTY" HANDKERCHIEF. 13x13". Rwb. 1964. $15.

26
"REPUBLICAN PARTY" HANDKERCHIEF. 13x13". Rwb. 1964. $15.

27
HUMPHREY SCARF. 32x32". With dark blue "H" designs over the center with bright green, white and blue border. $30.

28
"McGOVERN FOR PRESIDENT" BANDANNA. 30x31". Rw/black. 1972. $40.

29
"CARTER-MONDALE" BANDANNA. 28x28". White/bright green. 1980. $25.

4. Banks

Banks are in two categories, *mechanical* (one or more moving parts to perform a function) or *still* (without moving parts). Iron, white metal, and tin are the most common substances, with several versions formed in a combination of celluloid and tin or other metal. In recent years, glass and plastic variations have emerged. Bank forms include portrait bust figures or political symbols such as the elephant, donkey, Uncle Sam's hat, etc. Mechanical banks are usually finished in painted colors while portrait still banks are most frequently finished in a single solid metallic color to resemble bronze, copper or brass. Many cast iron banks, both mechanical and still, have been reproduced so caution is needed in that area but there are a large number of banks from other materials to choose from. While not as common as in the past, each election year still inspires the production of at least a few still banks.

1
"TAMMANY" cast iron mechanical bank of seated politician. Place coin in hand and arm moves to drop coin in slot as head nods. C. 1872. $400.

2
"AL SMITH" CELLULOID ELECTION CONTRIBUTION DIME BANK. 2 1/8" diameter in rwb. 1928. $150.

3
"F.D. ROOSEVELT" BANK 2x3x4.5" tall white metal with dark bronze finish. Coin slot is in the trap under the base. C. 1940. $40.

4
ELEPHANT GLAZED CERAMIC 2.5x3.5x5.5" tall depicting seated gray elephant holding a sign. C. 1936. $25.

5
JOHNSON 1.5x3" white plastic bank with portrait in blue and his name in red. 1964. $10.

6
GOLDWATER BANK. A mate to #5. 1964. $25.

7
WALLACE SILVERED CAST IRON BANK 3.5" tall fashioned like the Liberty Bell inscribed "Stand Up For America." 1968. $30.

1

2

3

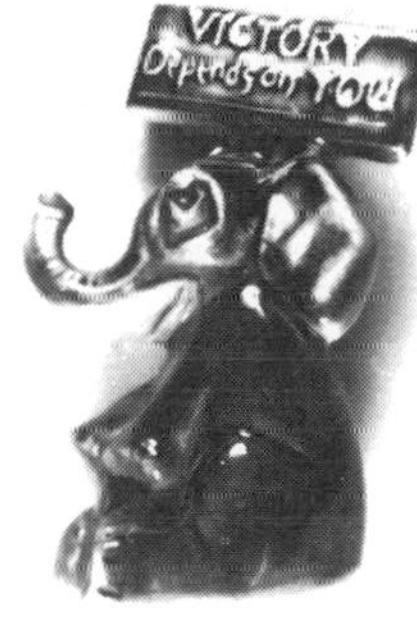

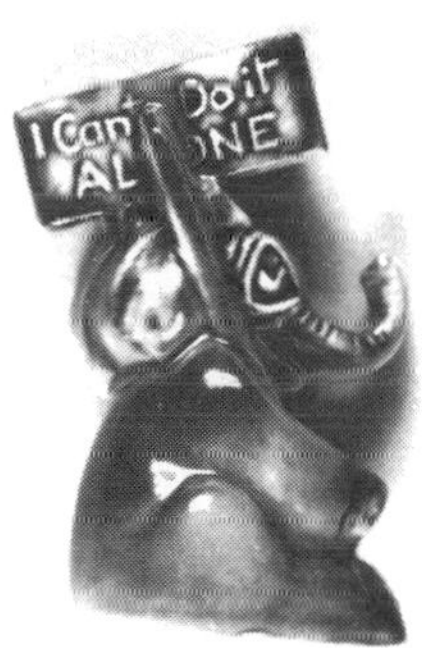

4

5

6

7

8

9

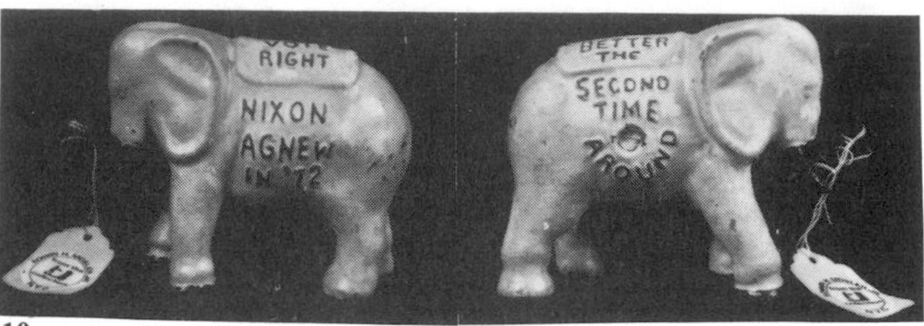

10

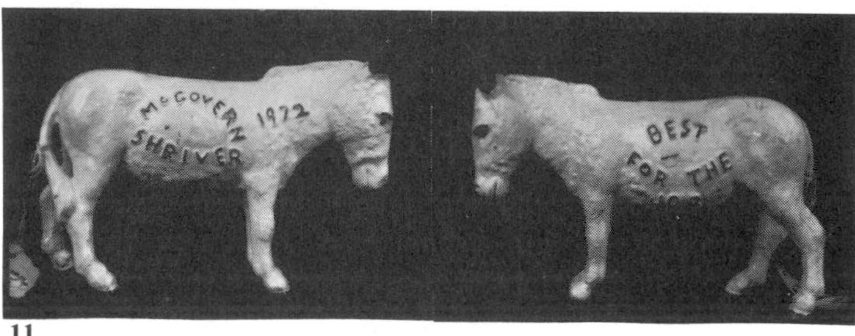

11

12

13

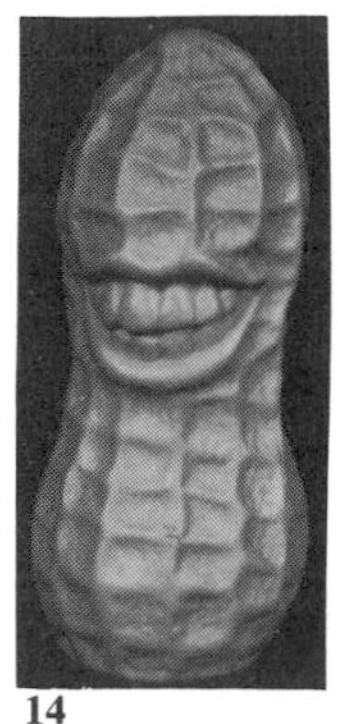
14

8
"NIXON AGNEW 68" 2.5" tall cast iron bank painted silver. 1968. $30.

9
"HUMPHREY MUSKIE 68" 1.5x4.5x4" cast iron bank similar to #8 but larger. 1968. $30.

10
NIXON "BETTER THE SECOND TIME AROUND" CAST IRON MECHANICAL BANK 3x7x4.5" tall. Elephant is mostly in white but with inscription on each side in red raised letters. Example shown has tag from the Mosler bank auction. 1972. $125.

11
McGOVERN "BEST FOR THE JOB" CAST IRON BANK. This item matches #8 but is not a mechanical bank. The cast iron donkey is 2.5x8x5.5" tall. 1972. $100.

12
McGOVERN bronzed white metal bank. 4" tall. 1972. $25.

13
"McGOVERN/SHRIVER" CANISTER BANK 5.5" tall. Bw/gray made of cardboard and tin. 1972. $20.

14
CARTER PEANUT BANK 5" diameter by 11.5" tall of beige vinyl designed like a smiling peanut. C. 1976. $15.

5. Biographies & Brochures

Campaign biographies in book or booklet form probably exist for all major candidates since the 1820s. The style of each is predictably sympathetic and frequently a glowing account of the individual's life, achievements and philosophies. Numerous candidates were the subject of multiple biographies during the campaign; William Henry Harrison, Zachary Taylor, and Abraham Lincoln lead the field. The 1800s also saw the introduction of the anti-campaign biography. Some of these castigate the candidate but others, in a more humorous vein, simply feature a title page with the candidate's name followed by blank pages. This device is still used and examples exist for candidates as diverse as Goldwater and McGovern. As the twentieth century moved on, campaign biographies became less popular. People became less inclined to read a several-hundred-page book about a candidate. The campaign brochure, usually 4 to 12 pages and with lots of photographs, became the printed tool to introduce the candidate to the voter. The demise of the extended campaign biography has been replaced with the post-presidential biography, now a tradition with modern day presidents. Most campaign biographies and brochures, even from the 1800s, are modestly priced compared to other campaign collectibles.

1
"BIOGRAPHIES OF MARTIN VAN BUREN AND RICHARD M. JOHNSON." 10x12.5" with 16 pages. 1833. $125.

2
HARRISON campaign biography published by Grigg & Elliott, Philadelphia. 92 pages. 1840. $60.

3
"THE HEROIC LIFE OF WILLIAM McKINLEY" published by DeWolfe, Fiske & Co., Boston. 48 pages. 7.5x9.5". 1902. $15.

1

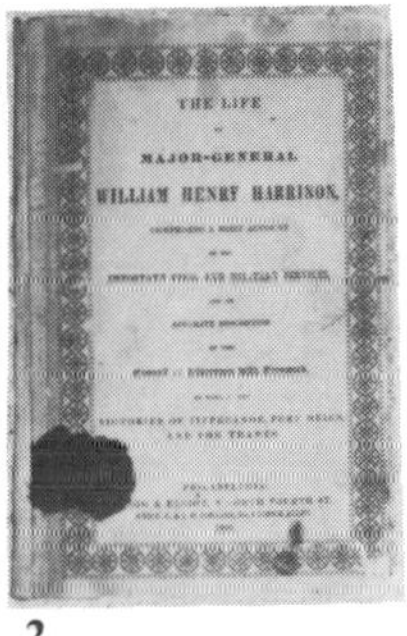

2

3

4
"THE FIRST BATTLE BY W. J. BRYAN A Story of the Campaign of 1896." Published by W. B. Conkey Company, Chicago, 1896. 6x9" with 632 pages. $25.

5
ROOSEVELT MINIATURE CAMPAIGN BOOK measuring 1.75x2.75 with bright yellow fabric cover. 1904. $30.

6
DAVIS. "Biography and Record of John W. Davis, Democratic Nominee for President." 32 pages. 3.5x9". 1924. $50.

7
BRYAN. "Speech of Acceptance of Governor Charles W. Bryan Democratic Nominee for Vice-President." A mate to #6. 1924. $30.

4

5

6

7

8
"DEWEY GETS THINGS DONE...The Man Who Gave New York State a Housecleaning." 3.25x6.25" pamphlet put out by the Republican National Committee. 16 pages. C. 1944. $8.

9
"A MAN NAMED STEVENSON" 5x7" with 16 pages published by The Democratic National Committee. 1952. $8.

10
"VETERANS FOR STEVENSON" 4x7" 4 page pamphlet with cartoon by Bill Mauldin. 4 pages. C. 1956. $15.

8

9

10

11

12

13

14

15

16

17

18

19

20

21

22

23

11
"KEEP AMERICA STRONG! WITH IKE AND DICK" 3x7" blue/white/orange folder. 1956. $10.

12
J.F.K. "OPERATION SUPPORT" 3.5x8.5" yellow/brown folder. 1960. $25.

13
"JOHN F. KENNEDY FOR U.S. SENATOR" CAMPAIGN BROCHURE 6.5x9" in rwb. 1952. $75.

14
"SENATOR JOHN F. KENNEDY" 1956 folder promoting him as vice-president. 6x9" bw/dark blue. $75.

15
J.F.K. "A TIME FOR GREATNESS" 4x9" folder that opens to 11x17" with many bw photos. 1960. $20.

16
"MEET LBJ" 8.5x12" magazine containing 89 photographs. 1964. $8.

17
PRO-GOLDWATER/ANTI-JOHNSON 3.5" bw/orange cardboard titled "Let's Compare." A cardboard wheel turns with quotes "From Each Candidate on Various Issues." 1964. $15.

18
"THE GOLDWATER CARTOON BOOK" 5.5x8" with full-page anti-Goldwater cartoons in bw. 1964. $10.

19
NIXON/AGNEW "ROW C" FLIER. 3.5x8" sheet which opens to 8x10.5" with endorsements by members of Row C, a New York political group. 1972. $3.

20
"NIXON'S THE ONE!" 4x8" two-sided campaign flyer put out by the Nixon/Agnew Campaign Committee. 1968. $3.

21
CARTER DOORHANGER. 3.5x9" hanger issued for New Hampshire Democratic primary. 1980. $4.

22
"WIN ONE FOR THE GIPPER!" bw folder 6x8" from the "Hudson County Democrats for Reagan." 1980. $5.

23
MONDALE BROCHURE about 3.5x9" titled "Why Women in the AFT Should Support Walter Mondale." 1984. $20.

6. Ceramics & Glass

Ceramic and glass political collectibles have existed from George Washington's era to the present. Among example products are creamers and pitchers, plates, flower jars, serving dishes, candy dishes, trays, glass tumblers, mugs, flasks, jugs, bottles, portrait tiles, paperweights, china matchboxes, toothpick holders and other utilitarian articles. Examples were produced both by well-known and anonymous makers. Most of the objects made prior to 1840 are actually commemorative in nature and issued after the candidate assumed office. From Harrison's 1840 "log cabin" campaign on, more objects were produced and actually used during the campaign. Of all the objects produced, plates are certainly the most abundant.

1
"A. LINCOLN" 3.5x4x5" tall pottery vase finished in dark brown w/solid black coloring on some raised designs. C. 1864. $600.

2
"JAMES A. GARFIELD" 6" clear glass plate with engraved frosted image on the underneath surface. 1880. $50.

3
"GARFIELD" 5x8x8" tall glazed white ceramic pitcher with large raised portrait on each side with his name below on a raised banner. 1880. $400.

4
GARFIELD "WE MOURN OUR NATION'S LOSS" pressed glass plate with raised bust. Clear glass is 11.5" diameter. 1881. $30.

5
"CLEVELAND/THURMAN" 8.5x9.5" rectangular clear glass with lightly frosted portraits at the center. 1888. $150.

6
"FOR PRESIDENT GROVER CLEVELAND" 8" white china plate with brown image and a thin gold band on the rim. 1888. $50.

7
"FOR PRESIDENT BENJAMIN HARRISON." Matches #6. 1888. $50.

8
"BENJ. HARRISON" 9" glazed plate in beige with dark brown portrait and leaf designs on the rim. C. 1888. $75.

9
McKINLEY 3x3" light blue glazed ceramic tile. 1896. $40.

10
McKINLEY/ROOSEVELT JUGATE GLASS 3.5" tall inscribed "Integrity, Inspiration, Industry." 1900. $70.

11
"WM. McKINLEY" 4" tall clear glass with frosted white portrait. 1896. $50.

12
"WM. McKINLEY" 3.75" tall clear glass with frosted image. C. 1896. $30.

1

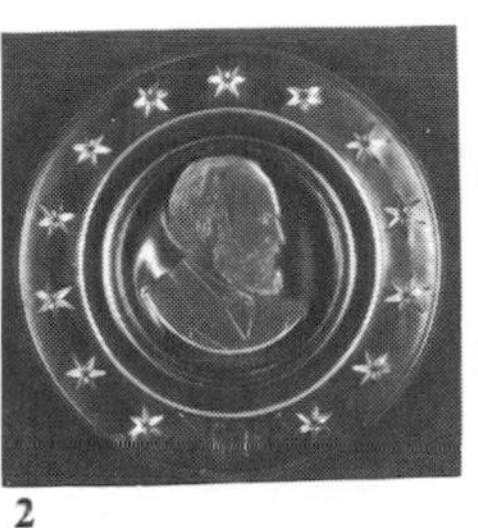
2

3

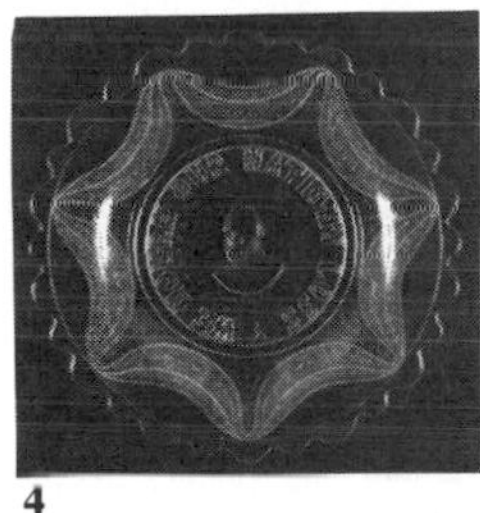
4

5

6

7

8

9

10

11

12

13

14

15

16

17

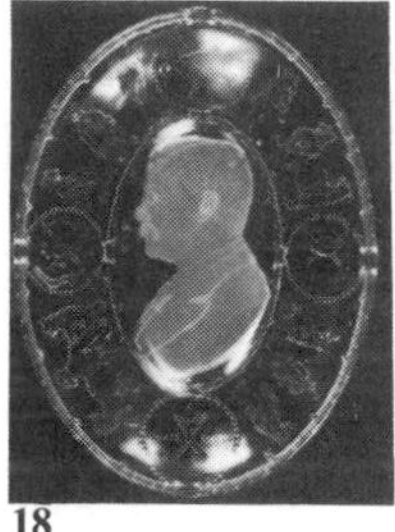

18

19

20

21

22

23

24

25

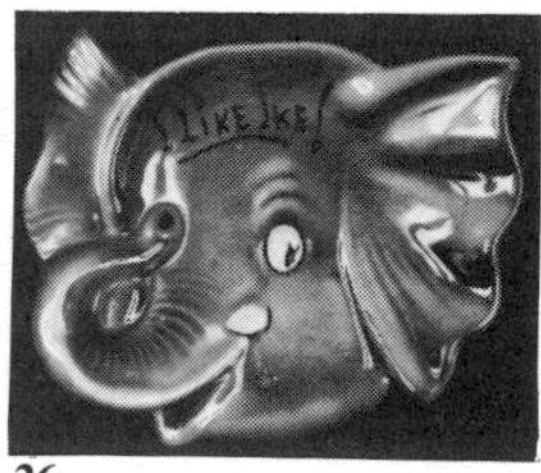

26

13
McKINLEY "PROTECTION AND PLENTY" 7.25" clear glass plate with frosted portrait. C. 1896. $35.

14
McKINLEY 5.5" pressed glass plate with a frosted white portrait. C. 1900. $35.

15
"GARRETT A. HOBART" 9" white glazed plate with browntone photo of McKinley's V. P. 1896. $40.

16
McKINLEY PITCHER 5x8x7" tall white china with full color portrait of McKinley on one side and depiction of "Old Glory" on the reverse. C. 1900. $50.

17
BRYAN/SEWELL "SIXTEEN TO ONE" 3.5" tall clear glass with frosted white portraits. 1896. $80.

18
ROOSEVELT 7.5x10" clear glass plate with large frosted portrait in the center surrounded by Teddy bears. 1904. $150.

19
"W. H. TAFT/J. S. SHERMAN" 9x11.5" white oval china platter with color portraits. 1908. $40.

20
"FOR PRESIDENT WILLIAM H. TAFT" 6" white china plate with brown photo image at center. 1908. $25.

21
"JOHN W. DAVIS" GLASS BERRY DISH marked "Compliments of Hazel-Atlas Glass Co." 4" diameter clear glass with 1.5" tall rim. 1924. $125.

22
COOLIDGE HOME SOUVENIR PITCHER 4.5x6x6" tall dark blue/white glazed ceramic. C. 1930s. $30.

23
"THE NEW DEAL" 4" tall tan pottery mug depicting Franklin Roosevelt. C. 1936. $20.

24
F.D.R. "3RD TERM" CERAMIC MUG 3x4x4" tall finished in medium blue color. 1940. $50.

25
EISENHOWER INAUGURATION 10.5" china plate in white with graytone portrait and inscription. 1953. $25.

26
"I LIKE IKE!" 5x5.5" glazed ceramic elephant head ashtray accented with bit of red on trunk and mouth. 1952. $30.

27
PRESIDENT AND MRS. EISENHOWER 9.25" white china plate with full color portrait. C. 1956. $15.

28
"PRESIDENT AND MRS. JOHN F. KENNEDY" 9" white china plate with full color illustration. C. 1961. $10.

29
"PRESIDENT AND MRS. JOHN F. KENNEDY" 5" tall white china pitcher. C. 1961. $60.

27

28

29

30
"PRESIDENT JOHN F. KENNEDY/ MRS. JOHN F. KENNEDY" salt and pepper set. 1.5x3x2" tall with color portraits. C. 1961. $30.

31
"JOHN F. KENNEDY, PRESIDENT/ ROBERT F. KENNEDY, SENATOR" 9" white china plate with color portraits from "Cape Cod, Mass." C. 1969. $20.

30

31

32
"LYNDON B. JOHNSON 36th PRESIDENT" 9" white china plate with image in black. C. 1964/1965. $20.

33
"RICHARD M. NIXON 37th PRESIDENT" 9" white china plate with full color portrait. C. 1969. $15.

34
"NIXON/AGNEW GOP 1969" 3x5x4" tall ceramic mug marked "Frankoma" (pottery). $25.

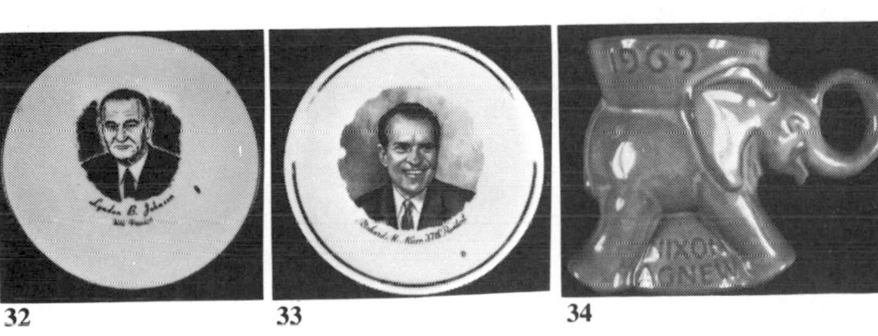
32 33 34

35
"JIMMY CARTER 39th PRESIDENT" 9.5" white china plate with browntone photo. C. 1976. $20.

36
"REPUBLICAN NATIONAL COMMEMORATIVE 1776-1976" whiskey bottle. Issued by Ezra Brooks-Heritage China for "Campaign '76." $25.

37
REAGAN/BUSH "A NEW BEGINNING" 10.5" plate with full color portraits. 1981. $35.

35

36

37

38
"REPUBLICAN NATIONAL CONVENTION AUGUST 20-23, 1984" 5" tall rwb ceramic mug with portraits of Reagan/Bush. $15.

39
"BOBBY FOR PRESIDENT" 4" tall white china mug in bw/rwb. 1968. $30.

40
"MUSKIE" rwb glass mug. 1972. $10.

38

39

40

7. Clocks & Watches

The earliest clocks, designed as shelf or mantle clocks, date to the 1840s. Varieties are known depicting Harrison's log cabin theme and there is a Henry Clay portrait clock. All these nineteenth century clocks are quite rare and expensive. The largest number of clocks are from the 1930s and depict Franklin Roosevelt. Both wind-up and electric models exist and some feature an animated dial. There are nearly 20 varieties, mostly made of bronzed white metal, bearing slogans such as "The Man Of The Hour" or "The New Deal." F.D.R. clocks are usually priced in the $100 to $200 range. Pocket watches are quite uncommon but one exists from 1888 with jugate portraits of Harrison and Morton engraved on the reverse. One 1896 pocket watch carries a McKinley slogan on the reverse. The most widely sought and valuable pocket watch is one from 1920 picturing both James Cox and Franklin Roosevelt on the dial. Its value, if sold at auction, would most likely exceed $25,000. Wrist watches are more recent collectibles, although an example does exist with a photo of Woodrow Wilson set into the watch case. In 1972, sparked partly by the revival of interest in Disney and other comic character watches, caricature watches were issued for Nixon, Agnew, Wallace, and McGovern. Since that time, the popularity of novelty watches usually inspires at least one or two examples each election year.

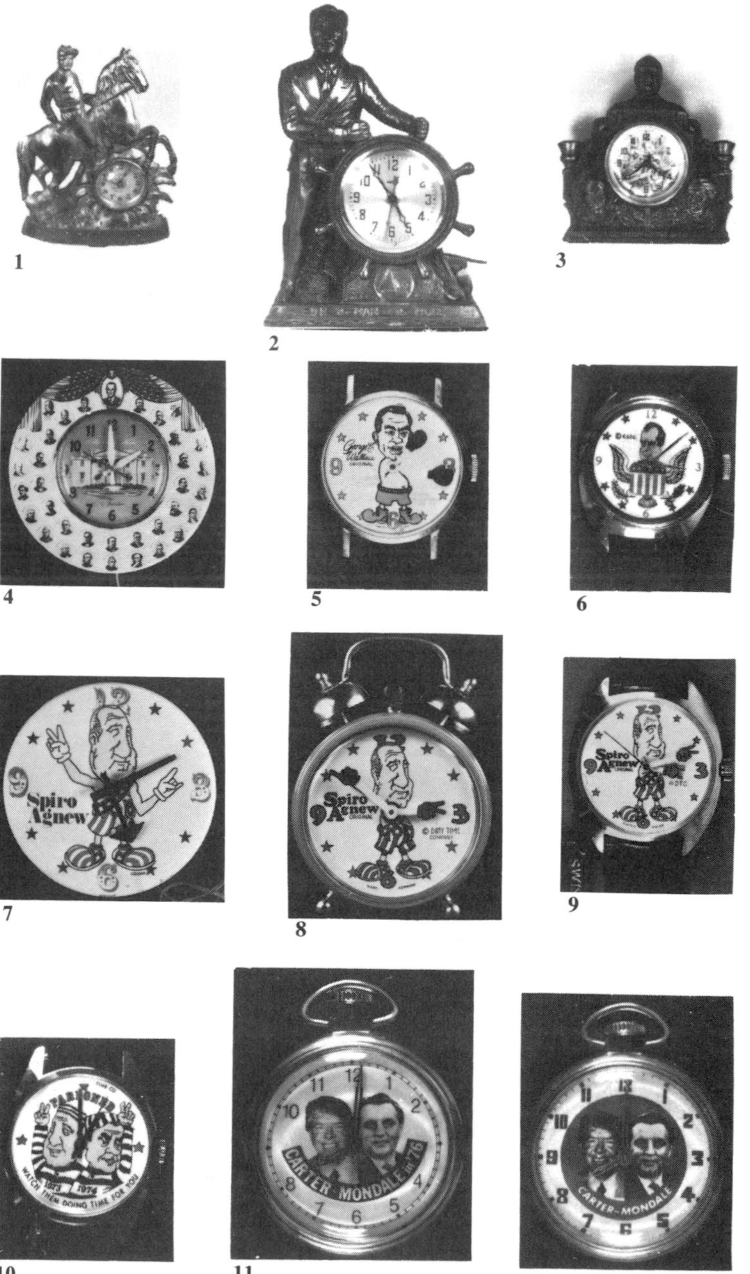

1
ROOSEVELT ROUGH RIDER 8x10" clock. Brass finish. C. 1904. $250.

2
"F.D.R. THE MAN OF THE HOUR" 4x9x13" tall white metal clock with copper finish. C. 1936. $150.

3
"THE SPIRIT OF THE U.S.A.-ROOSEVELT, GEN. H. S. JOHNSON, MISS F. PERKINS" white metal clock with copper finish. C. 1936. $175.

4
PRESIDENTIAL ELECTRIC CLOCK 10" diameter metal picturing Washington through L.B.J. C. 1964. $40.

5
"GEORGE C. WALLACE ORIGINAL" caricature wristwatch with rwb dial. 1970. $100.

6
NIXON WRISTWATCH substituting the eagle's head with a portrait of Nixon. C. 1968. $65.

7
"SPIRO AGNEW" rwb 9" celluloid-like electric clock. C. 1973. $50.

8
"SPIRO AGNEW" 1x2.5x3.5" tall alarm clock by "Dirty Time Co." C. 1972. $40.

9
"SPIRO AGNEW ORIGINAL" watch marked "DTC" (Dirty Time Co.). C. early 1970s. $50.

10
NIXON/AGNEW wristwatch captioned "Watch Them Doing Time For You." C. 1974. $100.

11
"CARTER/MONDALE IN '76" pocket watch in 2" silvered case. $45.

12
"CARTER/MONDALE" pocket watch in silvered metal case. C. 1976. $45.

8. Clothing, Hats & Uniforms

Campaign apparel offers an unusual collecting opportunity with a wide assortment of items depending on the collector's chosen degree of specialization. Parade uniforms and manufacturer's catalogues are a limited but fascinating specialty area. Several collectibles are based on the hat preference of candidates, notably Benjamin Harrison (beaver hat), Al Smith (brown derby), Estes Kefauver (coonskin cap). Felt beanie versions were produced for both major party candidates in the 1920s election years. Neckties have been a staple campaign item since the 1940s and date back to examples for Theodore Roosevelt and Woodrow Wilson. More recently, T-shirts have emerged as collectibles. Hosiery has been issued sporadically. Convention hats have always been popular, with construction ranging from paper and actual straw to later simulated straw of plastic or Styrofoam.

1
"JAMES A. GARFIELD" 5x5x3" deep wood collar box with the lid in brown thermo-plastic. 1880. $200.

2
BENJAMIN HARRISON beige heavy felt campaign hat. Also pictured is the inside label with portraits of Harrison and Morton. 1888. $250.

3
"WILSON/MARSHALL" black necktie 1.5" wide by 47" long. C. 1912. $65.

4
"CAMPAIGN OF 1896" 9.5x14.5" manufacturer's bw catalog sheet. Sheet shows 12 parade helmets mostly featuring the names or photos of "McKinley & Hobart." $75.

5
"SMILE WITH 'AL'- A CENTURY OF PROGRESS" 2x5" brown metal derby hat with elastic band and a printed cardboard on the front picturing the 1933 Chicago World's Fair logo. $75.

6
DEWEY NECKTIE in a dark rust shade with silk screened image in bw and yellow. C. 1948. $25.

7
"DEWEY IN '48" blue tie with illustrations of U.S. Capitol and Dewey in white. $30.

8
"TRUMAN IN '48" blue tie matching item #7. $60.

9
EISENHOWER necktie with 3.5x10" image consisting of bright yellow lightning bolt leading into a picture of the U.S. Capitol building. C. late 1940s. $45.

10
EISENHOWER dark purple necktie. Similar to #9, but rather than a photo of Ike, there is a brown/white illustration. C. late 1940s. $30.

1 2 3 4 5 6 7 8 9 10

11

12

13

15

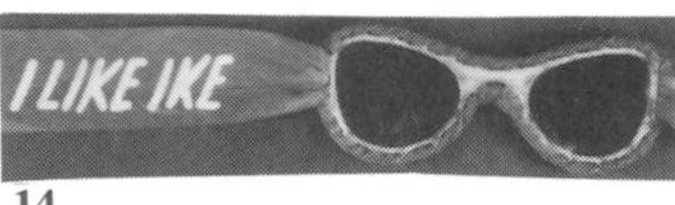

14

16

17

18

19

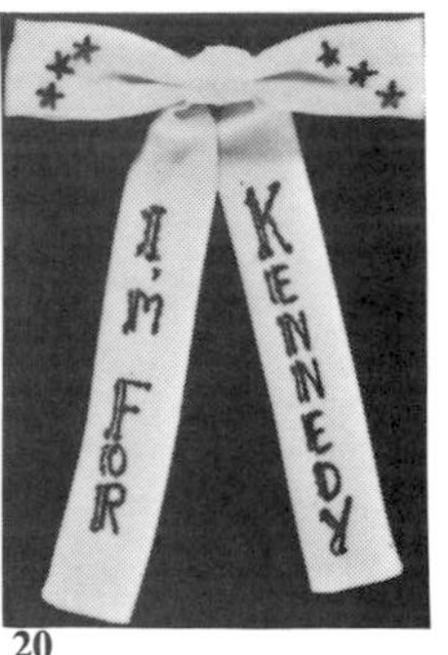

20

21

22

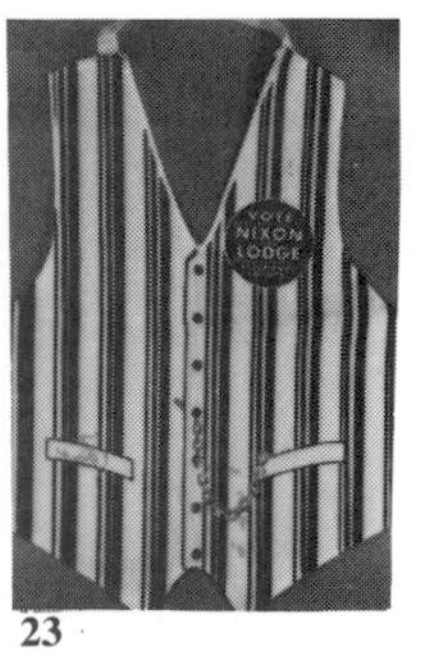

23

11
"I LIKE IKE" 10x13" felt bag with 8" handle and cut-out felt appliques in rwb and gray. C. 1956. $30.

12
"WIN WITH EISENHOWER" paper hat with red printing. C. 1952. $20.

13
"WIN WITH IKE" cardboard head visor in rwb. On the sides are six pictures of three different 7/8" Ike political buttons. These buttons say "I Like Ike, Ike in '56, Let's Back Ike." 1956. $12.

14
"I LIKE IKE" plastic frame sunglasses with 28" blue ribbon extensions to tie around the head. C. 1952. $35.

15
"I LIKE IKE" pair of gray socks with red motto. C. 1952. $20.

16
"ADLAI-JOHN" 2x6" rwb fabric/elastic garter with a white plastic 1.5" donkey mounted at the center. "John" refers to either John Sparkman the 1952 V.P. or John Kennedy a 1956 vice-presidential hopeful. $25.

17
STEVENSON "PEACE, PROSPERITY FOR ALL" green tie 3" wide by 52" long with his portrait in bw. C. 1952. $25.

18
"LET'S BACK JACK" necktie featuring a repeating slogan in black letters on tan background. 1960. $25.

19
"KENNEDY FOR PRESIDENT" white plastic campaign hat with a rwb/bw paper band picturing J.F.K. 1960. $40.

20
"I'M FOR KENNEDY" 4.5 x 6.5 " clip-on bow tie in white fabric with hand-painted designs. 1960. $75.

21
"I'M WORKING FOR NIXON AND LODGE" pair of 10" long yellow gardening gloves. 1960. $20.

22
"NIXON FOR PRESIDENT" white plastic campaign hat. Taped on the top of the hat is a rwb paper sticker which reads "Nixon Now '60." $20.

23
"VOTE NIXON/LODGE EXPERIENCE COUNTS!" rwb cloth vest. 1960. $35.

24
"NIXON FOR PRESIDENT" necktie in very dark gray with white lettering and small white elephant design. 1960. $8.

25
"L.B.J. FOR THE U.S.A." western style campaign hat in bright orange felt with red on white fabric band stapled around the crown. 1964. $15.

26
"U.S.A. LIKES L.B.J." white letters on red fabric tie. 1964. $5.

27
"L.B.J. ALL THE WAY" full-size fabric baseball-style hat in white with red brim. On the front is a dark blue design of a donkey wearing a western outfit. 1964. $8.

28
"GOLDWATER IN '64" 10x11.5x4" tall white Styrofoam hat with black on gold paper band around the side. Band has slogans plus two portraits of Goldwater. $25.

29
"GO GOLDWATER" pair of black on white cardboard eyeglasses. Front section is 2x6". Probably used at San Francisco convention. 1964. $20.

30
GOLDWATER actual size pair of pliable black plastic frames with raised gold letters on each temple "AuH2O." 1964. $25.

31
GOLDWATER pair of thick white cord neckties, each with a 1.5" across oval slide. One slide is in green plastic while the other is in white. Inside each is a gold elephant along with the gold lettering "AuH2O." 1964. EACH $8.

32
"WALLACE" white plastic hat with a bw paper portrait on the top and a rwb portrait band around the side. 1968. $8.

33
"McGOVERN/SHRIVER" 12x15" dark blue shoulder bag with names in red plus white shoulder strap. 1972. $25.

34
"McGOVERN/SHRIVER" 3x4" colorful fabric patch with rainbow design. 1972. $10.

24

25

28

27

26

29

30

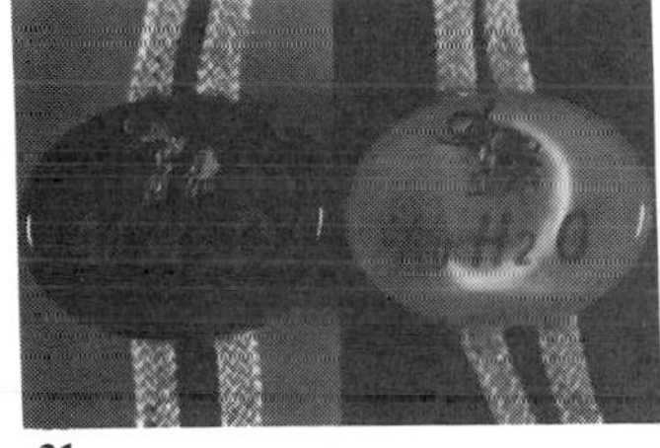
31

32

33

34

9. Clothing Buttons

Clothing buttons of a commemorative or inauguration nature are available from George Washington on, although this particular collectible has all but disappeared in recent years. The collector of early clothing buttons would be wise to be well-versed in this specialty as reproductions are quite common. Some commemoratives, although authentic, may be issued quite a few years later than the commemorated event or individual. Earliest examples were worn on outer coats, waist coats, breeches, lapels or collars. Design was usually engraved or incised on a brass or copper disk with the attachment shank soldered on the back. Beginning in 1840, most versions consisted of an embossed brass shell applied over a back shank. Rather inexpensive clothing buttons can be acquired for nineteenth century candidates such as William Henry Harrison (1840), Zachary Taylor (1848), and major party candidates from 1880 through 1896. Throughout the history of political clothing buttons, beautiful examples in porcelain or enameled metal have augmented those of traditional metals.

1
WASHINGTON $1\frac{5}{16}$" brass inauguration button inscribed "March The Fourth 1789 Memorable Era." 1789. $1500.

2
"GW" INSCRIBED 1789 INAUGURAL CLOTHING BUTTON. $1\frac{3}{8}$" diameter thin silvered copper disk. $1000.

3
HARRISON BRASS BUTTON. $\frac{3}{4}$". Depicts Log Cabin. 1840. $40.

4
"MARTIN VAN BUREN EXCELSIOR" $\frac{3}{4}$" brass clothing button with inscription on the reverse. 1840. $200.

5
ZACHARY TAYLOR brass $\frac{15}{16}$" portrait clothing button. 1848. $60.

6
"GARFIELD AND ARTHUR" $\frac{13}{16}$" brass clothing button. 1880. $25.

7
"BLAINE & LOGAN" $\frac{3}{4}$" brass button. Depicts plumed knight. 1884. $25.

8
"CLEVELAND AND HENDRICKS" $\frac{3}{4}$" brass clothing button. 1884. $20.

9
"HARRISON/MORTON" $\frac{3}{4}$" diameter brass button. 1888. $20.

10
ROOSEVELT $1\frac{1}{8}$" brass with bear at center. C. 1904. $12.

11
TAFT "BILLY POSSUM" brass clothing button. $1\frac{1}{8}$". 1908. $15.

12
HOOVER AND WIFE with celluloid-covered full color illustrations and brass rims. $1\frac{1}{2}$". C. 1932. PAIR $100.

13
F.D.R. AND WIFE. A matched pair to item #12. C. 1932. PAIR $100.

14
TRUMAN button with green fabric rim around bw photo. 1". 1948. $85.

10. Convention Items

Convention items consist of varied memorabilia from the individual party nominating conventions preceding national (and state) elections. Pinback buttons, delegate badges, press and news media badges and credentials, plus paper or fabric items generally constitute this collecting area. Paper items include posters, placards, programs, tickets, hats, pennants, fans and a long list of other possibilities. Fabric items include hats, pennants, ribbons, delegate sashes and cummerbunds, wall and ceiling hangers, and large banners. A convention item identified by year and/or location is generally considered more desirable.

1
REPUBLICAN NATIONAL CONVENTION engraved ticket. June, 1900. $18.

2
"SOCIALIST PARTY PLATFORM" four-page pamphlet from 1912 with jugate pictures of "Debs/Seidel." $35.

3
HOOVER "REPUBLICAN PARTY PLATFORM 1932" 24 page booklet with jugate cover. $20.

1

Socialist Party Platform

2

3

4
"REPUBLICAN NATIONAL CONVENTION" engraved appointment card. 6x9" stiff card in bw with a line to fill in the name of individual being appointed as a "Page" at the 1940 convention. $20.

5
DEMOCRATIC NATIONAL CONVENTION TICKET. 3x6.5" on colored stock issued for a "Guest." Chicago, 1940. $5.

6
"THAT GRAND OLD PARTY" 9x12" blue/white sheet music featuring Uncle Sam and "G.O.P." elephant. Issued for 1948 convention. $10.

REPUBLICAN NATIONAL CONVENTION

4

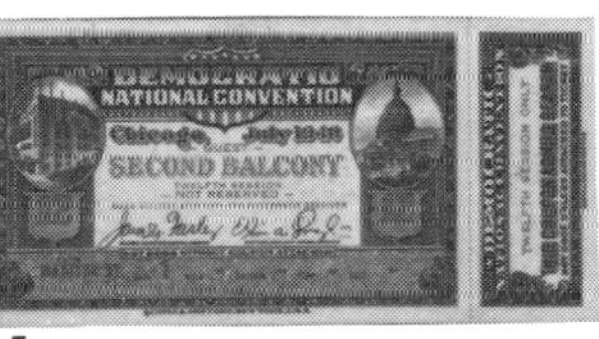

5

6

7
"OFFICIAL PROGRAM-DEMOCRATIC NATIONAL CONVENTION" 80 page 9x12" souvenir program from 1948 convention that nominated Truman. $45.

8
"REPUBLICAN NATIONAL CONVENTION OFFICIAL PROGRAM." 9x12" 92 page program from 1948 convention that nominated Dewey. $30.

9
"CENTENNIAL NATIONAL REPUBLICAN CONVENTION" 9x12" 160 page souvenir program. Front cover is bw/ orange with portraits of Ike and Lincoln. 1956. $30.

7

8

9

10
"REPUBLICAN NATIONAL CONVENTION" press ticket. San Francisco, 1956. $8.

11
DEMOCRATIC NATIONAL CONVENTION press ticket. Chicago, 1956. $6.

10

11

12

13

14

15

16

17

18

19

20

21

22

23

24

12
REPUBLICAN NATIONAL CONVENTION Sergeant-At-Arms certificate. 6x8.5" $12.

13
"REPUBLICAN NATIONAL CONVENTION-Press Messenger." Admission ticket. "Chicago, July 25, 1960." $8.

14
"REPUBLICAN NATIONAL CONVENTION OFFICIAL PROGRAM" 10x13" 168 page program from the Miami Beach 1968 convention. $15.

15
CBS NEWS TAG. 3x4.25" rwb laminated card for the 1968 Republican Convention. $10.

16
DEMOCRATIC CONVENTION 2.25x3.5" laminated card for 1968 News/Radio/TV press facilities. $10.

17
DEMOCRATIC CONVENTION cloth vest showing 3x3" rwb chest patch depicting 1968 Chicago convention logo. $30.

18
"REPUBLICAN NATIONAL CONVENTION" 8.5x11" 288 page convention souvenir book. Miami Beach, 1972. $10.

19
PRO-FORD "SHOOT OUT AT KANSAS CITY" 2.25" tan/brown/bw button from 1976 convention depicting Ford wearing white hat and Reagan wearing black hat. $8.

20
PRO-REAGAN mate to item #19 with hat colors reversed. $8.

21
DEMOCRATIC NATIONAL CONVENTION bw/green button. 1976. $4.

22
"ABC NEWS" CONVENTION BUTTONS. 3" with identical designs except one is rwb/black on white and the other is red/blue/black on yellow. 1976. EACH $5.

23
"REPUBLICAN NATIONAL CONVENTION-DOWN THE PIKE TO WASHINGTON-FULL SPEED AHEAD" 9" rwb/bw button. 1980. $8.

24
"REPUBLICAN NATIONAL CONVENTION OFFICIAL PROGRAM." 8.5x11" with 92 pages. New Orleans, 1988. $15.

11. Fans

Fans have existed since the 1800s as political collectibles with original distribution made mostly at campaign stops and conventions. The most common type is die-cut thin cardboard with either a thumbhole or attached wooden handle. A much scarcer version of political fan is the collapsible folding fan of stiff paper usually mounted on a webbing or struts of thin wood joined by a brass fastener. Fans, particularly the more common design variety, will frequently be printed on the reverse with an advertisement for a local sponsor. Folding umbrellas are also known in both paper and fabric. Fabric umbrellas were produced mostly in the late 1890s to early 1900s era and are quite scarce.

1
TAFT-SHERMAN/BRYAN-KERN jugates with cloud design below. Rwb cardboard with the four pictures on a stars and stripes background. 1908. $75.

2
"THE ROOSEVELT CREED" 9x14.5" cardboard with colorful portrait of T.R. Reverse has advertising for the Norfolk Lumber Co. C. 1916. $30.

3
"KEEP COOL-IDGE" rwb cardboard with portrait of Coolidge in the center. Reverse advertising for an ice cream company. 1924. $150.

4
COOLIDGE 9x15" cardboard with wood handle. Black letters on one side read "We Will Help To Keep Cool-idge." Opposite side has imprint of "Mifflin County Women's Coolidge Club, Lewistown, Pennsylvania 1924." $40.

5
COOLIDGE/DAVIS pictured on a bw/ blue cardboard issued by a coal dealer. Map of the U.S. depicts the states and their electoral votes. 1924. $50.

6
F.D.R. "OUR PRESIDENT" cardboard with a full color picture and an ad on the reverse for coffee. C. 1940. $25.

7
"OUR PRESIDENT AND HIS CABINET" 8x10" with a 6" wood handle. Bw/rwb cardboard with large oval portrait of F.D.R. plus smaller portraits of Vice President Garner and the members of F.D.R.'s famous cabinet. 1933. $50.

8
"LANDON FOR PRESIDENT" 8.5" cardboard in brown/yellow. 1936. $35.

9
"DEWEY" 10x10.5" diecut cardboard with white eagle on dark blue. C. 1944. $25.

10
"GOLDWATER FAN CLUB" cardboard with a tongue depressor handle. About 10" tall. 1964. $30.

1 2 3 4 5 6 7 8 9 10

12. Figural Items

Three-dimensional figures representing either the full figure or bust of the candidate are quite popular among collectors. Busts are much more common than full figures and metal is the most frequently used material but other materials used include bisque, china, wood, composition, soap, plaster, papier mache´, glass, marble, starched fabric, celluloid, plastic and vinyl. While obviously intended for display, some figures are also designed to be used as book ends, banks, dolls, paperweights, pencil holders, pitchers or wind-up toys.

1
"McKINLEY" white plaster bust 3.5x4.5x8" tall. C. 1900. $40.

2
ROOSEVELT 8x10.75" tall iron doorstop with brass finish. C. 1904. $100.

3
TAFT 3.5" tall bisque container possibly to hold cigars. C. 1908. $65.

4
AL SMITH 5.5x9.5" tall embossed copper wall plaque. Al's hat is inscribed with large numbers "1928." $130.

5
AL SMITH 3.5x7" plaster caricature. Greatly exaggerated nose and a 2" cigar protrudes from his mouth. 1932. $100.

6
"NRA/WE DO OUR PART/F.D. ROOSEVELT" 2.5x2.5x6" tall white metal bust with dark gold finish. The eagle is rwb. C. 1933. $100.

7
"FORWARD FRANKLIN D. ROOSEVELT" 2.25x3.5" tall white metal bust with bronze finish. 1933. $40.

8
EISENHOWER 7" tall glazed pitcher. Colorful and realistic. C. 1952. $75.

9
EISENHOWER 1.5x3x3.5" tall beige/tan ceramic salt and pepper set. Ike's head lifts off for one shaker while his body serves as the other. C. 1952. $20.

10
EISENHOWER 4.5x4.5x6.5" tall three-dimensional plaster bust in beige with light brown accenting. C. 1956. $35.

11
EISENHOWER 6" tall composition figure with head mounted on a spring. Colorful. C. late 1950s. $125.

12
"JFK" 2x3.5x4" tall salt and pepper set. Brown and white rocker has intials in gold and JFK is in black pants and necktie with a white shirt. 1962.

13
J.F.K. 6.75" composition bobbing head marked under the base "Japan." J.F.K. depicted in brown shoes and pants with yellow/green sweater. Caption reads "I Don't Care If You Are Attorney General, You Were Off Side!!" C. 1961. $300.

14
"J.F. KENNEDY" 4x4x13.5" tall solid plaster bust finished in gold with a base that depicts a PT-boat, Liberty Bell and Presidential Seal. C. 1964. $40.

15
"LBJ HIMSELF...BY REMCO" 5.5" vinyl figure of LBJ with "LBJ" campaign button that snaps onto his chest. 1964. $30.

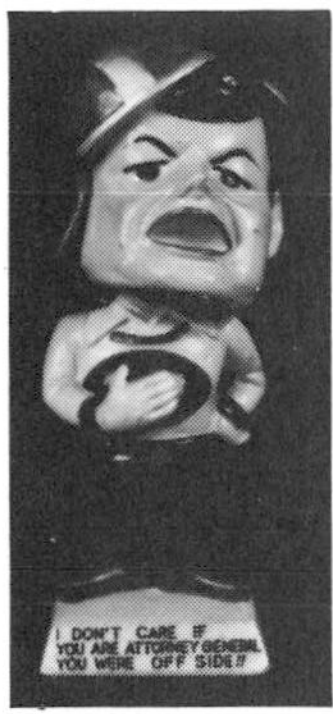

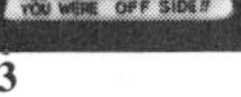

13

14

15

16
JOHNSON BOTTLE STOPPER. Realistically colored composition with cork stopper below. C. 1960s. $25.

17
"DICK/SPIRO" 2.5" tall soft rubber figures depicting each holding a small name sign. Done in tan rubber with some detailing in black or brown. C. 1972. $20.

18
NIXON 5x7.5" card holding a vinyl and plastic novelty figure of Nixon titled "Tricky Dick (Who Can Figure Him Out) Try To Pull His Leg And He'll Fool You Every Time." 1972. $15.

16

17

18

19
NIXON 4" tall full-dimensional soft vinyl plastic figure in dark tan/fleshtone with black suit. C. 1972. $20.

20
REAGAN/BUSH-CARTER/MONDALE 4.5x7x2" deep gray china donkey and 6x5x3.5" deep gray elephant. Donkey has a green and white litho button inscribed "Carter/Mondale" and the elephant has blue and white litho button inscribed "The Time Is Now/Reagan/ Bush." 1980. EACH $20.

19

20

21
DUKAKIS/BUSH 3" tall figures joined together in sitting position with bodies covered in black fabric. Shoes, hands, heads and hats are done in hard plastic and nicely colored. 1988. $15.

21

13. Inauguration Items

Inauguration items are those produced specifically to commemorate this quadrennial event. Such items exist for each president beginning with George Washington, but items produced for inaugurations prior to 1896 tend to be rather scarce. Very few inauguration collectibles exist for presidents assuming the office upon the death of the elected president. Typical inauguration collectibles include invitations, tickets, programs, badges, buttons, ribbons, medals and medalets, banners, posters, speech copies, mugs, matches, napkins, and, at least since 1948, District of Columbia Metropolitan Police badges and car license plates.

1

2

3

4

5

6

7

8

9

10

11

1
JACKSON 1829 INAUGURATION WOOD BOX WITH PORTRAIT UNDER GLASS. 3x7x11" overall while under the glass at the center is a 3x4" bw lithographed paper portrait of Jackson wearing glasses. Inscription below portrait reads "Andrew Jackson. Born May. 15. 1767. IN. 1829." $3000.

2
"HARRISON/MORTON" 5x10" fabric ribbon in bw with a pair of rwb flags and a sewn-on outer edge of light blue fringe. 1889. $100.

3
McKINLEY'S 1901 INAUGURATION silvered brass card case 2x3". $140.

4
TAFT/SHERMAN 1909 OFFICIAL INAUGURAL PROGRAM. 32 pages. $50.

5
TAFT "INAUGURAL SOUVENIR 1909" 8.5x11" booklet. $35.

6
WILSON "OFFICIAL SOUVENIR PROGRAM/SECOND INAUGURATION." 8x11" with 32 pages. 1917. $75.

7
F.D.R. FIRST INAUGURATION. Framed souvenir with jugate photos. 8x11". 1933. $75.

8
F.D.R. 1937 INAUGURATION ticket with stub. 2.5x6". $40.

9
F.D.R./WALLACE INAUGURAL PROGRAM 8.5x11" with rwb/brown cover and 56 pages. 1941. $50.

10
TRUMAN "OFFICIAL INAUGURAL PROGRAM 1949" 8.5x11" with 72 pages. $40.

11
TRUMAN INAUGURATION 2.5x4.5" ticket. 1949. $20.

12
"INAUGURATION CEREMONIES PROGRAM" 6x9" with 8 pages inside printed on one side only. Front cover has small embossed Presidential Seal. "January 20, 1949." $125.

13
"PRESIDENTIAL INAUGURATION 1953" official program about 8.5x11" with 52 pages. $20.

14
EISENHOWER "INAUGURATION CEREMONIES PROGRAM" 6x9" with 8 sheets of paper on inside printed on one side only. Cover has embossed Presidential Seal in gold plus rwb ribbon binding. 1953. $35.

15
"DWIGHT DAVID EISENHOWER MCMLIII" 2.75" brass medal from first inauguration. $15.

16
"A MARCH TO EISENHOWER Souvenir of Inauguration 1953" rwb sheet music about 8x11" with 4 pages. $10.

17
EISENHOWER INAUGURATION 8x11" 48 page program. Front cover is in bw/gold with design by Norman Rockwell. 1957. $35.

18
"OFFICIAL INAUGURATION PROGRAM, JANUARY 20, 1961" about 8.5x11" with 64 pages. $50.

19
J.F.K./L.B.J. INAUGURAL INVITATION 8.5x11" with Inaugural Seal embossed in gold. 4 blank pages inside. January 20, 1961. $35.

20
J.F.K. "SOUVENIR OF WASHINGTON D.C. INAUGURAL" large white and green cardboard periscope 3x4x16" tall. J.F.K.'s name and picture appear on two sides while the other two sides show the Capitol. 1961. $45.

21
"JOHN FITZGERALD KENNEDY" 2.75" brass inaugural medal. 1961. $50.

22
L.B.J. INAUGURAL INVITATION 8.5x11" with the Presidential Seal in gold. $10.

23
NIXON/AGNEW 1973 OFFICIAL INAUGURATION 3x7" ticket that has jugate pictures in bw of Nixon and Agnew on one side plus Presidential Seal, dates, etc. on the other side. $12.

12

13

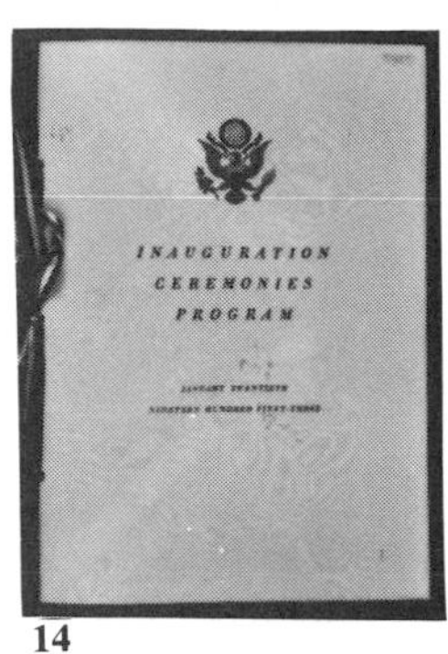

14

15

16

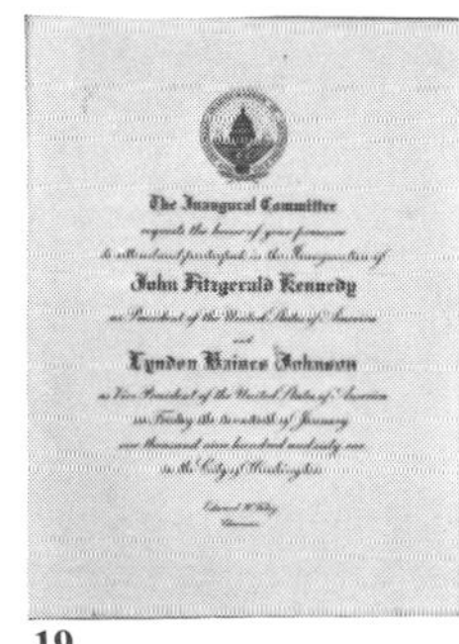

17

18

19

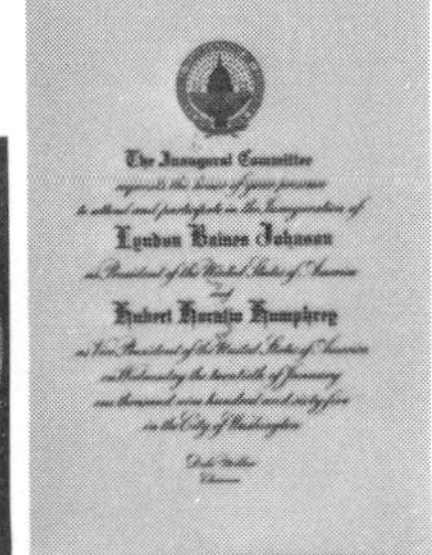

20

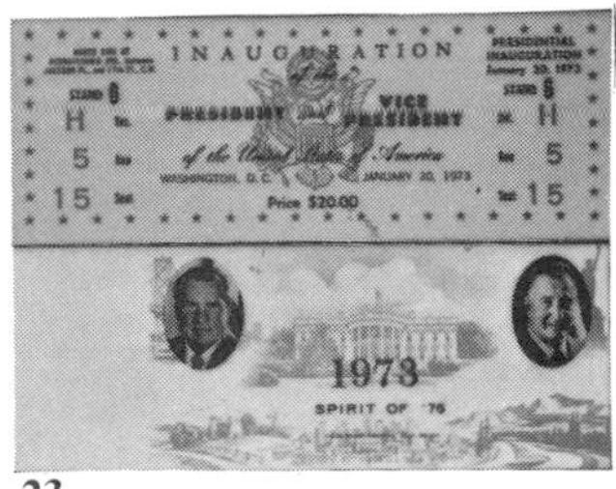

21

22

23

24

25

26

27

28

29

30

31

32

33

24
NIXON INAUGURATION 6x12" license plate in red/blue on silvery reflective background. 1973. $20.

25
NIXON CHINA MUG 2.5x3" tall dark blue china with gold bands and gold logo inscribed "Inauguration of President Nixon and Vice-President Agnew." C. 1972. $12.

26
JIMMY CARTER OFFICIAL INAUGURAL MEDAL. Bronze. 1976. $20.

27
CARTER "INAUGURATION 1977" license plate. $15.

28
"REAGAN INAUGURATION" 3x4" ABC News press pass from January 20, 1981 inauguration. Features full color picture of Reagan with colorful typography, all sealed in plastic and with a chain for wearing around the neck. $20.

29
REAGAN INAUGURATION 8.5x11" stiff paper invitation for the 1981 event. At top is the inauguration symbol embossed in gold. $15.

30
REAGAN/BUSH WASHINGTON POST 11x21" advertising poster in rwb showing pictures of the candidates with an announcement for the "Special Inauguration Sections of the Post." 1985. $10.

31
REAGAN INAUGURAL 6x12" metal license plate in red/gold/silver/blue from 1985. Has the Inaugural Seal on the left with the names "Reagan-Bush 1985." $15.

32
"PRESIDENT RONALD REAGAN Inauguration Jan. 20, 21, 1985" 2.5" diameter metal yo-yo with black/gray celluloid sides. 1985. $15.

33
REAGAN INAUGURATION MUSICAL CARD 6x8" with clear cellophane cover. Front has gold "Reagan-Bush" 1985 inauguration logo while the inside has a Ronald Reagan quote plus a full color photo of Reagan and Bush. When the card is opened, the Star Spangled Banner plays and a pair of small red lights glow on each man's necktie. $30.

14. Jugate Buttons

Any campaign item picturing two candidates is known as a jugate. Jugate buttons picturing a party's presidential and vice-presidential nominees are the overwhelming favorite of collectors. For major party candidates since 1896 there are both very common and very rare jugates. Because there were few varieties produced and small quantities of those that were produced, jugates for Theodore Roosevelt/Hiram Johnson (1912), Warren Harding/Calvin Coolidge (1920), James Cox/Franklin Roosevelt (1920) and John Davis/Charles Bryan (1924) are all valued close to $1000 or more. The highest prices paid in the hobby are for Cox/Roosevelt jugates. In 1991, several changed hands in both private and auction transactions ranging from $37,000 to a record high of $50,000. Fortunately for most collectors, lower and moderately priced jugates are available for all but the above four campaigns. Rarity and condition being equal, a number of other factors contribute to a jugate's desirability and value. If the inscriptions on the jugate include the captions "For President" and "For Vice-President," the candidates' names, the date of the election, and/or a campaign slogan; collectors will view that jugate more favorably than examples with less detail. Particularly desired are jugates with inscriptions identifying specific groups supporting the candidate, jugates intended for specific single day events or for use in specific localities, and, probably most desired of all, jugates with a great amount of color and imaginative graphic design. The size of the button is also a consideration. Most collectors prefer buttons 1 3/4" or smaller. In recent years, manufacturers have tended to prefer larger buttons so collectors may not have much choice. Generally, from 1948 through 1968 smaller-sized jugates are preferred while from 1896 through 1944 larger jugates (over 2") are for the most part highly prized because of their rarity.

1
McKINLEY/HOBART National Wheelmen's Club $1\frac{1}{4}$" bw/rwb. 1896. $330.

2
"McKINLEY AND HOBART" $\frac{7}{8}$" bw/rwb. 1896. $15.

3
McKINLEY/ROOSEVELT Dinner Bucket. $1\frac{1}{4}$" bw/brown. 1900. $80.

4
McKINLEY/ROOSEVELT $1\frac{3}{4}$" bw/fleshtone/gold. 1900. $50.

5
McKINLEY/ROOSEVELT 1" bw/rwb/gold. 1900. $30.

6
"BRYAN & SEWALL Victory 1896" $1\frac{1}{2}$" bw/red. 1896. $230.

7
"BRYAN/SEWALL 16 to 1" $\frac{7}{8}$" bw/blue. 1896. $30.

8
BRYAN/STEVENSON Constitution and Flag. $1\frac{1}{4}$" bw/rwb/silver. 1900. $80.

9
"BRYAN/STEVENSON" $1\frac{3}{4}$" bw/rwb/silver. 1900. $65.

10
BRYAN/KERN $\frac{7}{8}$" color. 1908. $40.

11
ROOSEVELT/FAIRBANKS $1\frac{1}{4}$" multicolor. 1904. $300.

12
ROOSEVELT/FAIRBANKS $\frac{7}{8}$" browntone. 1904. $12.

13
ROOSEVELT/FAIRBANKS $1\frac{1}{4}$" multicolor. 1904. $110.

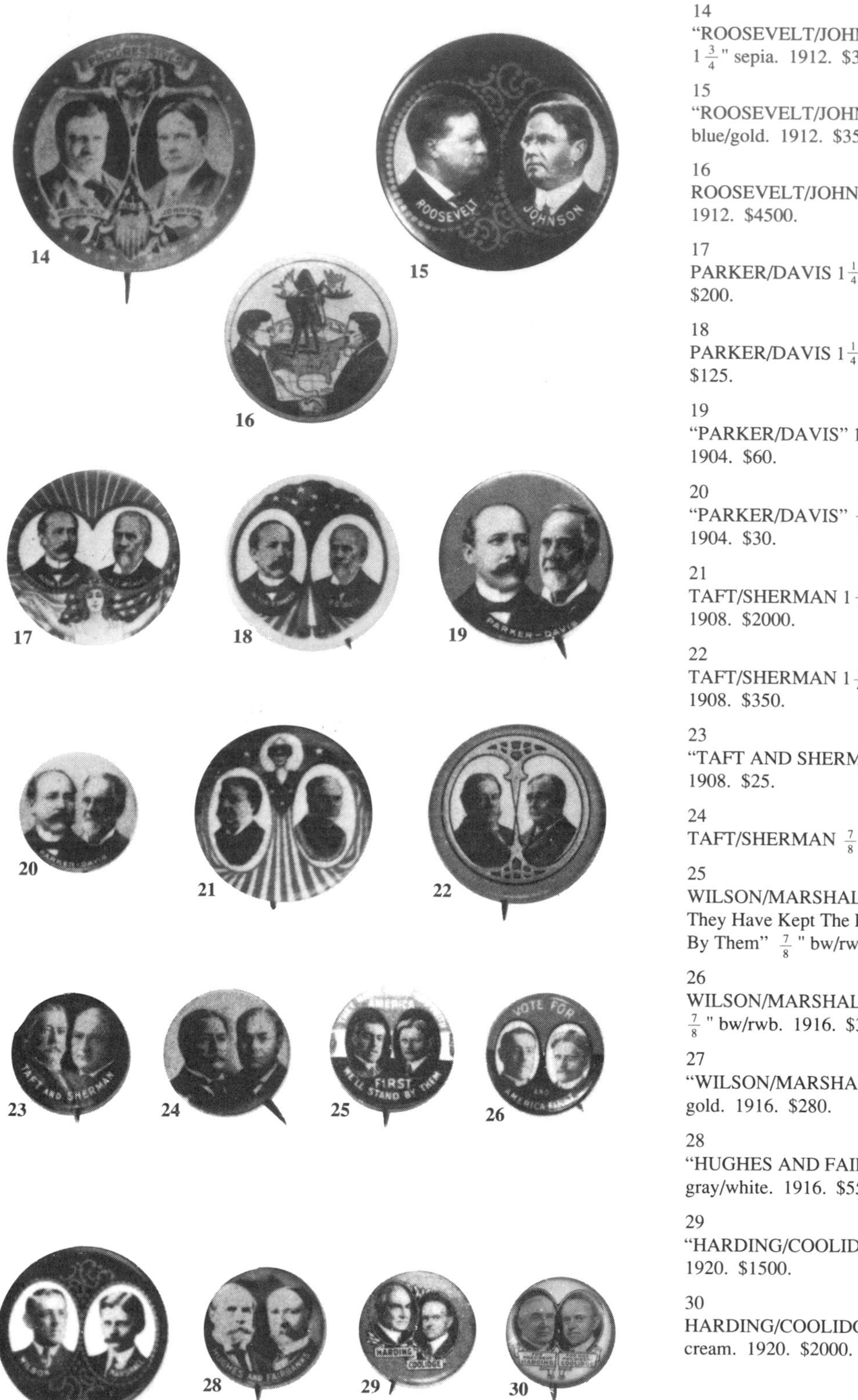

14
"ROOSEVELT/JOHNSON Progressives" $1\frac{3}{4}$" sepia. 1912. $3500.

15
"ROOSEVELT/JOHNSON" $1\frac{3}{4}$" bw/blue/gold. 1912. $3500.

16
ROOSEVELT/JOHNSON $1\frac{1}{4}$" sepia. 1912. $4500.

17
PARKER/DAVIS $1\frac{1}{4}$" multicolor. 1904. $200.

18
PARKER/DAVIS $1\frac{1}{4}$" multicolor. 1904. $125.

19
"PARKER/DAVIS" $1\frac{1}{4}$" bw/flesh/gold. 1904. $60.

20
"PARKER/DAVIS" $\frac{7}{8}$" multicolor. 1904. $30.

21
TAFT/SHERMAN $1\frac{1}{4}$" multicolor. 1908. $2000.

22
TAFT/SHERMAN $1\frac{1}{4}$" multicolor. 1908. $350.

23
"TAFT AND SHERMAN" $\frac{7}{8}$" bw. 1908. $25.

24
TAFT/SHERMAN $\frac{7}{8}$" bw. 1908. $20.

25
WILSON/MARSHALL "America First-They Have Kept The Faith We'll Stand By Them" $\frac{7}{8}$" bw/rwb. 1916. $35.

26
WILSON/MARSHALL "America First" $\frac{7}{8}$" bw/rwb. 1916. $30.

27
"WILSON/MARSHALL" $1\frac{1}{4}$" bw/blue/gold. 1916. $280.

28
"HUGHES AND FAIRBANKS" $\frac{7}{8}$" gray/white. 1916. $55.

29
"HARDING/COOLIDGE" $\frac{7}{8}$" browntone. 1920. $1500.

30
HARDING/COOLIDGE $\frac{7}{8}$" sepia/cream. 1920. $2000.

31
"COX AND ROOSEVELT" 1$\frac{1}{4}$" bw. 1920. $50,000.

32
"COX AND ROOSEVELT" $\frac{7}{8}$" bw. 1920. $20,000.

33
COX/ROOSEVELT $\frac{7}{8}$" sepia. 1920. $25,000.

34
"VOTE FOR COX AND ROOSEVELT Americanize America" $\frac{7}{8}$" bw. 1920. $40,000.

35
"COOLIDGE/DAWES" 1$\frac{3}{4}$" bw/blue/gold. "1924." $2000.

36
"COOLIDGE AND DAWES" $\frac{7}{8}$" bw. 1924. $240.

37
COOLIDGE/DAWES $\frac{7}{8}$" bw/rwb. 1924. $65.

38
COOLIDGE/DAWES $\frac{7}{8}$" bw. 1924. $40.

39
"DAVIS/BRYAN CLUB St. Joseph, Mo." 1$\frac{1}{2}$" bw. 1924. $6000.

40
"DAVIS AND BRYAN" 1$\frac{1}{4}$" bw. 1924. $9000.

41
"DAVIS AND BRYAN Nebraska" 1$\frac{1}{4}$" bw. 1924. $5000.

42
"LA FOLLETTE/WHEELER" $\frac{7}{8}$" bw. 1924. $400.

43
"HOOVER/CURTIS" 1$\frac{1}{4}$" bw/rwb/gold. 1928. $1950.

44
"HOOVER AND CURTIS" $\frac{7}{8}$" bw. 1928. $145.

45
"HOOVER/CURTIS" $\frac{7}{8}$" bw. 1928. $110.

46
"HOOVER/CURTIS" 1$\frac{1}{2}$" long bw/rwb. 1928. $75.

47
"SMITH/ROBINSON" 1$\frac{1}{4}$" bw/rwb/gold. 1928. $1200.

48
"SMITH/ROBINSON" $\frac{7}{8}$" bw/rwb/gold. 1928. $150.

46

47

48

49

50

51

52

53

54

55

56

57

58

59

60

61

62

63

64

65

49
"ROOSEVELT/GARNER" $\frac{7}{8}$" bw. 1932. $250.

50
"ROOSEVELT/GARNER" 1$\frac{1}{4}$" rwb. 1936. $40.

51
"ROOSEVELT/WALLACE" 1$\frac{1}{4}$" brown/rwb. 1940. $40.

52
"ROOSEVELT/WALLACE" 1" bw/rwb litho. 1940. $20.

53
ROOSEVELT/WALLACE $\frac{7}{8}$" bw litho. 1940. $85.

54
"ROOSEVELT/TRUMAN" 1$\frac{1}{2}$" sepia. 1944. $125.

55
LANDON/KNOX 1$\frac{1}{4}$" bw/rwb. 1936. $85.

56
"LANDON/KNOX/GOP" 1$\frac{1}{4}$" brown/yellow/white. 1936. $35.

57
"LANDON/KNOX/GOP" $\frac{7}{8}$" brown/white/yellow with brass sunflower petal backing. 1936. $25.

58
"LANDON AND KNOX" $\frac{7}{8}$" bw. 1936. $125.

59
"I'M FOR WILLKIE AND McNARY" $\frac{7}{8}$" bw. 1940. $100.

60
WILLKIE/McNARY $\frac{7}{8}$" rwb litho. 1940. $165.

61
"DEWEY/BRICKER" $\frac{3}{4}$" rwb litho. 1944. $40.

62
"DEWEY/BRICKER" 1$\frac{1}{4}$" rwb. 1944. $225.

63
"DEWEY/WARREN" 1$\frac{1}{4}$" bw. 1948. $20.

64
"DEWEY/WARREN" $\frac{7}{8}$" bw. 1948. $30.

65
"TRUMAN/BARKLEY" $\frac{7}{8}$" blue/white. 1948. $200.

66
"EISENHOWER-NIXON" 4" bw. 1952. $75.

67
"IKE AND DICK JUNIOR CLUB" $2\frac{1}{4}$" litho. 1952. $35.

68
"IKE/DICK They're For You" $1\frac{3}{8}$" multicolor litho. 1952. $15.

69
"LET'S BACK IKE & DICK" $1\frac{3}{8}$" rwb litho. 1952. $15.

70
"STEVENSON/SPARKMAN Vote Straight Democratic" 4" rwb. 1952. $300.

71
"STEVENSON/SPARKMAN" $3\frac{1}{2}$" bw/rwb. 1952. $70.

72
STEVENSON/KEFAUVER "Vote Democratic" $3\frac{1}{2}$" bw/rwb. Kefauver with glasses. 1956. $55.

73
STEVENSON/KEFAUVER $3\frac{1}{2}$" bw/rwb. Similar to item #72. Depicts Kefauver without glasses. 1956. $50.

74
STEVENSON/KEFAUVER "Vote Straight Democratic/General Election 1956" 4" rwb. $500.

75
KENNEDY/JOHNSON "For America! For President!!" $3\frac{1}{2}$" bw/rwb. 1960. $150.

76
"KENNEDY & JOHNSON Leaders of Our Country and a Friendly World" $3\frac{1}{2}$" bw/rwb. 1960. $30.

77
"KENNEDY/JOHNSON New Leadership" $1\frac{3}{8}$" bw/rwb. 1960. $20.

78
"NIXON/LODGE" $3\frac{1}{2}$" bw/rwb/gold. 1960. $15.

79
"NIXON-LODGE Experience Counts" $3\frac{1}{2}$" bw/rwb. 1960. $15.

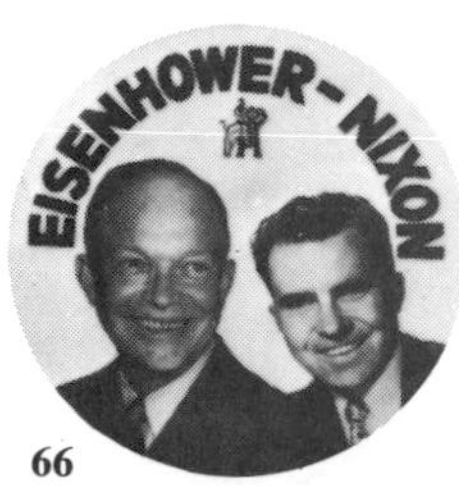

66

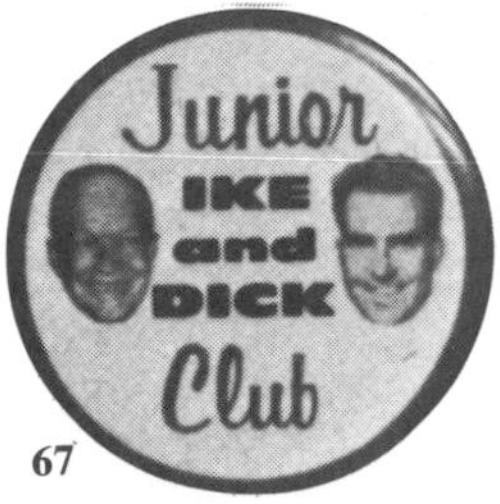

67

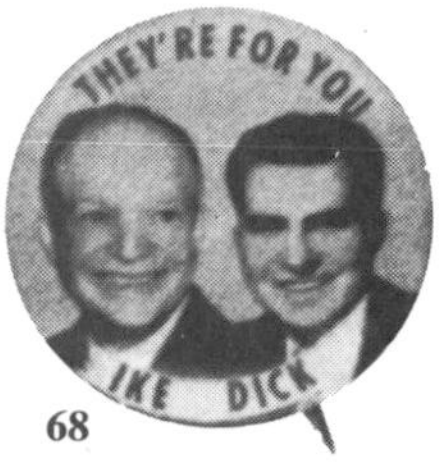

68

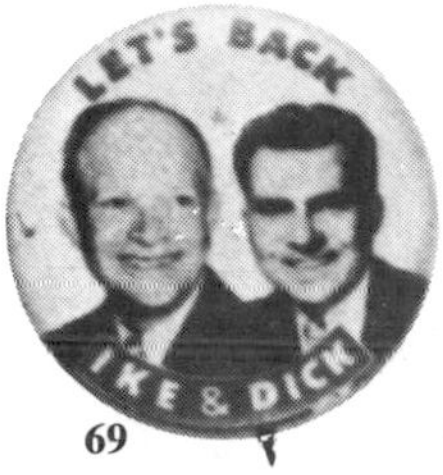

69

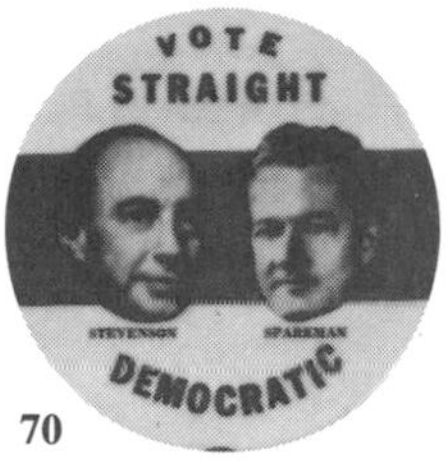

70

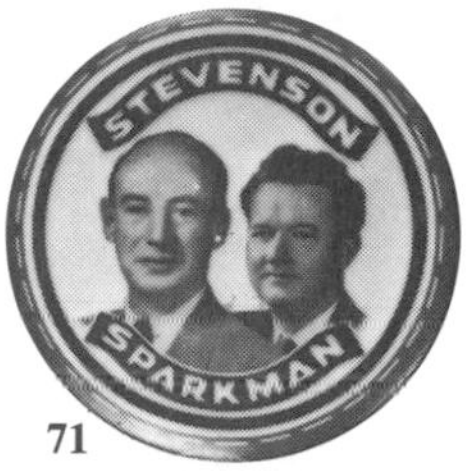

71

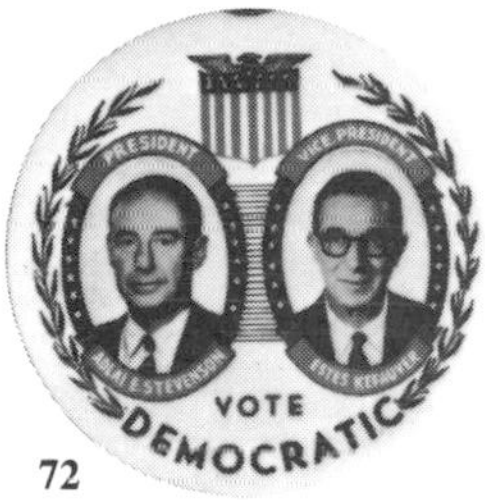

72

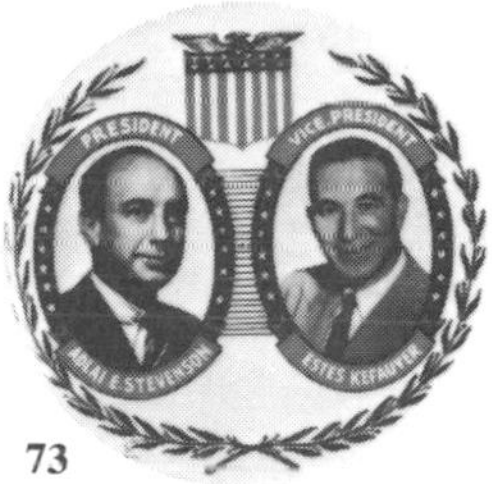

73

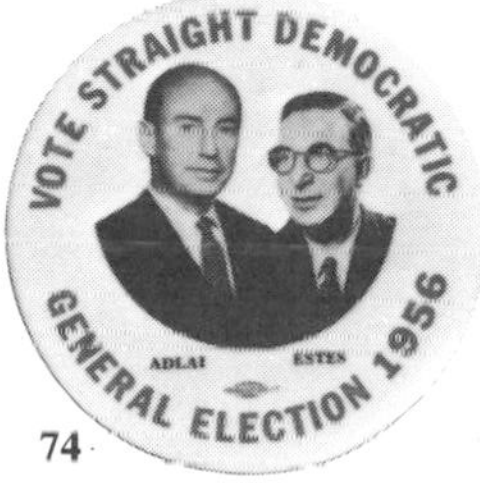

74

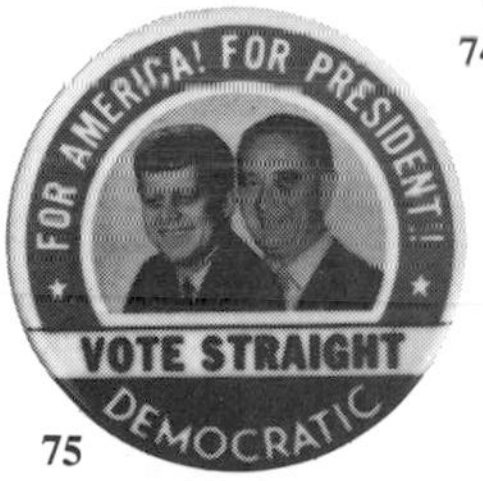

75

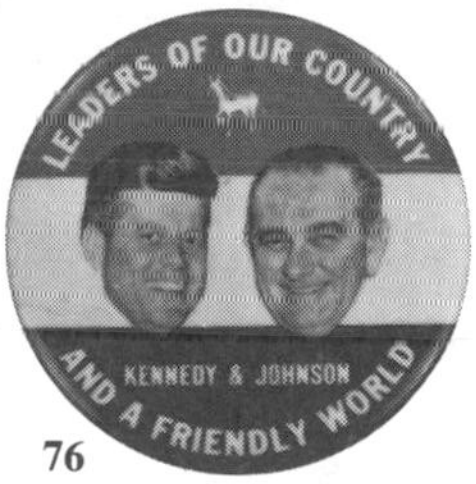

76

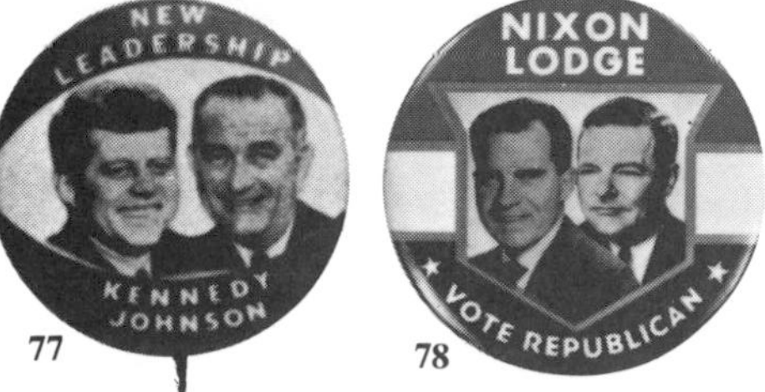

77

78

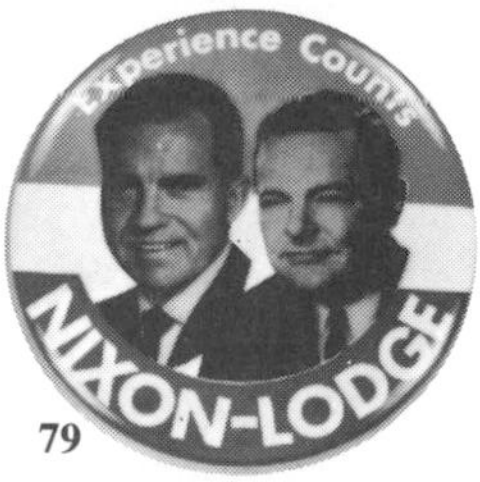

79

80

81

82

83

84

85

86

87

88

89

90

91

92

80
"NIXON/LODGE" $\frac{7}{8}$ " bw/rwb litho. 1960. $8.

81
NIXON/AGNEW New Leadership" 1 $\frac{3}{4}$ " bw/rwb. 1960. $5.

82
"JOHNSON/HUMPHREY 'The Choice Is Clear'" 1 $\frac{1}{2}$ " bw/rwb. 1964. $8.

83
"CITIZENS FOR JOHNSON & HUMPHREY" 1 $\frac{1}{2}$ " bw/rwb. 1964. $6.

84
"GOLDWATER/MILLER The Winning Team" 1 $\frac{3}{8}$ " bw/rwb litho. 1964. $5.

85
GOLDWATER/MILLER "A Choice Not An Echo" 1 $\frac{3}{4}$ " rwb. 1964. $5.

86
"HUMPHREY/MUSKIE" 1 $\frac{3}{4}$ " bw/rwb. 1968. $3.

87
"HUMPHREY/MUSKIE" 1 $\frac{1}{2}$ " bw/rwb. 1968. $5.

88
"WALLACE/LEMAY Stand Up For America" $\frac{7}{8}$ " bw/rwb. "1968." $6.

89
"McGOVERN/SHRIVER" 1 $\frac{1}{2}$ " bluetone/rwb. "1972." $60.

90
"CARTER-MONDALE In '76" 4" multicolor. $6.

91
"CARTER/MONDALE For America's Third Century, Why Not Our Best?" 2 $\frac{1}{4}$ " bw/green litho. 1976. $8.

92
"CARTER-MONDALE In '76" 1 $\frac{3}{4}$ " bw/green. $3.

93
"FORD-DOLE In '76" 4" multicolor. $6.

94
"FORD-DOLE In '76 Victory For The American People" 2$\frac{1}{4}$" bw/rwb. $8.

95
"FORD/DOLE Republican 1976" 1$\frac{3}{4}$" rwb/yellow. $12.

96
"REAGAN-BUSH In '80 The Time Is Now" 1$\frac{3}{4}$" bw/rwb. $5.

97
"RE-ELECT RON AND GEORGE" 2$\frac{1}{4}$" bw/rwb. "1984." $5.

98
"MONDALE-FERRARO America Needs New Leadership" 3$\frac{1}{2}$" bw/rwb. "1984." $5.

99
"MONDALE/FERRARO '84 America Needs New Leadership" 1$\frac{1}{2}$" bw/rwb. $5.

100
"MONDALE/FERRARO" 2$\frac{1}{2}$" multicolor. "1984." $5.

93

94

95

96

97

98

99

100

15. Single Picture Buttons

Second to jugates in popularity among collectors are single picture buttons. Every campaign produces a wider selection of single picture buttons than jugates. Most of the factors that make one jugate more valuable than another also apply to single picture buttons. However, some of the most imaginative designs are found on single picture buttons probably because the button designer was not constrained by the dual portrait format found on jugates. Cartoon images, caricatures of the candidate, interesting design elements, and intense color can combine to push a number of single picture buttons over the $1000 level. Buttons in that price range are by far the exception, however, and single picture buttons for all major party candidates except Cox (1920) and Davis (1920) can be purchased in the price range of $1 to $25. The most common Cox picture button is now around $250 while the most common Davis picture button is about $150. There are still many common and less colorful picture buttons from the McKinley (1896) to Wilson (1916) era available for $25 or less but many single picture buttons $1\frac{1}{4}$" or larger from this "Golden Age" that do have nice color and design are quickly climbing toward the $100 or $200 mark.

1
"McKINLEY" $1\frac{1}{4}$" bw/rwb. 1896. $25.

2
McKINLEY $1\frac{3}{4}$" bw/rwb/gold. 1900. $70.

3
McKINLEY $1\frac{1}{4}$" bw/rwb/gold with rosy tinted cheeks. 1900. $80.

4
BRYAN $1\frac{1}{4}$" bw/rwb/silver. 1900. $25.

5
BRYAN $1\frac{1}{4}$" multicolor. 1908. $105.

6
BRYAN "COMMONER/Guarantee of Bank Deposits" $1\frac{1}{4}$" bw/rwb. 1908. $340.

7
ROOSEVELT "EQUALITY" design representing T.R.'s invitation of Booker T. Washington to the White House. $1\frac{1}{4}$" multicolor. 1904. $4000.

8
ROOSEVELT "STAND PAT" $1\frac{1}{4}$" bw/red. 1904. $325.

9
ROOSEVELT $1\frac{1}{4}$" multicolor. 1904. $110.

10
ROOSEVELT $1\frac{1}{4}$" multicolor. 1904. $75.

11
PARKER $1\frac{1}{4}$" multicolor. 1904. $225.

12
PARKER $1\frac{1}{4}$" multicolor. 1904. $100.

13
TAFT 4" multicolor. 1908. $250.

14
TAFT $1\frac{1}{4}$" bw. 1908. $30.

15
TAFT $1\frac{1}{4}$" bw/rwb/gold. 1908. $50.

16
"COMMERCIAL TRAVELERS FOR TAFT" $1\frac{1}{4}$" bw/tan. 1908. $1000.

17
"WIN WITH WILSON" $1\frac{1}{4}$" multicolor. 1916. $35.

18
WILSON "The Man of the Hour" $1\frac{1}{4}$" bw/blue/yellow. C. 1912. $420.

19
WILSON "He Proved The Pen Mightier Than The Sword" $\frac{7}{8}$" bw/blue. C. 1916. $30

20
"HUGHES" $1\frac{1}{8}$" rwb/brown. One of the first litho buttons. 1916. $145.

21
HUGHES $\frac{7}{8}$" bw. 1916. $30.

22
HARDING $\frac{7}{8}$" browntone. 1920. $12.

23
HARDING $\frac{7}{8}$" browntone photo with blue/white rim. 1920. $15.

24
HARDING $\frac{7}{8}$" browntone photo with red/white rim. 1920. $15.

25
COX $1\frac{1}{4}$" bw. 1920. $250.

26
COX $1\frac{1}{8}$" sepia with brass rim. 1920. $350.

27
"KEEP COOLIDGE" $\frac{7}{8}$" bw. 1924. $25.

28
COOLIDGE $1\frac{3}{4}$" bw/rwb. 1924. $340.

29
COOLIDGE $1\frac{1}{4}$" bw. 1924. $250.

30
DAVIS $\frac{7}{8}$" bw. 1924. $125.

31
DAVIS $\frac{7}{8}$" bw. 1924. $300.

32
DAVIS $\frac{7}{8}$" bw. 1924. $150.

33
HOOVER $1\frac{1}{4}$" bw. 1928. $45.

34
HOOVER $1\frac{1}{4}$" bw. 1928. $45.

35
HOOVER $1\frac{3}{4}$" bw/rwb. C. 1932. $300.

36
SMITH $1\frac{1}{4}$" bw. 1928. $25.

37
SMITH $1\frac{1}{4}$" bw/rwb. 1928. $60.

38
SMITH $1\frac{1}{2}$" bw. 1928. $350.

39
ROOSEVELT $1\frac{3}{4}$" bw/rwb. 1932. $135.

40
ROOSEVELT 9" multicolor/dark green background. C. 1936. $200.

41
ROOSEVELT "LABORS NON-PARTISAN LEAGUE" $1\frac{1}{4}$" bw/rwb. C. 1936. $20.

42
"WE WANT ROOSEVELT" $3\frac{1}{2}$" bw/rwb. C. 1940. $40.

43
"RE-ELECT ROOSEVELT" $1\frac{1}{8}$" blue/white litho. C. 1940. $10.

44
ROOSEVELT "We Are Going To Win This War And Win The Peace That Follows" $1\frac{1}{4}$" rwb. 1944. $30.

45
LANDON 1$\frac{1}{4}$" bw/rwb. 1936. $30.

46
LANDON $\frac{7}{8}$" bw. 1936. $30.

47
LANDON 1$\frac{3}{4}$" brown/white/yellow. 1936. $15.

48
WILLKIE 9$\frac{1}{2}$" bw/rwb. 1940. $300.

49
WILLKIE 1$\frac{3}{4}$" bw/rwb. 1940. $35.

50
WILLKIE 1$\frac{1}{4}$" rwb/brown. 1940. $15.

51
DEWEY 1$\frac{1}{4}$" rwb. C. 1944. $8.

52
DEWEY 1$\frac{1}{4}$" bw/rwb. 1948. $8.

53
DEWEY 1$\frac{3}{4}$" bw. 1948. $12.

54
TRUMAN 1$\frac{3}{4}$" bw. 1948. $35.

55
TRUMAN 3$\frac{1}{2}$" bw/rwb/gold. 1948. $90.

56
TRUMAN 3$\frac{1}{2}$" bw/rwb. 1948. $15.

57
TRUMAN 1$\frac{1}{4}$" bw/rwb. 1948. $25.

58

59

60

61

62

63

64

65

66

67

68

69

70

58
"U.S. FOR IKE" 9" bw/rwb. C. 1952. $85.

59
"PEACE AND PROSPERITY WITH EISENHOWER" $3\frac{1}{2}$" bw/rwb. 1956. $11.

60
EISENHOWER $3\frac{1}{2}$" blue/white. C. 1956. $12.

61
"I LIKE IKE Peace Progress Prosperity" $1\frac{3}{4}$" bw/rwb. C. 1956. $8.

62
"I'M FOR STEVENSON 'How We'd Like Harry'" $2\frac{1}{2}$" bw/reddish-orange shows Truman with lips buttoned shut. 1952. $25.

63
"ALL THE WAY WITH ADLAI" $\frac{7}{8}$" bw/red litho. C. 1952. $12.

64
STEVENSON $1\frac{3}{8}$" bw/red litho. 1956. $10.

65
"ADLAI Best In View" $1\frac{1}{2}$" bw/rwb. 1956. $85.

66
"STEVENSON Our Next President" $1\frac{3}{4}$" bw/rwb. 1952. $8.

67
KENNEDY $3\frac{1}{2}$" bw/rwb. 1960. $15.

68
"YOUTH FOR KENNEDY" 4" bw/rwb litho. 1960. $250.

69
"ON THE RIGHT TRACK WITH JACK" $1\frac{3}{4}$" rwb. 1960. $30.

70
KENNEDY $2\frac{1}{4}$" bw/blue. 1960. $400.

1789–1892 LAPEL DEVICES

"GW/Long Live The President" Washington Inaugural clothing button, 1789. **$2000.** "Harrison & Reform" sulphide brooch, 1840. **$700.** "Harrison & Reform" hand-painted brooch, 1840. **$1000.** "Henry Clay" brass shell medalet, 1844. **$225.** "Abraham Lincoln" ferrotype with Hamlin on reverse, 1860. **$450.** "Abraham Lincoln" ferrotype with Johnson on reverse, 1864. **$1100.** "A. Lincoln, 1864" ferrotype portrait on brass star. **$1000.** "U.S. Grant" ferrotype portrait on brass star, 1868. **$500.** "Grant/Colfax" jugate ferrotype portraits, 1868. **$750.** "Seymour/Blair" jugate ferrotype portraits, 1868. **$750.** Seymour ferrotype with velvet rim, 1868. **$175.** Garfield cardboard photo, 1880. **$200.** Blaine 'plummed knight' brass shell stickpin, 1884. **$200.** "Blaine" brass horseshoe pin, 1884. **$100.** Tilden ferrotype on silvered brass shell, 1876. **$400.** Cleveland cardboard photo on eagle brass shell, 1888. **$125.** Harrison cardboard photo on brass shell, 1888. **$150.** Cleveland cardboard photo on brass shell broom, 1888. **$100.** Cleveland cardboard photo on flag and eagle brass shell, 1888. **$150.** Cleveland/Thurman "A Public Office Is A Public Trust" brass shell rooster stickpin with large cardboard jugate photo, 1888. **$600.** Harrison/Morton jugate cardboard photos on brass shell, 1888. **$250.** Harrison cardboard photo on brass shell broom, 1888. **$100.**

1896–1916 THE GOLDEN AGE OF BUTTONS

McKinley/Roosevelt jugate 1¾″, 1900. **$450.** McKinley/Roosevelt "Commerce and Industries" jugate 1¼″, 1900. **$350.** McKinley "Do You Smoke?" factory/dinner pail, 2″, 1900. **$3000.** Bryan 1¼″, 1908. **$125.** Bryan "16 to 1," 1¼″, 1896. **$100.** McKinley ⅞″, 1900. **$45.** McKinley ⅞″, 1896. **$40.** McKinley 1″, 1896. **$40.** Bryan "No Compromise" ⅞″, 1896. **$35.** "Bryan/Kern" jugate ⅞″, 1908. **$35.** "Nebraska For Bryan" ⅞″, 1908. **$75.** T. Roosevelt "Rough Rider" 1¼″, c. 1900. **$225.** "Roosevelt's Rough Riders Reunion" 1¾″, 1900. **$750.** T. Roosevelt brass mechanical with opening mouth, 1¾″ tall, c. 1900. **$400.** "Theodore Roosevelt For President" 1¼″, 1904. **$1000.** "Roosevelt's Rough Riders Reunion" 1¼″, 1904. **$500.** T. Roosevelt/Fairbanks jugate 1¼″, 1904. **$350.** T. Roosevelt "Welcome" 1¼″, c. 1904. **$2000.** T. Roosevelt "Stand Pat!" 1¼″, 1904. **$325.** Parker/Davis "Shure Mike" jugate 1¼″, 1904. **$700.** "Alton B. Parker/H. G. Davis" jugate 1¼″, 1904. **$200.** "Alton B. Parker" 1¼″, 1904. **$400.** Taft 1¼″, c. 1912. **$200.** Taft 1¼″, 1908. **$85.** Taft 1¼″, 1908. **$85.** Hughes ⅞″, 1916. **$35.** "Wilson" 1¼″, 1912. **$85.** "Win With Wilson" 1¼″, 1916. **$35.**

1920–1944 POST WORLD WAR I THROUGH WORLD WAR II BUTTONS

Harding brass mechanical nose thumber 1¾″ tall, 1920. **$200.** "Warren G. Harding" 1¼″, 1920. **$200.** "For Vice-President Franklin D. Roosevelt" 1¼″, 1920. **$2000.** "Coolidge-Dawes Club/Albany County" jugate 1″, 1924. **$475.** "Hoover" 1″ oval, c. 1928. **$50.** Smith 1¼″, 1928. **$25.** "Our Veldt Rose/Roseveldt" ⅞″, c. 1936. **$750.** Let (FDR)/Freedom Democracy Remain" 1″, 1940. **$75.** "Sweeping The Depression Out" (F.D.R.) 1¼″, c. 1936. **$65.** F. D. Roosevelt with birthstone design 2″, 1936. **$400.** F.D.R./Anti-Landon "We Can't Eat Sunflowers" 2″, 1936. **$700.** "Our President" F.D.R. 1¼″, 1940. **$25.** "Labor's Choice" F.D.R. 1¼″, 1944. **$125.** "Landon On The New Deal" (Anti-F.D.R.) 1¼″, 1936. **$2500.** "Landon/Knox" ⅞″ jugate with brass frame, 1936. **$30.** "Land On Washington" 1¼″, 1936. **$2500.** Willkie/Anti-Eleanor Roosevelt 1⅝″, litho, 1940. **$65.** "Willkie/McNary" litho jugate 1″, 1940. **$150.** "Every 'Buddy' For Willkie" 1″, 1940. **$150.** Willkie porcelain oval 1½″ tall, 1940. **$150.** "Joe (Louis) And I Want Willkie" 1¼″, 1940. **$350.** "Willkie McNary and Chemurgy" 1¼″, 1940. **$400.** "Dewey/Bricker" jugate 1¼″, 1944. **$225.**

POST WORLD WAR II BUTTONS

Truman/Barkley jugate 1¼″, 1948. **$300.** Dewey/Warren jugate 1¼″, 1948. **$35.** Dewey/Anti-Truman 8 Ball 1½″ litho, 1948. **$2600.** Dewey/Anti-Truman 1¾″, 1948. **$1150.** Stevenson/Sparkman jugate 1⅜″ litho, 1952. **$30.** "Eisenhower/Nixon" jugate 1¼″, 1952. **$400.** "My Friend Ike" (brown and white hands) 1⅛″ litho, 1956. **$50.** "For Vice-President" Nixon ⅞″, c. 1952. **$125.** Nixon/Lodge jugate 1⅜″ litho, 1960. **$8.** "All The Way With J.F.K." 1¼″, 1960. **$100.** "LBJ/Let's Back Johnson" 1¼″, 1964. **$8.** "Goldwater/Miller" jugate 1⅛″ litho, 1964. **$5.** "HHH (Humphrey) Fills The Prescription" 1½″, 1968. **$15.** "Nixon/Agnew" jugate 1½″, 1968. **$8.** "McGovern/Eagleton" 1⅛″ litho, one of two known original name button designs issued prior to Eagleton's withdrawal, 1972. **$8.** "McGovern" 1½″, 1972. **$3.** "McGovern/Shriver" jugate 1¾″, 1972. **$3.** "Elect Ford/ Don't Settle For Peanuts" 1¾″, 1976. **$3.** Carter "The Grin Will Win" 1¾″, 1976. **$3.** Carter as Uncle Sam/ peanut man 1⅜″ litho, 1976. **$3.** Reagan "Let's Make America Great Again" 1¾″, 1980. **$3.** "Mondale/Ferraro" 1¾″, 1984. **$3.** "Dukakis/Bentsen" jugate 1¾″, 1988. **$3.** "Bush/Quayle" jugate 2″, 1988. **$5.**

RIBBONS AND RIBBON BADGES

The "100th Anniversary" of Washington's birth, 2 × 9″, 1832. **$200.** "Henry Clay. Pride of America," 3¼ × 8½″, 1844. **$175.** "Grant And Colfax," 2⅜ × 5½″, 1872. **$500.** Blaine/Logan, 2⅝ × 7″, 1884. **$200.** Cleveland/Hendricks with paper photos, 2½ × 6″, 1884. **$100.** Harrison/Morton, 2½ × 7½″, 1888. **$250.** Harrison with celluloid photo, 2¾ × 8½″, 1888. **$150.** "McKinley and Hobart" with celluloid jugate, 2½ × 9½″, 1896. **$150.** McKinley "Our Standard" 2½ × 6½″ with brass hanger bar, 1896. **$300.** T. Roosevelt "He's Good Enough For Me. . ." 3 × 9½″, 1904. **$200.**

FIGURAL POLITICAL COLLECTIBLES

Jimmy Carter 'peanut' battery operated AM plastic radio, 7½″ tall, c. late 1970s. **$50.** "Win With Barry" Goldwater boxed plastic doll with litho "Barry" button by Remco, 6″ tall, 1964. **$40.** "F.D.R. The Man Of The Hour" animated white metal wind-up clock by United Electric Clock Corp., 4 × 9 × 14″ tall, 1933. **$150.** Johnson/Humphrey metal figures by "Heritage Pewter," 3½″ tall, 1964. **$25.** "Nixon For President" bobbing head elephant with bag of chocolate 'coin' candy, 7¾″ tall, 1960. **$50.** McKinley "Protection To American Industry" papier mâché parade horn, 2 × 9½ × 14″ long, 1896. **$500.** Truman painted white metal figure with matchbox holder, 2¼ × 4 × 6″ tall, 1948. **$300.** "Land-on Roosevelt 1936" anti-F.D.R. painted cast iron bank, 2½ × 3 × 5″ long, 1936. **$450.** Taft glazed china pitcher, 5″ tall, 1908. **$125.** Franklin D. Roosevelt painted plaster bookend, 3 × 4 × 8¼″ tall, c. 1930s. **$160.** "Dewey" painted white metal figure, 7″ tall, c. 1948. **$150.** "JFK" in rocking chair glazed china salt and pepper sets, 2 × ¾″ tall, c. 1962. **$35.**

NINETEENTH CENTURY CAMPAIGN ITEMS

"Full Dinner Pail" glass miniature with wire and wood handle and tin cup, 4½" tall, 1896. **$400.** "The Full Dinner Pail" actual lunch pail with slogan in stenciled letters, 5½ × 8¼ × 8" tall, 1896. **$400.** Bryan cane with white metal head, 34" long, 1896. **$150.** Benjamin Harrison cane with white metal head, 34" long, c. 1888-1892. **$200.** McKinley cane with white metal head, 34" long, 1896. **$150.** Cleveland and Thurman cotton bandana, 21½ × 24½", 1888. **$250.** Political parade torch, 3½" diameter × 6" tall on 4' pole, c. 1880s. **$100.** McKinley

glazed china plate, 8", c. 1896. **$50.** Cleveland glazed china plate, 8", 1884. **$55.** McKinley "An Honest Dollar" brass shell badge with extensive text on back label, 5" diameter, 1896. **$125.** Abraham Lincoln cardboard photo in brass frame ¾ × 1" on original card 2⅜ × 4", 1864. **$300.** McKinley brass gold bug for parade horse's saddle blanket, 5½" long, 1896. **$150.**

TWENTIETH CENTURY CAMPAIGN ITEMS

Willkie-McNary campaign fund raiser window card, 10½ × 13½″, 1940. **$50.** Theodore Roosevelt lithographed tin serving tray, 13½ × 16½″, 1904. **$400.** "Vote Truman For President" celluloid pin back and easel back button, 9″, 1948. **$2000.** "Gerald R. Ford For President/76" cane with alum. handle, 35″, 1976. **$25.** "Calvin Coolidge" paper label on 8½″ cigar, 1924. **$75.** "Jimmy Carter 1976 For President" cane with painted metal peanut-shaped handle, 33″ shaft. **$25.** "Alton B. Parker" lithographed tin tray "Spokane, Wash." 13½ × 16½″, 1904. **$500.** Bryan-Taft who will win fan, 7¾ × 14″ tall, 1908. **$75.** T. Roosevelt "The Bull Moose Song" sheet music, 10½ × 13½″, 1912. **$40.** "Keep Cool with Coolidge" sheet music, 9 × 12″, 1924. **$40.** "Franklin D. Roosevelt" English "Ivorex" wall plaque, 4 × 5″, c. 1940. **$100.** Willkie fabric wall banner, 9 × 12″, 1940. **$25.** Taft/Sherman lithographed tin plate, Republican presidents, 9½″, 1908. **$250.** F.D.R. hard rubber head, rocks when chin is pushed, reverse "Going To Run 3rd Term/Just Tap My Chin." Of course he nods "yes." 2½ × 3½ × 2″ deep, 1940. **$100.**

71
"NIXON IN NOVEMBER" 6" bw/rwb. 1960. $75.

72
"KEEP DICK ON THE JOB" 3 1/2" bw/rwb. 1960. $60.

73
"NIXON MAN OF STEEL" 3 1/2" bw/rwb. 1960. $125.

74
"NIXON'S THE ONE!" 3 1/2" bw/rwb. 1968. $5.

75
"NIXON'S THE ONE" cartoon of Nixon leading Humphrey and Wallace in a race. 1 1/2" bw/rwb. 1968. $35.

76
"LET'S BACK JOHNSON IN '64" 1 1/4" bw/rwb. $7.

77
"WIN WITH JOHNSON" 1 3/4" bw/rwb. 1964. $6.

78
GOLDWATER 9" bw/gold. 1964. $100.

79
"I'M A TEENAGER FOR BARRY" 3 1/2" bw/red/yellow. 1964. $35.

80
"YAF BACKS BARRY" 3 1/2" bw/red. 1964. $25.

81
GOLDWATER "AuH2O 1964" 3 1/2" bw/yellow. $10.

82
HUMPHREY 1 1/2" bw/rwb. 1968. $3.

83
"WALLACE School Bus" 1 1/2" bw/blue/orange. 1968. $8.

84
WALLACE 1 3/8" bw/rwb litho. 1968. $4

85
"ROBIN McGOVERN" 4" bw/green. 1972. $60.

71

72

73

74

75

76

77

78

79

80

81

82

83

84

85

86
"McGOVERN" $1\frac{3}{4}$ " bw. 1972. $5.

87
"'MY NAME IS JIMMY CARTER AND I'M RUNNING FOR PRESIDENT'" $1\frac{3}{4}$ " bw/green. 1976. $2.

88
"THE COMING OF CARTER" $2\frac{1}{4}$ " multicolor. 1976. $8.

89
"PRESIDENT FORD '76" $1\frac{3}{4}$ " bw/blue. $4.

90
FORD $1\frac{3}{4}$ " bw/rwb. "1976." $6.

91
"REAGAN Hot-Lites" $3\frac{1}{2}$ " full color battery operated button with blinking lights. 1984. $10.

92
REAGAN "FRITZ BUSTERS" $2\frac{1}{4}$ " bw/red. 1984. $3.

93
MONDALE $2\frac{1}{4}$ " multicolor. 1984. $4.

94
FERRARO "America's First Woman Vice-Pres." $3\frac{1}{2}$ " bw/rwb. 1984. $4.

16. Coattail Buttons

Political items picturing or naming a candidate for a high office in combination with one or more candidates for lower offices are known as coattail items. In the case of presidential campaign buttons, the presidential candidate is often paired with his party's candidate for the U.S. Senate or governorship of a particular state. Two portraits would make the button a *jugate coattail*. Occasionally, some combination of national and state candidates will result in three portraits on one button in which case the button would be known as a *trigate coattail*. Because coattail buttons are meant to be distributed in a limited geographic area, they are generally produced in limited numbers and are often scarce. Coattail buttons appeal to many collectors and are of special interest to collectors who specialize in buttons related to a particular state.

1
"McKINLEY/TANNER" $\frac{7}{8}$" bw/rwb. 1896. $35.

2
"McKINLEY/TANNER" $\frac{7}{8}$" bw/rwb. "Illinois 1896." $35.

3
"McKINLEY AND SCOFIELD" $\frac{7}{8}$" bw/rwb. 1896. $40.

4
"WM. McKINLEY/R.M. LA FOLLETTE" 1$\frac{1}{4}$" bw/rwb. 1900. $250.

5
"McKINLEY/ROOSEVELT/BLISS" 1$\frac{1}{4}$" sepia. 1900. $120.

6
"ROOSEVELT/MEAD" 1$\frac{1}{4}$" bw/rwb. 1904. $140.

7
"ROOSEVELT/FAIRBANKS/CASSELL Republicans Must Elect A President And Control Congress" 1$\frac{1}{4}$" bw. 1904. $1[illegible]

8
"TAFT AND JACOBSON" $\frac{7}{8}$" bw. 1908. $40.

9
"PRESIDENT WILSON/SENATOR REED Vote For Champions Of 8 Hour Law" 1" bw. 1916. $140.

10
HUGHES/FAIRBANKS and two other candidates. "Good Luck Good Times Vote Republican Ticket" 1" bw/green. 1916. $250.

11
"HUGHES/WILLIS/HERRICK" Ohio trigate $\frac{7}{8}$" bw. 1916. $48.

12
"COOLIDGE/FULLER/GILLETTE" $\frac{7}{8}$" bw. 1924. $50.

13
COOLIDGE/DAVIS $\frac{7}{8}$" bw. 1924. $45.

14
"COOLIDGE/WEEKS" $\frac{7}{8}$" bw. 1926 Vermont governor's campaign. $300.

15
"DAVIS/SMITH" $\frac{7}{8}$" blue/white. 1924. $225.

1

2

3

4

5

6

7

8

9

10

11

12

13

14

15

16
"HOOVER/ALLEN/YOUNG" $\frac{7}{8}$" bw/rwb/silver. 1928. $65.

17
"HOOVER-COOPER" $\frac{3}{4}$" bw litho. 1928. $25.

18
"HOOVER/SMALL" $\frac{3}{4}$" rwb litho. 1932. $20.

19
"SMITH/WAGNER" $\frac{7}{8}$" blue/white. 1928. $30.

20
"ECONOMIC SECURITY/ROOSEVELT/CURLEY" 2 $\frac{1}{4}$" bw/rwb. 1932. $350.

21
"WORK AND WAGES/ROOSEVELT/CURLEY" 2 $\frac{1}{4}$" bw/rwb. 1932. $300.

22
"ROOSEVELT/BLOOD Economic Security" 1" bw/red. 1932. $300.

23
ROOSEVELT/LAUSCHE 2 $\frac{1}{4}$" bw. 1944. $750.

24
ROOSEVELT/McALISTER 1" bw. 1932. $200.

25
"ROOSEVELT AND SHOLTZ" $\frac{7}{8}$" rwb. 1932. $60.

26
"GARNER/ROOSEVELT/STARK" $\frac{7}{8}$" blue/white. 1936. $15.

27
"FOR CONGRESS HONEYMAN WITH ROOSEVELT" $\frac{3}{4}$" blue/white litho. C. 1936. $14.

28
"ROOSEVELT-LEHMAN American Labor Party" $\frac{3}{4}$" blue/white litho. C. 1936. $10.

29
"CLARK/ROOSEVELT/PARK" 1" blue/white. C. 1936. $16.

30
"CLARK/ROOSEVELT/WILSON" 1" blue/white. C. 1936. $16.

31
"ROOSEVELT/DAVEY" $\frac{3}{4}$" rwb litho. C. 1936. $5.

32
"MINTON/ROOSEVELT/SCHRICKER" $\frac{7}{8}$" rwb. C. 1940. $2.

33
"ROOSEVELT/CROMWELL" $\frac{7}{8}$" rwb. 1940. $18.

34
"NEELY/ROOSEVELT/KILGORE" 1" white/blue. 1940. $10.

35
"VOTE/HARRIMAN/ROOSEVELT/CIO" $\frac{7}{8}$" blue and white litho. C. 1944. $12.

36
"LANDON/HAIGIS/KNOX" 1$\frac{1}{4}$" blue/white/yellow. 1936. $65.

33

34

35

36

37
"LANDON/WHITE/BARROWS Elect All Three" $\frac{7}{8}$" rwb. 1936. $14.

38
"MEMBER LANDON LEGORE CLUB" $\frac{7}{8}$" yellow/brown. 1936. $18.

39
"ELECT BOTH/LANDON/DOUTRICH" $\frac{7}{8}$" rwb. 1936. $14.

40
"LANDON AND BARBOUR" $\frac{7}{8}$" rwb. 1936. $18.

37

38

39

40

41
"WILLKIE/VANDERBILT" 1" rwb. 1940. $125.

42
"WILLKIE/BREWSTER/SEWALL" $\frac{7}{8}$" blue/white. 1940. $10.

43
"DEWEY/DAWSON/BRICKER" $\frac{3}{4}$" rwb litho. 1944. $4.

41

42

43

44
"DEWEY/CREIGHTON/WARREN" 1$\frac{1}{4}$" rwb. 1948. $9.

45
"IKE FOR PRESIDENT/BUTLER FOR SENATOR" 1$\frac{1}{8}$" brown/white. C. 1952. $15.

46
"I LIKE IKE AND CLYDE" 1$\frac{1}{8}$" rwb litho. C. 1952. $12.

44

45

46

47
"LET'S BACK IKE/McCUSKER FOR CONGRESS" 1" rwb litho. 1954. $15.

48
"IKE/MORTON COOPER/ROBSION" 1" red/white litho. C. 1952. $12.

49
"IKE AND PIKE" $\frac{7}{8}$" rwb. C. 1952. $7.

50
"IKE/BEARDSLEY/NIXON" $\frac{3}{4}$" rwb litho. 1952. $5.

47

48

49

50

51

52

53

54

55

56

57

58

59

60

61

62

63

64

51
"STEVENSON/MARLAND/KILGORE" 1 1/8" rwb litho. 1952. $12.

52
"STEVENSON/WILLIAMS/MOODY Vote Democratic" 7/8" green/white litho. 1952. $8.

53
KENNEDY/VANDEN HEUVEL 1 3/4" bw/rwb. 1960. $155.

54
"SWAINSON/KENNEDY/ McNAMARA" 7/8" rwb litho. 1960. $15.

55
"KENNEDY PRESIDENT/ HARRINGTON CONGRESS" 7/8" red/ white litho. 1960. $30.

56
"JOHNSON/BERMAN" 1 1/2" bw/rwb. 1964. $25.

57
"LBJ & BERMAN" 1" dark blue on white litho tab. 1964. $10.

58
"JOHNSON/KERNER A Winning Team" 1 1/2" rwb litho. 1964. $6.

59
"BIG 3/JOHNSON/KERNER/ KIMBALL" 1 3/4" long red/white litho tab. 1964. $18.

60
"JOHNSON/HUMPHREY-KENNEDY" 3 1/2" rwb. 1964. $20.

61
"JOHNSON WANTS KENNEDY" 3 1/2" bw/rwb. 1964. $25.

62
"LBJ FOR THE USA Tydings/Sickles/ Hanson" 1 3/4" rwb litho. 1964. $12.

63
"NEW YORK STUDENTS FOR JOHNSON/HUMPHREY/KENNEDY IN '64" 1 3/4" rwb. 1964. $50.

64
"JOHNSON/HUMPHREY/KENNEDY." Same as item #63 except color is white/ blue/orange. $30.

65
"I'M ON THE JOHNSON, HUMPHREY, KENNEDY TEAM" $1\frac{3}{4}$" blue/white. 1964. \$15.

66
"JOHNSON/KENNEDY" $1\frac{1}{4}$" blue/white. 1964. \$15.

67
"JOHNSON/KENNEDY" $1\frac{1}{8}$" rwb litho. 1964. \$8.

68
"GOLDWATER/MILLER/SCOTT" $2\frac{1}{2}$" bw/blue. 1964. \$50.

69
"NIXON-AGNEW-FARGHER" $1\frac{1}{2}$" bw/rwb. 1968. \$6.

70
"NIXON/HUDNUT" $2\frac{1}{4}$" rwb. 1972. \$5.

71
"HUMPHREY/MUSKIE/CLARK" $1\frac{3}{4}$" rwb. 1968. \$15.

72
"CARTER/MOYNIHAN/SCHEUER" $1\frac{3}{4}$" green/white. 1976. \$10.

73
"CARTER/MONDALE/MOYNIHAN" $1\frac{3}{4}$" rwb. 1976. \$3.

74
"CARTER/METCALFE" $1\frac{3}{4}$" purple/white/orange. 1976. \$4.

75

76

77

78

79

80

81

82

75
"CARTER/MOYNIHAN/NOLAN/AYLWARD/VAN BUREN" $1\frac{3}{4}$" blue/white. 1976. $10.

76
"CARTER/MONDALE/HARTKE/CONRAD" cloverleaf $2\frac{1}{8}$" bw/green. 1980. $15.

77
"REAGAN & O'NEAL 'Play In Peoria'" $2\frac{1}{4}$" bw/yellow/brown. 1980. $15.

78
REAGAN/LOUSMA $2\frac{1}{4}$" bw/blue. 1984. $18.

79
"REAGAN/WELDON" $2\frac{1}{4}$" rwb. 1984. $6.

80
"REAGAN/WELDON" $1\frac{3}{4}$" rwb. 1984. $3.

81
"MONDALE/FERRARO/JAY ROCKEFELLER/CLYDE SEE" $2\frac{1}{2}$" bw/blue/gold. "1984." $5.

82
"MONDALE/FERRARO/WOLPE/LEVIN Be Emphatic Vote Straight Democratic" $2\frac{1}{4}$" rwb. 1984. $20.

17. Name Buttons

Name buttons may feature the presidential candidate's first name, nickname, last name, initials, or perhaps the last names of both the presidential and vice-presidential candidates. Name buttons may include one or two words such as "Vote" or "For President." There may also be some simple design element such as stars and stripes or a colored area in the shape of a specific state. Name buttons from the early twentieth century are actually rather uncommon, although not very valuable, because pictures were so preferred. The introduction of the litho button in 1920 made the style popular and today this is the style most often produced first and used as free hand-outs by the candidate. Many name buttons sell for $1 to $3 and even pre-1920 examples seldom exceed $15. Like picture buttons, examples for Cox and Davis are scarcer. The standard Cox name button sells around $35 while a Davis name button is usually $75 or more. Many candidates named Davis ran for office. A few that just say Davis really are for John W. Davis, but the majority are for local candidates. If the button says "For President," "Davis and Bryan," or "Davis/Smith" (Al Smith running for New York governor) the button is certainly referring to John W. Davis.

1
McKINLEY $\frac{7}{8}$" bw. Issued by High Admiral Cigarettes. 1896. $20.

2
BRYAN $\frac{5}{8}$" blue/white. 1908. $50.

3
ROOSEVELT "For President" (rose) "Velt" 1$\frac{1}{4}$" multicolor. 1904. $260.

4
ROOSEVELT. (rose) "VELT" 1$\frac{1}{4}$" multicolor. 1904. $248.

5
ROOSEVELT $\frac{5}{8}$" rwb. 1904. $15.

6
ROOSEVELT $\frac{3}{4}$" white/blue. "1912." $20.

7
ROOSEVELT 1$\frac{1}{4}$" blue/white/yellow. 1912. $55.

8
PARKER/DAVIS 1$\frac{1}{4}$" rwb. 1904. $85.

9
TAFT $\frac{7}{8}$" rwb. 1908. $10.

10
TAFT $\frac{3}{4}$" red/white. 1908. $12.

11
WILSON $\frac{7}{8}$" white/maroon. C. 1912. $10.

12
WILSON $\frac{7}{8}$" rwb. C. 1916. $15.

13
HUGHES/FAIRBANKS $\frac{7}{8}$" rwb. 1916. $30.

14
HUGHES $\frac{7}{8}$" rwb 1916. $75.

15
HUGHES $\frac{7}{8}$" rwb. 1916. $10.

16
HARDING/COOLIDGE $\frac{7}{8}$" rwb litho. 1920. $8.

1

2

3

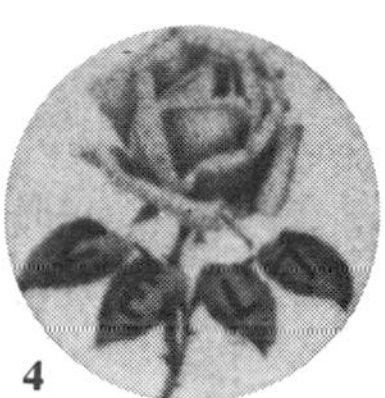
4

5

6

7

8

9

10

11

12

13

14

15

16

17

18

19

20

21

22

23

24

25

26

27

28

29

30

31

32

33

34

35

17
HARDING/COOLIDGE $\frac{3}{4}$" rwb litho. 1920. $8.

18
HARDING $\frac{3}{4}$" rwb. 1920. $40.

19
COX/ROOSEVELT $\frac{3}{4}$" rwb. 1920. $65.

20
COX/ROOSEVELT $\frac{5}{8}$" rwb. 1920. $65.

21
COX $\frac{1}{2}$" red/white litho. 1920. $50.

22
COOLIDGE/DAWES $\frac{7}{8}$" rwb. 1924. $15.

23
COOLIDGE/DAWES $\frac{7}{8}$" rwb. 1924. $45.

24
DAVIS/BRYAN $\frac{3}{4}$" rwb litho. 1924. $75.

25
HOOVER 1" rwb. 1928. $60.

26
HOOVER/CURTIS $\frac{3}{4}$" blue/white litho. 1928. $10.

27
SMITH 1" rwb. 1928. $45.

28
SMITH/ROBINSON $\frac{7}{8}$" rwb. 1928. $12.

29
ROOSEVELT 1$\frac{1}{4}$" rwb. C. 1940. $40.

30
ROOSEVELT. (rose) "Velt" 1" pink/white/green. 1936. $125.

31
ROOSEVELT/GARNER $\frac{7}{8}$" gold/blue. 1936. $20.

32
ROOSEVELT/WALLACE $\frac{3}{4}$" rwb litho. 1940. $10.

33
ROOSEVELT/TRUMAN 1" rwb litho. 1944. $45.

34
LANDON $\frac{7}{8}$" rwb. 1936. $15.

35
LANDON/KNOX 1$\frac{1}{4}$" brown/yellow with diecut felt sunflower petal back. 1936. $15.

36
LANDON $1\frac{1}{4}$" brown/yellow with diecut felt sunflower petal back. 1936. $30.

37
LANDON $1\frac{1}{4}$" brown/yellow. 1936. $25.

38
WILLKIE/McNARY $1\frac{1}{4}$" brown/yellow. 1940. $8.

39
WILLKIE. "WILL" (key) $1\frac{1}{4}$" blue/white. 1940. $15.

40
WILLKIE 1" long rwb. 1940. $6.

41
DEWEY/BRICKER $2\frac{1}{8}$" white/blue. 1944. $10.

42
DEWEY/WARREN $1\frac{1}{8}$" rwb litho. 1948. $10.

43
TRUMAN/BARKLEY $\frac{3}{4}$" rwb litho. 1948. $15.

44
TRUMAN/BARKLEY $\frac{7}{8}$" rwb litho. 1948. $25.

45
TRUMAN $\frac{7}{8}$" rwb litho. 1948. $15.

46
TRUMAN 2" brown/gold. 1948. $175.

36

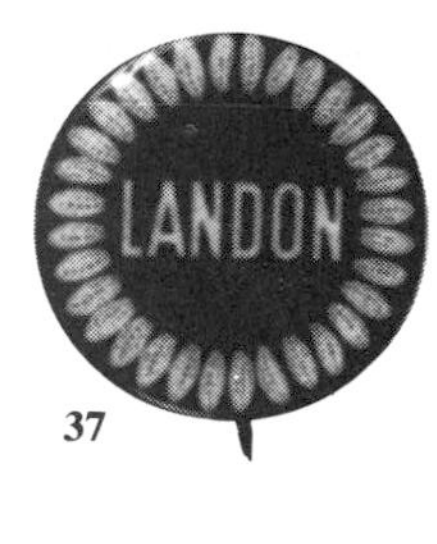

37

38

39

40

41

42

43

44

45

46

47

48

49

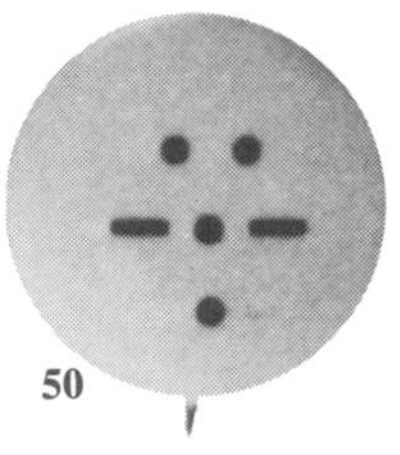
50

51

52

53

54

55

56

57

58

59

60

47
EISENHOWER 1 $\frac{1}{4}$ " red/gold/blue from a set of 48 different state buttons. 1952. $25.

48
EISENHOWER 1 $\frac{1}{4}$ " blue/white. 1952. $15.

49
EISENHOWER 1 $\frac{1}{2}$ " rwb/pink. C. 1956. $100.

50
EISENHOWER 1 $\frac{1}{4}$ " blue/white Morse Code for "Ike." 1956. $20.

51
STEVENSON 1 $\frac{1}{2}$ " red/white issued by "ADA" (Americans for Democratic Action). C. 1956. $20.

52
STEVENSON/KEFAUVER $\frac{7}{8}$ " white/blue litho. 1956. $3.

53
KENNEDY/JOHNSON 2 $\frac{3}{4}$ " long rwb. 1960. $25.

54
KENNEDY 1 $\frac{1}{4}$ " blue/white. 1960. $25.

55
NIXON 1 $\frac{1}{4}$ " blue/white. 1960. $5.

56
JOHNSON 2 $\frac{1}{4}$ " rwb. 1964. $5.

57
GOLDWATER/MILLER 1 $\frac{1}{4}$ " rwb. 1964. $3.

58
GOLDWATER 1 $\frac{1}{4}$ " rwb. 1964. $2.

59
GOLDWATER 1 $\frac{1}{4}$ " black/gold (chemical symbols for gold and water). 1964. $15.

60
GOLDWATER (anti-L.B.J. reference to political scandal) 1 $\frac{1}{2}$ " rwb. 1964. $10.

61
NIXON 2" rwb. C. 1972. $5.

62
NIXON 1 $\frac{3}{4}$ " blue/white. 1968. $15.

63
NIXON/AGNEW 2" rwb litho. 1968. $4.

64
NIXON 1 $\frac{3}{4}$ " rwb litho from Illinois. 1968. $7.

65
HUMPHREY 1 $\frac{1}{2}$ " rwb litho. 1968. $2.

66
HUMPHREY/MUSKIE 1 $\frac{1}{2}$ " rwb. "1968." $2.

67
HUMPREY 1 $\frac{3}{4}$ " orange/black. 1968. $4.

68
McGOVERN/EAGLETON 1 $\frac{3}{8}$ " white/blue litho. One of the four or five items actually in circulation before Eagleton left the ticket. 1972. $8.

69
McGOVERN 1 $\frac{1}{2}$ " rwb. 1972. $3.

70
McGOVERN/SHRIVER 1 $\frac{3}{4}$ " white/blue. 1972. $3.

71
McGOVERN (anti-Nixon) 1 $\frac{1}{4}$ " black/green. 1972. $3.

72
CARTER/MONDALE 1 $\frac{1}{4}$ " green/white. 1976. $3.

61 62 63 64 65 66 67 68 69 70 71 72

73

74

75

76

77

78

79

80

81

82

73
CARTER $1\frac{3}{4}$" rwb litho. 1976. $2.

74
CARTER $1\frac{3}{4}$" bw/green. "1980." $3.

75
FORD/DOLE $1\frac{3}{4}$" blue/white. 1976. $4.

76
FORD/DOLE $1\frac{3}{4}$" rwb from Texas. 1976. $5.

77
FORD $1\frac{3}{4}$" white/blue from Illinois. 1976. $6.

78
FORD $1\frac{3}{4}$" rwb. 1976. $8.

79
REAGAN $1\frac{1}{2}$" rwb litho from Wisconsin. 1980. $3.

80
REAGAN $1\frac{3}{4}$" black/yellow. C. 1980. $4.

81
MONDALE/FERRARO $1\frac{3}{4}$" blue/white litho with yellow lightning bolt. 1984. $8.

82
FERRARO $1\frac{1}{2}$" white/blue. 1984. $5.

18. Slogan Buttons

Every political campaign hopes to develop a catchy slogan to grab the attention of the electorate. Probably the best known slogan is the classically concise phrase "I Like Ike" from 1952. Other slogans abound (see Appendix III) and many appear on buttons. Various types of slogan button exist. Some refer to campaign issues, some signify the support of a state, county, city or other geographical region, and some signify the support of a specific group such as a labor union, ethnic group, or a myriad of other organizational possiblities. A primary factor in recent times that stimulated issuance of geographical and organizational slogan buttons was the legislation enacted in 1974 that placed monetary limits on campaign spending. National committees devote most of that money to the mass media and paying for campaign buttons became a low priority. In 1976, at the local level, however, demand for buttons was intense. The void was filled with an incredible variety of buttons issued by regional and issue-oriented organizations. Many of these special interest groups are known as Political Action Committees (PACs) of which the largest number are labor unions. The trend that began in 1976 carried through 1988, giving collectors lots of items to collect and presenting challenges as many of these buttons were issued in limited numbers.

1
McKINLEY $1\frac{1}{4}$" bw. 1896. $35.

2
BRYAN $1\frac{1}{4}$" bw. 1896. $60.

3
McKINLEY $1\frac{1}{4}$" multicolor. 1900. $70.

4
McKINLEY/ROOSEVELT $1\frac{1}{4}$" bw/red. 1900. $210.

5
ROOSEVELT $1\frac{1}{4}$" rwb. 1912. $200.

6
ROOSEVELT $\frac{7}{8}$" bw. 1912. $140.

7
ROOSEVELT $\frac{7}{8}$" red/white. 1912. $20.

8
TAFT $\frac{7}{8}$" rwb. 1908. $15.

9
WILSON $\frac{7}{8}$" blue/white. 1912. $15.

10
WILSON $\frac{7}{8}$" rwb. C. 1916. $20.

11
WILSON $\frac{5}{8}$" blue/white. C. 1916. $20.

12
HUGHES $\frac{7}{8}$" blue/white. 1916. $55.

13
HARDING $3\frac{1}{2}$" rwb. 1920. $500.

14
HARDING $\frac{5}{8}$" rwb. 1920. $20.

15
COX $\frac{5}{8}$" blue/white. 1920. $40.

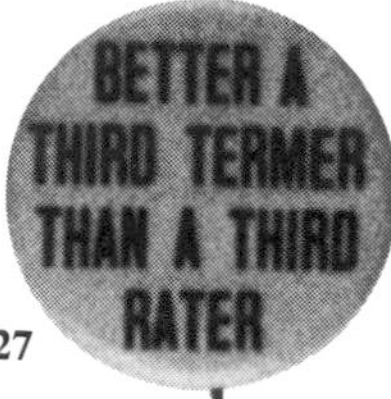

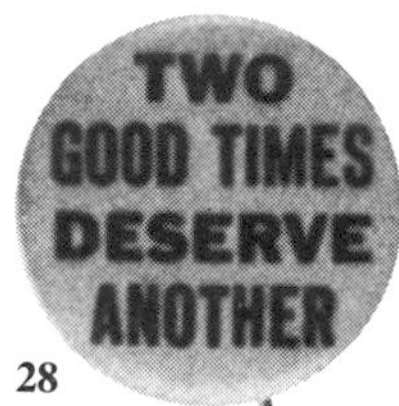

16
COOLIDGE $\frac{7}{8}$" blue/white. 1924. $30.

17
COOLIDGE $\frac{3}{4}$" rwb. 1924. $20.

18
HOOVER 1 $\frac{1}{4}$" blue/white. C. 1932. $40.

19
HOOVER $\frac{7}{8}$" rwb. 1928. $20.

20
HOOVER $\frac{7}{8}$" blue/white. 1928. $20.

21
SMITH $\frac{7}{8}$" blue/white. 1928. $250.

22
SMITH $\frac{7}{8}$" red/white litho. 1928. $50.

23
SMITH $\frac{7}{8}$" green/white. 1928. $50.

24
ROOSEVELT 1" rwb. 1932. $55.

25
ROOSEVELT $\frac{7}{8}$" rwb. 1936. $12.

26
ROOSEVELT $\frac{3}{4}$" rwb litho. 1936. $10.

27
ROOSEVELT 1 $\frac{1}{4}$" blue/white. 1940. $8.

28
ROOSEVELT 1 $\frac{1}{4}$" blue/white. 1940. $8.

29
LANDON $\frac{7}{8}$" white/brown/yellow. 1936. $40.

30
LANDON/KNOX $\frac{7}{8}$" white/blue/yellow. 1936. $20.

31
WILLKIE 1 $\frac{3}{4}$" blue/white. 1940. $35.

32
WILLKIE 1 $\frac{1}{4}$" blue/white. 1940. $6.

33
WILLKIE 1 $\frac{1}{4}$" red/white. 1940. $6.

34
WILLKIE $1\frac{1}{4}$" bw. 1940. $25.

35
WILLKIE $1\frac{1}{4}$" bw. 1940. $12.

36
DEWEY $1\frac{1}{4}$" blue/white. C. 1944. $15.

37
DEWEY $1\frac{1}{4}$" blue/white. C. 1948. $25.

38
DEWEY $1\frac{1}{4}$" rwb. C. 1948. $25.

39
TRUMAN $1\frac{1}{4}$" red/white. 1948. $25.

40
TRUMAN $1\frac{1}{4}$" blue/white. 1948. $25.

41
TRUMAN $\frac{7}{8}$" blue/white. 1948. $180.

42
EISENHOWER $1\frac{1}{4}$" rwb. 1952. $10.

43
EISENHOWER $1\frac{1}{2}$" rwb. 1956. $175.

44
EISENHOWER $1\frac{1}{2}$" rwb/gray. 1956. $25.

45
EISENHOWER $1\frac{1}{4}$" blue/yellow. 1952. $12.

46
STEVENSON 6" rwb. 1956. $100.

47
STEVENSON $1\frac{3}{4}$" blue/white. 1952. $25.

48
STEVENSON $1\frac{1}{4}$" blue/white. 1952. $12.

34

35

36

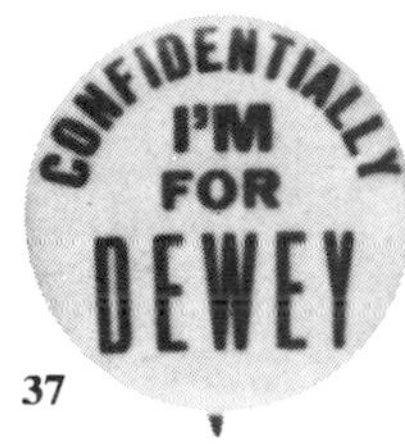

37

38

39

40

41

42

43

44

45

46

47

48

49

50

51

52

53

54

55

56

57

58

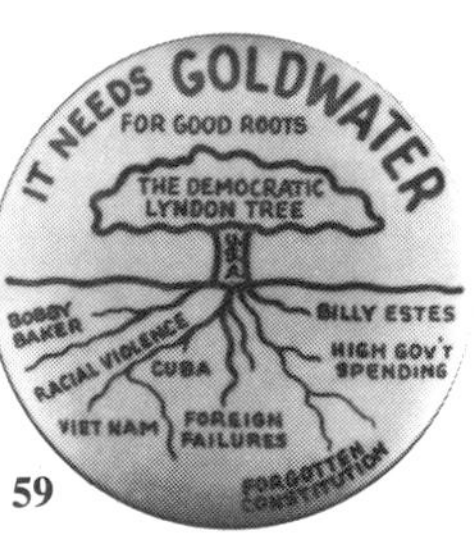

59

60

61

62

49
KENNEDY 1 $\frac{3}{4}$" rwb. 1960. $150.

50
KENNEDY 1 $\frac{3}{8}$" blue/white litho. 1960. $25.

51
NIXON 4" rwb. 1960. $200.

52
NIXON 1 $\frac{3}{4}$" green/white litho. 1960. $12.

53
NIXON $\frac{7}{8}$" rwb litho. 1960. $5.

54
JOHNSON 1 $\frac{3}{4}$" rwb litho. 1964. $12.

55
JOHNSON 1 $\frac{3}{4}$" rwb litho. 1964. $12.

56
JOHNSON 1 $\frac{3}{4}$" orange/black. 1964. $10.

57
JOHNSON 1 $\frac{1}{2}$" black/yellow (chemical symbols for urinate on Goldwater). 1964. $60.

58
GOLDWATER/MILLER 1 $\frac{3}{4}$" rwb. 1964. $20.

59
GOLDWATER 3 $\frac{1}{2}$" black/gold. 1964. $100.

60
GOLDWATER 1 $\frac{1}{2}$" red/white. 1964. $10.

61
NIXON 1 $\frac{1}{8}$" red/yellow litho. 1968. $2.

62
NIXON 1 $\frac{3}{4}$" rwb. 1968. $8.

63
HUMPHREY 3 $\frac{1}{2}$" bw/green with plastic flashing eyes. 1968. $50.

64
HUMPHREY/MUSKIE 2 $\frac{1}{8}$" rwb. 1968. $15.

65
HUMPHREY 1 $\frac{3}{4}$" black/orange. 1968. $8.

66
McGOVERN 1 $\frac{3}{4}$" rwb. 1972. $3.

67
McGOVERN 1 $\frac{3}{4}$" rwb. 1972. $3.

68
McGOVERN 3" bw/red flasher button. 1972. $4.

69
McGOVERN 3 $\frac{1}{2}$" bw. 1972. $15.

70
CARTER 2 $\frac{1}{2}$" rwb/black. 1976 refers to *Playboy* magazine interview. EACH $2.

63

64

65

66

67

68

"Those who have had a chance for four years and could not produce peace, should not be given another chance."
Richard Nixon
October 9th, 1968

69

70

71

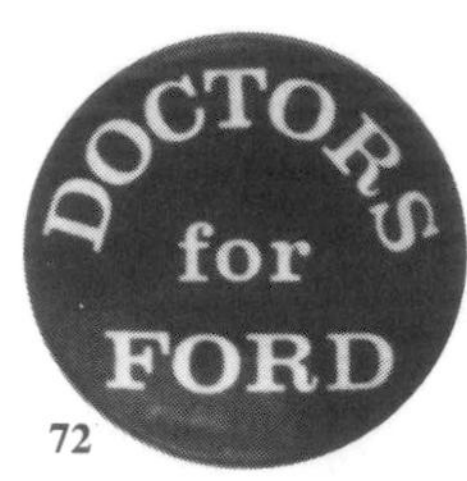

72

73

74

75

76

77

78

79

71
CARTER 1 $\frac{3}{4}$ " bw/green. 1976. $6.

72
FORD 1 $\frac{3}{8}$ " white/red litho. 1976. $2.

73
FORD 1 $\frac{3}{8}$ " bw/red litho. 1976. $2.

74
REAGAN 1 $\frac{3}{4}$ " blue/white. 1980. $8.

75
REAGAN 1 $\frac{1}{8}$ " rwb litho. 1980. $7.

76
REAGAN 1 $\frac{3}{4}$ " white/red. 1984. $5.

77
REAGAN 1 $\frac{3}{4}$ " white/blue. 1984. $5.

78
MONDALE/FERRARO 1 $\frac{1}{2}$ " multicolor. 1984. $5.

79
DUKAKIS 2 $\frac{1}{4}$ " rwb. 1988. $5.

19. Specific Event Buttons

It is almost a sure thing that a button issued for a specific single day event was produced in a relatively small quantity. Inauguration buttons, covered in the following section, are the major exception. The older a single day button is, the greater the chance that it is actually a rarity. Buttons dated for events occuring during the campaign are the most highly valued. After a president assumes office, buttons are occasionally issued for specific events, most often visits to some locality outside Washington. These buttons are also highly regarded and older issues can be quite valuable.

1
"McKINLEY St. Louis, June 18, 1896." $\frac{7}{8}$ " bw lapel stud from National Convention. $50.

2
"McKINLEY & PROSPERITY Oct. 9, 1896." $\frac{3}{4}$ " multicolor lapel stud. $30.

3
"McKINLEY/ATLANTA PEACE JUBILEE" 1 $\frac{3}{4}$ " bw/rwb from Dec. 14-15, 1898. $125.

4
"TEDDY'S TERRORS" 1 $\frac{3}{4}$ " bw/green from Los Angeles Rough Riders convention. C. early 1900s. $450.

5
ROOSEVELT "At Concord State Fair" 1 $\frac{1}{4}$ " bw/yellow. 1902. $175.

6
ROOSEVELT "Presidential Roundup Nov. 8, 1904." 1 $\frac{1}{4}$ " multicolor. $200.

7
ROOSEVELT "Georgia Day, Jamestown" Exposition. 2 $\frac{1}{4}$ " multicolor. 1907. $500.

8
"W. H. TAFT Notification Day July 28-'08/Cincinnati." 1 $\frac{1}{4}$ " rwb/gold. $120.

9
TAFT "At Spokane Sept. 28, 1909." 1 $\frac{1}{4}$ " bw/red/green. $120.

10
"WESLEYAN TAFT DAY Middletown/ Nov. 12, '09." 1 $\frac{1}{4}$ " multicolor. $50.

11
TAFT AND WILHELM II JUGATE. "6th Annual German Day, Aug. 8, 1910-Compliments of the Du Bois Art Studio/ Utica, N.Y." 1 $\frac{1}{2}$ " brown/white with colorful tinting. $200.

12
"TAFT The Gunnison Tunnel Opening/ Montrose, Colo." 1 $\frac{1}{2}$ " tall multicolor. C. 1910. $300.

1 2 3 4 5 6 7 8 9 10 11 12

13
"PRESIDENT HARDING'S PACIFIC COAST TOUR" $1\frac{1}{4}$" rwb with sepia photo. 1923. $400.

14
"HOMETOWN COOLIDGE CLUB PLYMOUTH VERMONT" $\frac{7}{8}$" bw/rwb/green. 1924. $225.

15
"HOOVER'S 80th BIRTHDAY-AUG. 10, 1954." $1\frac{3}{4}$" red/white. $30.

16
SMITH $1\frac{1}{4}$" bw with fabric ribbons reading "Sept. 2, 1928/Al Smith Day." $300.

17
F.D.R. "New Deal In Penna./Nov. 6, 1934." $\frac{7}{8}$" bw/rwb/gold. $20.

18
"DEWEY DAY" $\frac{5}{8}$" red/white. C. 1944. $20.

19
TRUMAN/CHURCHILL. "Westminister College/Fulton, Mo. 1946" 2" white/blue/orange. $300.

20
EISENHOWER. "Ike For President In 1964/Of The United States Golf Assn." $2\frac{1}{4}$" rwb. $30.

21
"WE WANT PAT TOO" $1\frac{1}{4}$" bw/rwb with "Pat Nixon Day" 9/1/1960 ribbon. $25.

22
GOLDWATER. "Prescott, Arizona Welcomes Barry/Sept. 3-1964." $15.

23
GOLDWATER. "I Sponsored a G-11 Tea Party" $1\frac{1}{2}$ " black/gold. 1964. $350.

24
FORD. "Colorado Welcomes V.P. Gerald Ford/April 5, 1974" $1\frac{3}{4}$ " bw/rwb. $15.

25
CARTER. "Welcome President Jimmy Carter/March 16-17, 1977/Clinton, Mass." $1\frac{3}{4}$ " green/white. $5.

26
MONDALE. $1\frac{3}{4}$ " blue/gray/white. 1977. $5.

27
"WELCOME GOV. REAGAN/CEDAR RAPIDS, IA." $1\frac{3}{4}$ " bw/blue. 1979. $5.

28
REAGAN 3" yellow/red/black for "June 3 Primary." 1980. $5.

29
"ABC NEWS/REAGAN IN EUROPE" $2\frac{1}{8}$ " rwb/black. 1985. $10.

30
"MONDALE/FERRARO" 2" white/blue. "New York Victory Night." 1984. $5.

22 23

24

25

26

27

28

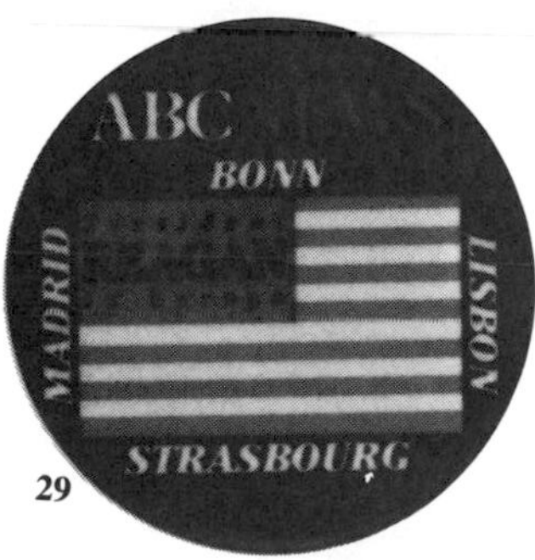

29

30

20. *Inauguration Badges & Buttons*

For many years, presidential inaugurations inspired souvenir objects to commemorate the event (see Section 13). Surprisingly, the introduction of buttons in 1896 did not immediately produce many inauguration buttons as the ribbon badge (see Section 31) was the larger and more favored souvenir. A few buttons are known for Taft, Wilson, Coolidge, Hoover, Franklin Roosevelt, and Truman. Beginning with Eisenhower, inauguration buttons became more common, mostly in the $3\frac{1}{2}$" size; and by the time of Johnson's inauguration in 1964 many varieties were being produced for sale by vendors to the large public audience attending the parade and ceremonies. Most items from 1964 to 1988 can be acquired for modest prices.

1
McKINLEY $1\frac{3}{4}$" double-sided celluloid with hanger bar (missing fabric ribbon). 1897. $125.

2
ROOSEVELT $3\frac{1}{2}$" sepia button with rwb ribbon hanger. March 4, 1905. $150.

3
ROOSEVELT $3\frac{1}{2}$" sepia with rwb ribbon. March 4, 1905. $150.

4
WILSON $1\frac{1}{4}$" bw/rwb/gold. March 4, 1913. $200.

5
WILSON $1\frac{1}{4}$" bw. 1917. $150.

6
WILSON $2\frac{1}{4}$" tall brass badge. March 4, 1913. $40.

7
HARDING brass portrait set in silvered brass badge with rwb ribbon. 1920. $125.

8
COOLIDGE $1\frac{1}{4}$" blue/yellow/tan with rwb shield. March 4, 1925. $400.

9
HOOVER brass/red enamel keystone with fabric ribbon and "Pennsylvania" brass bar. March 1929. $125.

10
HOOVER $1\frac{1}{4}$" bw/rwb. 1929. $55.

11
ROOSEVELT $2\frac{1}{8}$" bw/rwb with rwb ribbon and brass bar. March 4, 1933. $400.

12
ROOSEVELT $1\frac{3}{4}$" bw/rwb button with $5\frac{1}{2}$" ribbon. January 20, 1937. $100.

13
ROOSEVELT $1\frac{1}{4}$" bw. January 20, 1941. $30.

14
ROOSEVELT $1\frac{1}{4}$" bw. January 20, 1941. $60.

15
ROOSEVELT/WALLACE 3" tall silvered brass District of Columbia Metropolitan Police badge. 1941. $350.

16
TRUMAN/BARKLEY $2\frac{1}{4}$" rwb jugate with purple ribbon. January, 1949. $500.

17
TRUMAN 2x$6\frac{1}{2}$" fabric and metal badge with $1\frac{3}{4}$" gold-colored metal pendant. January 20, 1949. $150

8 9 10 11 12 16 13 15 14 17

18

19

20

21

22

23

24

25

26

27

28

18
TRUMAN brass hanger with pink ribbon with gold lettering. January 20, 1949. $50.

19
TRUMAN/BARKLEY jugate $1\frac{3}{4}$" rwb/gold. 1949. $450.

20
TRUMAN $1\frac{1}{2}$ x2 $\frac{3}{4}$" with brass hanger and rwb ribbon with $1\frac{1}{8}$" brass medalet picturing Truman. 1949. $50.

21
TRUMAN $1\frac{3}{4}$" bw. January 20, 1949. $25.

22
TRUMAN $1\frac{3}{4}$" bw with rwb rim. January 20, 1949. $20.

23
TRUMAN $1\frac{1}{4}$" bw with rwb rim. January 20, 1949. $80.

24
TRUMAN $2\frac{1}{8}$" blue/white. January 20, 1949. $180.

25
EISENHOWER/NIXON 3" jugate in rwb/gold with purple ribbon and brass hanger. January 20, 1953. $150.

26
EISENHOWER $1\frac{3}{4}$" bw/rwb button with brass medalet and 5" white/red ribbon. January 20, 1953. $20.

27
EISENHOWER $2\frac{1}{4}$ x2 $\frac{1}{2}$" bw flasher button with ribbon. 1953. $12.

28
EISENHOWER 4" rwb button with blue/white ribbon. 1953. $50.

29
EISENHOWER $1\frac{3}{4}$ " bw button with 4" blue ribbon with gold lettering. January 20, 1957. $30.

30
KENNEDY $1\frac{3}{4}$ " bw/gold button with blue/gold ribbon. January 20, 1961. $50.

31
KENNEDY 6" multicolor with rwb rim. 1961. $30.

32
KENNEDY/JOHNSON $1\frac{3}{4}$ " bw/rwb. 1961. $30.

33
KENNEDY $1\frac{3}{4}$ " rwb/gold. January 20, 1961. $12.

34
KENNEDY $1\frac{3}{4}$ " bw. January 20, 1961. $30.

35
JOHNSON $3\frac{1}{2}$ " rwb/bw with blue/white ribbon. January 20, 1965. $15.

36
JOHNSON/HUMPHREY $3\frac{1}{2}$ " bw/rwb. 1965. $20.

37
JOHNSON $1\frac{5}{8}$ " bw litho with blue/ white ribbon and gold plastic donkey. January 20, 1965. $15.

38
NIXON 2" rwb with gold ribbon and blue lettering. January 20, 1969. $20.

39
CARTER $1\frac{3}{4}$ " rwb/yellow. January 20, 1977. $3.

40
REAGAN $2\frac{1}{2}$" multicolor. January 20, 1981. $5.

21. Third Party Buttons

While the Democratic and Republican parties have dominated the political scene since 1856, a large number of other groups with diverse philosophies fielded candidates as part of the democratic process. Some collectors ignore these "also rans" while others specialize in a particular party or all the third party items they can find. Because of limited budgets, many older third party buttons are scarce. Third parties with the longest histories of issuing buttons are the Prohibition, Socialist, and Communist Parties. Third parties that made an impact on the outcome of an election, or at least won electoral votes, include Theodore Roosevelt's Progressive Party (1912), Robert La Follette's Progressive Party (1924), Strom Thurmond's States' Rights Party (1948), and George Wallace's American Independent Party (1968). Of all the third party candidates, Eugene Debs, the four-time Socialist candidate, is the top favorite among collectors and even the most common single picture buttons exceed \$100. Prior to 1968, the vast majority of third party buttons were actually paid for and distributed by the various parties. Beginning in 1968, some third party buttons have been produced by individuals or button manufacturers to meet collector demand for buttons. While made during the campaign, since these buttons were not authorized third party issues, some collectors choose to avoid these buttons.

1
JAMES WEAVER People's Party. 1892. $\frac{3}{4}$ " bw lapel stud. \$150.

2
JOSEPH SIBLEY Silver Party. 1896. $1\frac{1}{4}$ " bw/rwb. \$60.

3
WHARTON BARKER People's Party. 1900. $1\frac{1}{4}$ " bw. \$250.

4
JOHN WOOLEY/HENRY METCALF Prohibition. 1900. $1\frac{1}{4}$ " bw/rwb. \$200.

5
EUGENE DEBS/BENJAMIN HANFORD Socialist Party. 1904. $1\frac{1}{4}$ " multicolor. \$550.

6
EUGENE DEBS Socialist Party. 1904. $\frac{7}{8}$ " bw/red. \$150.

7
SILAS SWALLOW/GEORGE CARROLL Prohibition Party. 1904. $1\frac{1}{4}$ " sepia. \$250.

8
SILAS SWALLOW Prohibition Party. 1904. $\frac{7}{8}$ " bw/rwb/gold. \$75.

9
EUGENE CHAFIN/AARON WATKINS Prohibition Party. 1908. $\frac{7}{8}$ " bw. \$40.

10
EUGENE DEBS/BENJAMIN HANFORD Socialist Party. 1908. $1\frac{1}{4}$ " bw/red/green. \$300.

11
EUGENE CHAFIN/AARON WATKINS Prohibition. 1912. $\frac{7}{8}$ " bw/blue. \$60.

12
EUGENE DEBS/EMIL SEIDEL Socialist Party. 1912. $\frac{7}{8}$ " bw/red. \$175.

13
EUGENE DEBS/EMIL SEIDEL Socialist Party. 1912. $\frac{7}{8}$ " sepia. \$500.

14
JAMES HANLEY/IRA LANDRITH Prohibition. 1916. $\frac{7}{8}$ " bw/rwb. \$50.

15
ALLAN BENSON/GEORGE KIRKPATRICK Socialist Party. 1916. $\frac{7}{8}$" bw/rwb. $100.

16
EUGENE DEBS Socialist Party. In prisoner clothing. "For President Convict No. 9653." 1920. 1" bw/red. $1500.

17
ROBERT LA FOLLETTE Progressive Party. 1924. $\frac{7}{8}$" bw. $35.

18
ROBERT LA FOLLETTE/BURTON WHEELER Progressive Party. 1924. $\frac{3}{4}$" rwb litho. $15.

19
WILLIAM FOSTER/JAMES FORD Communist. 1932. 1" bw/red litho. $210.

20
WILLIAM LEMKE/THOMAS O'BRIEN Union Party. 1936. $\frac{3}{4}$" blue/white litho. $35.

21
EARL BROWDER/JAMES FORD Communist Party. 1936. $\frac{7}{8}$" bw/red litho. $60.

22
BROWDER/FORD Communist Party. 1940. 1" bw/red litho. $35.

23
NORMAN THOMAS/MAYNARD KRUEGER Socialist Party. 1940. 1" bw/red. $40.

24
HENRY WALLACE Progressive Party. 1948. $2\frac{1}{4}$" blue/white. $60.

25
HENRY WALLACE Progressive Party. 1948. $1\frac{1}{4}$" bw. $20.

26
HENRY WALLACE Progressive Party. 1948. $1\frac{1}{4}$" blue/white. $10.

27
HENRY WALLACE/GLEN TAYLOR Progressive. 1948. $1\frac{1}{8}$" blue/white litho. $15.

28
HENRY WALLACE Progressive Party. 1948. $\frac{7}{8}$" blue/white. $100.

29
STROM THURMAN/FIELDING WRIGHT States' Rights Democratic Party. 1948. $\frac{7}{8}$" rwb litho. $15.

30
THOMAS ANDREWS/THOMAS WERDEL States' Rights Party. 1956. $1\frac{1}{2}$" rwb. $35.

15

16

17

18

19

20

21

22

23

24

25

26

27

28

29

30

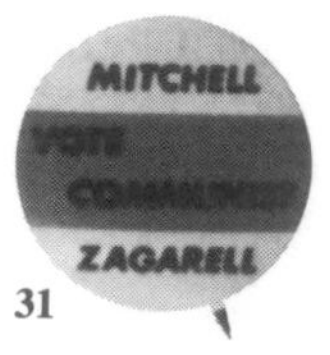

31

32

33

34

35

36

37

38

39

31
CHARLENE MITCHELL/MICHAEL ZAGARELL Communist Party. 1968. $\frac{7}{8}$" bw/red litho. $4.

32
DICK GREGORY/BENJAMIN SPOCK Peace and Freedom Party issued prior to party name change and selection of V.P. candidate (see next item). 1968. $1\frac{1}{4}$" red/blue. $25.

33
DICK GREGORY/MARK LANE Freedom & Peace Party. 1968. $1\frac{1}{4}$" bw/red. $5.

34
FRED HALSTEAD Socialist Workers Party. 1968. $1\frac{3}{4}$" bw/green. $6.

35
PAUL BOUTELLE (for V.P.) Socialist Workers Party. 1968. $1\frac{3}{4}$" bw/pink. $4.

36
HENNING BLOMEN/GEORGE TAYLOR Socialist Labor Party. 1968. $1\frac{1}{2}$" bw/red. $12.

37
YOUTH INTERNATIONAL PARTY (YIPPIES). No official candidates. Group leaders were Abbey Hoffman/Jerry Rubin. 1972. 2" black/blue/orange. $15.

38
JOHN SCHMITZ American Independent Party. 1972. $1\frac{3}{4}$" bw/rwb. $4.

39
JOHN SCHMITZ American Independent Party. 1972. $1\frac{3}{4}$" rwb. $5.

40
LINDA JENNESS/ANDREW PULLEY Socialist Workers Party. 1972. $1\frac{1}{2}$" bw/green. $5.

41
LINDA JENNESS Socialist Workers Party. 1972. $1\frac{1}{2}$" bw/green. $5.

42
ANDREW PULLEY (for V.P.) Socialist Workers Party. 1972. $1\frac{1}{2}$" bw/blue. $5.

43
GUS HALL/JARVIS TYNER Communist Party. 1972. 3" bw/red/yellow. $8.

44
BENJAMIN BUBAR/EARL DODGE Prohibition Party. 1976. $2\frac{1}{4}$" bw/rwb litho. $10.

45
GUS HALL/JARVIS TYNER Communist Party. 1976. $2\frac{1}{4}$" bw/red. $5.

46
FRANK ZEIDLER/J. QUINN BRISBEN Socialist Party. 1976. $2\frac{1}{4}$" rwb litho. $5.

47
PETER CAMEJO Socialist Workers Party. 1976. $1\frac{3}{4}$" bw/orange. $5.

48
WILLIE MAE REID (for V.P.) Socialist Workers Party. 1976. $1\frac{3}{4}$" bw/orange. $5

40

41

42

43

44

45

46

47

48

49

50

51

52

53

54

55

56

57

49
LYNDON LAROUCHE U. S. Labor Party. 1976. $1\frac{1}{2}$" blue/white litho. $5.

50
BARRY COMMONER Citizen Party. 1980. $1\frac{3}{4}$" rwb. $15.

51
JOHN ANDERSON/PATRICK LUCEY National Unity Campaign. 1980. $1\frac{3}{4}$" bw/rwb. $15.

52
"ANDERSON." National Unity Campaign. $2\frac{1}{4}$" rwb. 1980. $12.

53
JOHN ANDERSON National Unity Campaign. $1\frac{1}{4}$" blue/white. 1980. $10.

54
EDWARD CLARK/DAVID KOCH Libertarian Party. 1980. $1\frac{3}{4}$" bw/green. $25.

55
SONIA JOHNSON/RICHARD WALTON Citizens Party. 1984. $1\frac{3}{4}$" white/green. $10.

56
LYNDON LAROUCHE Independent Party. 1984. 2" blue/white. $5.

57
GUS HALL/ANGELA DAVIS Communist Party. 1984. 2" long bw/red. $10.

22. *Hopeful Buttons*

Prior to the balloting at national conventions, all the potential candidates are known as hopefuls or favorite sons. Some may actually have a chance of being nominated, others would need a miracle; but one and all alike may have buttons promoting his nomination. After the balloting, the losers generally become historical footnotes unless they land the vice-presidential position, achieve the nomination in future years, or, having once been nominated for president, become a hopeful at a future convention. Any of these circumstances would make that candidate's buttons more sought after than most other hopeful buttons. Not many collectors specialize in hopefuls so prices tend to be quite reasonable but it is a fascinating area and buttons exist for such well-known personalities as William Randolph Hearst, Huey Long, Henry Ford, and, more recently, Nelson Rockefeller, Eugene McCarthy, Robert and Ted Kennedy, and Jesse Jackson.

1
WILLIAM B. ALLISON. 1896. $1\frac{3}{4}$" bw celluloid on rwb ribbon hanger. $100.

2
MATTHEW QUAY. 1896. 3x$5\frac{1}{2}$" with 2" sepia on bw hanger with rwb ribbon. $20.

3
HORACE BOIES. 1896. $1\frac{1}{4}$" bw. $30.

4
LEVI P. MORTON. 1896. $\frac{7}{8}$" bw lapel stud. $20.

5
THOMAS REED. 1896. $\frac{7}{8}$" bw lapel stud. $40.

6
CHAMP CLARK. 1912. $\frac{7}{8}$" bw. $38.

7
CHAMP CLARK "They Gotta Quit Kickin' My Dawg Aroun'." 1912. $\frac{7}{8}$" red/white. $30.

8
HIRAM JOHNSON. 1920. $\frac{5}{8}$" bw/rwb. $20.

9
HIRAM JOHNSON. 1920. $\frac{7}{8}$" rwb. $12.

10
CHARLES CURTIS. 1928. $1\frac{1}{4}$" bw. $30.

11
JOHN GARNER. 1932. $\frac{7}{8}$" bw. $15.

12
JOHN GARNER. 1932. $\frac{3}{8}$" bw litho. $15.

13
JOHN GARNER. 1932. $\frac{7}{8}$" blue/white litho. $10.

14
HAROLD STASSEN. C. 1948. $1\frac{3}{4}$" rwb/yellow. $9.

1 2 3 4 5 6 7 8 9 10 11 12 13 14

15

16

17

18

19

20

21

22

23

24

25

15
ROBERT TAFT. C. 1948. $1\frac{1}{4}$" bw. $25.

16
ROBERT TAFT (anti-Taft button). C. 1948. $1\frac{1}{2}$" rwb litho. $7.

17
ROBERT A. TAFT. C. 1952. $1\frac{3}{4}$" brown/white. $15.

18
EARL WARREN. 1948. 6" blue/orange. $25.

19
DOUGLAS MacARTHUR. 1948. $1\frac{1}{4}$" bw/rwb. $10.

20
DOUGLAS MacARTHUR. 1948. 1" rwb. $10.

21
ALBAN BARKLEY. 1952. 3" rwb. $8.

22
AVERELL HARRIMAN. 1952. 4" bw. $15.

23
ESTES KEFAUVER. 1952. 3" black/orange. $10.

24
ROBERT KERR. 1952. $2\frac{1}{2}$" brown/white. $15.

25
AVERELL HARRIMAN. C. 1956. $2\frac{1}{4}$" blue/white litho. $15.

26
STUART SYMINGTON. 1956. $3\frac{1}{2}$" rwb. $8.

27
MARGARET CHASE SMITH. 1964. $1\frac{3}{4}$" blue/pink. $12.

28
NELSON ROCKEFELLER. 1964. $1\frac{1}{4}$" rwb. $5.

29
EUGENE McCARTHY. 1968. $1\frac{3}{4}$" bw/rwb. $15.

30
EUGENE McCARTHY. 1968. $1\frac{1}{4}$" bw/rwb. $15.

31
EUGENE McCARTHY. 1968. $1\frac{1}{8}$" bw litho. $8.

32
EUGENE McCARTHY. 1968. $1\frac{3}{8}$" blue/white litho. $4.

33
ROBERT KENNEDY. 1968. 4" bw/red/yellow. $30.

34
ROBERT KENNEDY. 1968. $3\frac{1}{2}$" bw/rwb. $25.

35
ROBERT F. KENNEDY. 1968. $1\frac{3}{4}$" bw/rwb. $25.

36
ROBERT F. KENNEDY. 1968. $1\frac{3}{4}$" bw/rwb. $18.

37
ROBERT KENNEDY. 1968. $1\frac{1}{2}$" blue/white. $20.

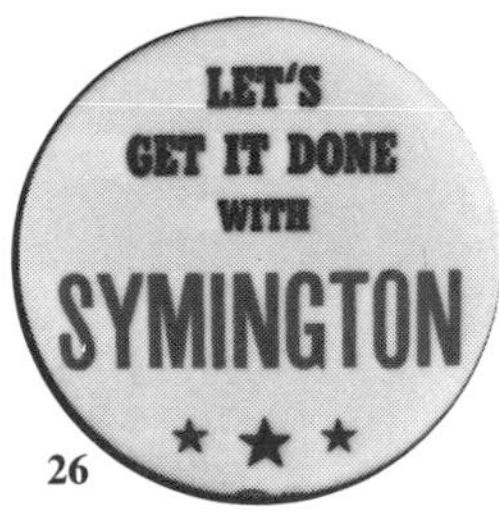

26

27

28

29

30

31

32

33

34

35

36

37

38

39

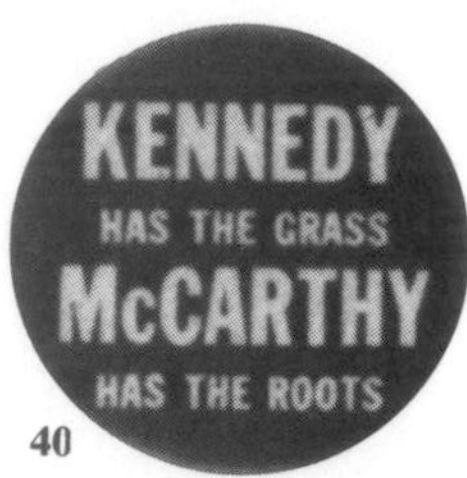

40

41

42

43

44

45

46

47

48

49

38
ROBERT KENNEDY. 1968. $1\frac{3}{8}$" blue/white litho. $20.

39
ROBERT KENNEDY. 1968. $1\frac{1}{2}$" blue/white. $20.

40
ROBERT KENNEDY (anti)/EUGENE McCARTHY. 1968. $1\frac{1}{2}$" white/green. $25.

41
ROBERT F. KENNEDY. 1968. $1\frac{1}{4}$" rwb. $8.

42
ROBERT KENNEDY. 1968. $1\frac{1}{2}$" blue/white. $8.

43
NELSON ROCKEFELLER. 1968. $1\frac{1}{2}$" bw/yellow. $12.

44
GEORGE ROMNEY. 1968. $1\frac{3}{4}$" rwb. $4.

45
MARK HATFIELD. 1968. $1\frac{3}{4}$" bw/red. $8.

46
EDWARD KENNEDY. 1972. $1\frac{3}{4}$" blue/white/gold. $10.

47
SHIRLEY CHISHOLM. 1972. $1\frac{3}{4}$" bw/red. $20.

48
EDMUND MUSKIE. 1972. $3\frac{1}{2}$" bw/green. $8.

49
HENRY JACKSON. 1976. $1\frac{3}{4}$" bw. $12.

50
LLOYD BENTSEN. 1976. $1\frac{1}{2}$" bw/rwb. $6.

51
LLOYD BENTSEN. 1976. $1\frac{1}{8}$" rwb litho. $6.

52
MORRIS UDALL. 1976. $1\frac{1}{2}$" bw/rwb. $3.

53
JERRY BROWN. 1976. $1\frac{3}{4}$" pink/red. $5.

54
NELSON ROCKEFELLER. 1976. $1\frac{1}{2}$" rwb. $8.

55
EDWARD KENNEDY. 1980. $1\frac{3}{4}$" bw/red. $3.

56
EDWARD KENNEDY. 1980. $1\frac{3}{4}$" bw/rwb. $3.

57
EDWARD KENNEDY (anti-Kennedy button). C. 1980. $2\frac{1}{4}$" rwb. $15.

58
FRANK CHURCH. 1976. $1\frac{1}{2}$" brown/white. $5.

59
FRANK CHURCH. 1976. $1\frac{1}{2}$" brown/white. $5.

60
HAROLD STASSEN. 1980. $1\frac{3}{4}$" red/white. $15.

50

51

52

53

54

55

56

57

58

59

60

23. Cardboard Photo Portraits

In the development of lapel devices featuring the candidate's photograph, the cardboard photo followed the ferrotype (see Section 25). These were the first paper photos, mounted on a thin piece of cardboard to provide some rigidity. Cardboard photos, more precisely known as albumen prints because egg white was used as a protective glaze, appeared first in the 1864 campaign. They were set into frames referred to as shell badges, stamped, and often die-cut into various shapes from thin sheets of brass or copper. Sometimes the metal was given a thin plating to produce a silver color rather than a brass finish. Albumen prints are produced in sepia tones and susceptible to fading so any examples that have survived to today should be shielded from any intense light. Shell badges with cardboard photos grew in popularity and by 1880 all but replaced ferrotypes. They, in turn, all but disappeared with the introduction of celluloid buttons in 1896. A few of the most common Blaine, Cleveland, and Benjamin Harrison shell badges with cardboard photos sell for under $100 but the majority of examples in nice condition will range between $100 and $300.

7

8

9

1
LINCOLN PHOTO in $1\frac{1}{2}$ x 2" brass frame mounted on $2\frac{1}{2}$ x 4" (carte de visite size) card. 1864. $600.

2
LINCOLN PHOTO in 1x$1\frac{1}{4}$ " brass frame with rwb ribbon attachment and stickpin. 1864. $400.

3
McCLELLAN IN MILITARY UNIFORM in $\frac{3}{4}$ x1" brass frame. No pin. 1864. $250.

4
GRANT PHOTO in 1x$1\frac{1}{4}$ " brass frame with rwb fabric ribbon and brass eagle hanger. 1868. $250.

5
GRANT PHOTO IN MILITARY UNIFORM set in white metal frame designed like the flag surmounted by eagle with stickpin. 1868. $160.

6
"GRANT" PHOTO stickpin in 1" brass frame with dark blue outer and pale purple inner inset paper circles. 1868. $175.

7
"SEYMOUR/BLAIR" PHOTO in $\frac{3}{4}$ x 1" brass frame with stickpin. 1868. $400.

8
HORACE GREELEY PHOTO 1" tall brass frame stickpin. 1872. $300.

9
"HORACE GREELEY" PHOTO set in circular brass rim with stickpin. 1872. $300.

10
"HAYES/WHEELER" PHOTO set in a $\frac{3}{4}$ x 1" brass frame with $1\frac{1}{2}$ " stickpin on the reverse. 1876. $375.

11
"HAYES/WHEELER" PHOTO in $\frac{7}{8}$ " brass rim with paper insert. 1876. $400.

12
"TILDEN/HENDRICKS" PHOTO set in a $\frac{3}{4}$ x 1" brass frame with $1\frac{1}{2}$ " stickpin on the reverse. 1876. $400.

13
"TILDEN/HENDRICKS" PHOTO set in a $\frac{7}{8}$ " brass frame with purple insert. 1876. $400.

14
GARFIELD/ARTHUR PHOTOS on $1\frac{1}{2}$ x $1\frac{1}{2}$ " brass shell pin with rwb ribbon. 1880. $700.

15
ARTHUR PHOTO in $\frac{3}{4}$ x 1" brass frame with stickpin reverse. Item is c. 1880. He assumed office after Garfield's assassination. $300.

16
BLAINE/LOGAN PHOTOS set in $1\frac{1}{4}$ x $1\frac{5}{8}$ " brass shell pin. 1884. $250.

17
BLAINE PHOTO on 1" brass shell pin with stickpin on reverse. 1884. $75.

18
CLEVELAND/HENDRICKS 1" brass charm with sepia photos under glass. Hendricks is on the back. 1884. $75.

19
CLEVELAND/THURMAN PHOTOS on $1\frac{1}{2}$ x $1\frac{1}{2}$ " brass shell with stickpin on reverse. 1888. $200.

20
CLEVELAND/THURMAN on 1" lapel stud with red metallic rim. 1888. $175.

21
CLEVELAND PHOTO on 1" diameter brass shell with stickpin. 1888. $100.

22
CLEVELAND PHOTO surrounded by $\frac{7}{8}$ x $1\frac{1}{8}$ " brass horsehoe inscribed "Our Next President." 1888. $125.

23
CLEVELAND PHOTO on $\frac{3}{4}$ " diameter white metal stickpin with floral designs. 1888. $50.

24
CLEVELAND/THURMAN PHOTOS on $1\frac{1}{2}$ x $2\frac{1}{4}$ " brass shell pin with ribbon. 1888. $250.

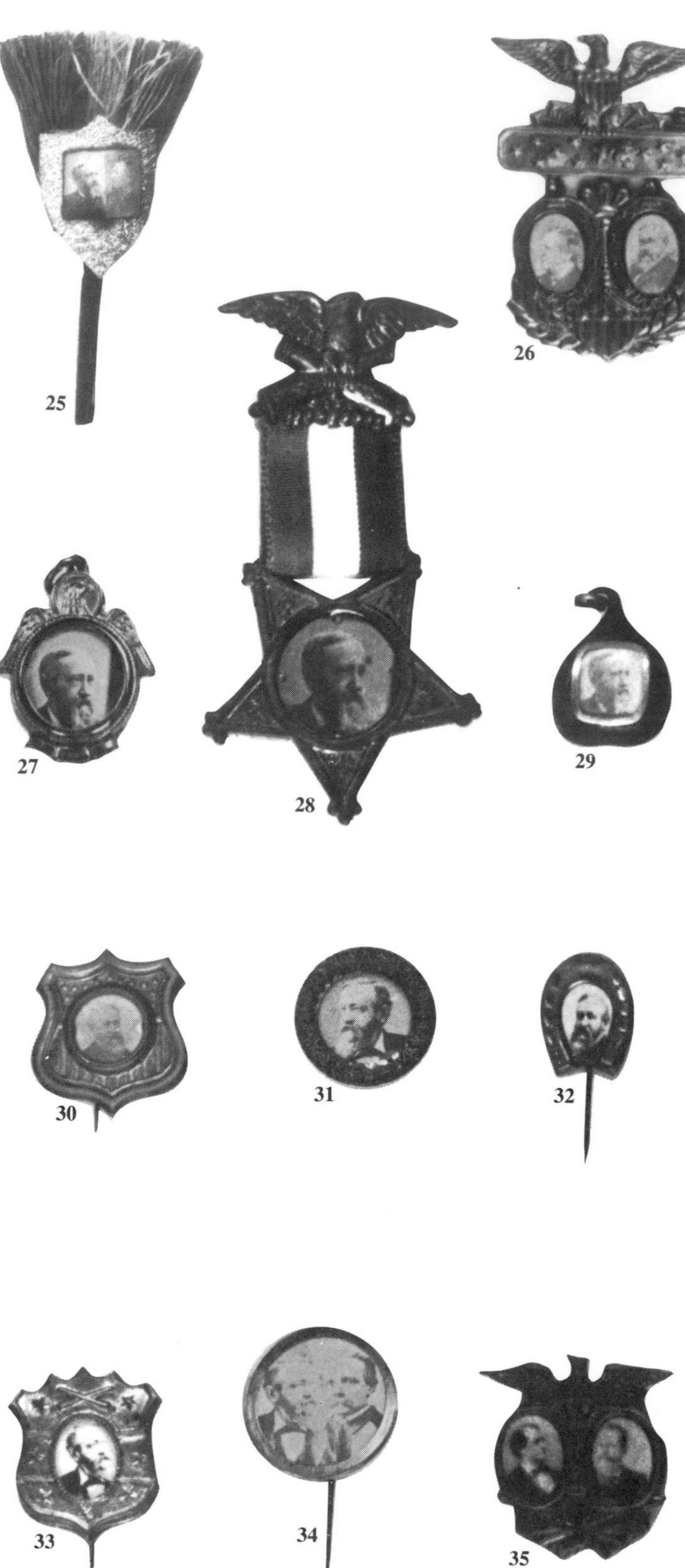

25
HARRISON/MORTON PHOTO on 3" broom pin with rwb bristles, brass shield and a blue wooden handle. 1888. $250.

26
HARRISON/MORTON PHOTOS on $1\frac{1}{2}$ x $2\frac{1}{4}$" embossed brass shell pin with eagle, star, shield, horseshoe motifs. 1888. $200.

27
HARRISON PHOTO in brass $1\frac{1}{4}$" tall eagle shaped watch chain charm with photos under glass. Morton is on reverse. 1888. $100.

28
HARRISON PHOTO on brass shell with rwb ribbon and brass hanger designed to resemble a Civil War Union Army Veterans badge. 3" long. 1888. $125.

29
HARRISON WATCH CHAIN CHARM with photo set in the front of the metal charm shaped and colored to represent a chestnut (Ohio Buckeye). 1" tall. 1888. $100.

30
HARRISON PHOTO on $1\frac{1}{4}$ x $1\frac{1}{4}$" brass shell stickpin. 1888. $90.

31
HARRISON PHOTO on 1" brass stud with ornate rim. Rim matches item #20. 1888. $100.

32
HARRISON PHOTO on $\frac{3}{4}$" brass shell stickpin with horseshoe shaped frame. 1888. $125.

33
HARRISON PHOTO on 1x$1\frac{1}{4}$" brass shell stickpin decorated with stars and crossed cannons. $120.

34
HARRISON/REID PHOTO in 1" silvered tin frame with stickpin on the reverse. 1892. $200.

35
BRYAN/SEWALL PHOTOS on $1\frac{1}{2}$ x $1\frac{1}{2}$" brass shell pin with flag and eagle designs. 1896. $200.

24. Convention Badges

Evolving from nineteenth century convention ribbons and ribbon badges, the mostly metal convention badge started becoming the standard in 1908. These badges have a bar pin across the top segment so they can be worn as the person's credential for accessing convention activities. The metal parts of the badge usually have a brass, bronze or silver finish. Sometimes the badge is embellished with a ribbon or celluloid accent. During World War II, some, if not all, of the 1944 badges were made of gold-colored plastic because of restrictions on the use of metal. Beginning in the 1960s plastic cards began to be used for some types of credentials and this trend was expanded in recent years as security measures became more stringent. The traditional convention badges carry some sort of designation such as "Delegate," "Alternate," "Press," or "Assistant Sergeant At Arms." This last designation was an honorary title and badges with this inscription tend to be more common. Collectors who specialize in a particular candidate would acquire the appropriate badge for the convention that nominated the candidate, but few collectors specialize in building a collection of convention badges. Although they do not picture candidates, convention badges are elaborate and well-made and a group of them presents an impressive assemblage.

1
REPUBLICAN CONVENTION SOUVENIR $2\frac{3}{4}$ " tall metal badge with bronze finish and brass cut-out of McKinley at center. Philadelphia, 1900. $50.

2
REPUBLICAN STATE CONVENTION "Delegate" badge with $1\frac{1}{4}$ " bw celluloid of Roosevelt set in a brass rim. $4\frac{1}{2}$ " tall. Sioux Falls, S.D., 1904. $70.

3
DEMOCRATIC "OFFICIAL" $2\frac{1}{2}$ x 7" ribbon badge with a $1\frac{1}{2}$ x $2\frac{3}{4}$ " long multicolor cello depicting Bryan with ears of corn and inscription "Two of America's Great Essentials to Peace and Prosperity Known the World Over." Denver, 1908. $750.

4
DEMOCRATIC "DELEGATE" badge 2x4" tall brass with rwb enamel accent and ribbon. Baltimore, 1912. $50.

5
REPUBLICAN "ASSISTANT SERGEANT AT ARMS" $2x4\frac{1}{2}$ " tall brass with rwb enamel and portrait of Lincoln. Ribbon is missing. Chicago, 1912. $50.

6
DEMOCRATIC "DELEGATE" 2x4" brass badge with rwb ribbon and enamel accents. St. Louis, 1916. $40.

7
REPUBLICAN BADGE WITH INDIVIDUAL'S NAME. "Abraham Lincoln" fob suspended from a rwb fabric hanger. 4" tall. Chicago, 1920. $50.

8
DEMOCRATIC "ALTERNATE" 2x3" silvered brass with blue enamel depicting Jefferson. San Francisco, 1920. $60.

9
DEMOCRATIC "DELEGATE" 2x4" badge from the convention which nominated John W. Davis. New York, 1924. $50

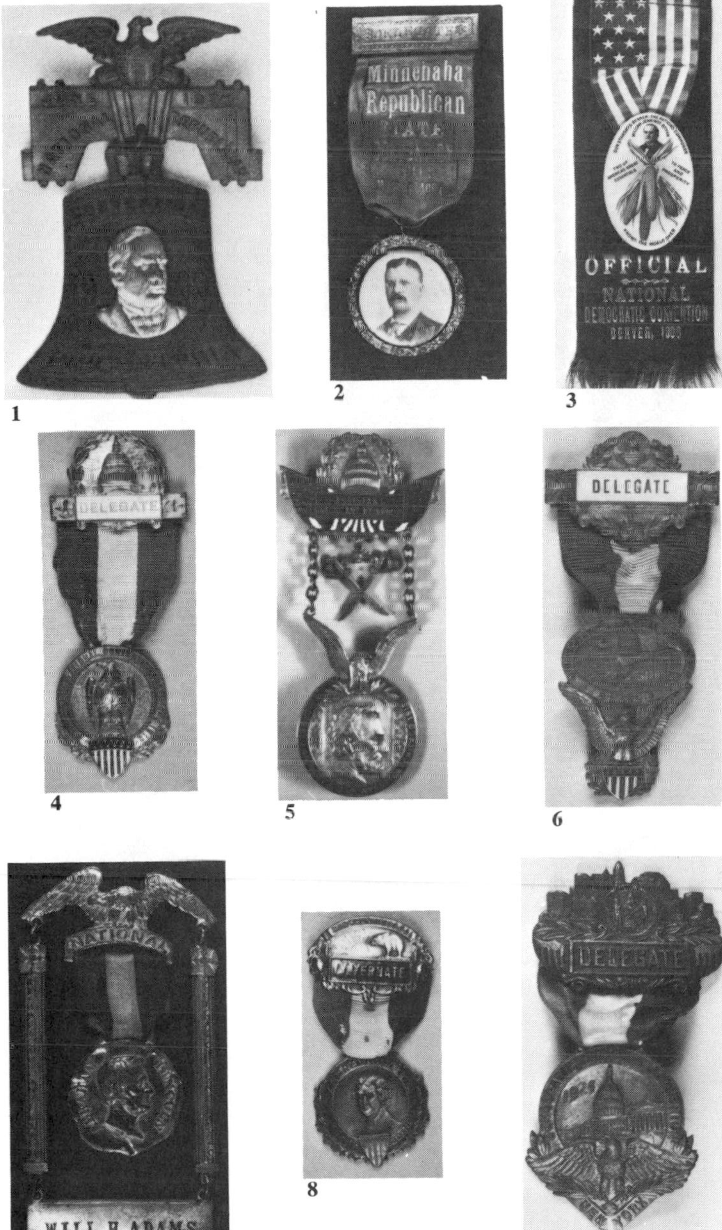

1 2 3 4 5 6 7 8 9

10

11

12

10
REPUBLICAN "DELEGATE" 2x5" rwb enamel/brass badge complete with rwb fabric. Depicts likeness of George Washington underneath an eagle. Chicago, 1932. $35.

11
DEMOCRATIC "DELEGATE" badge $4\frac{1}{2}$ " tall with red fabric ribbons. Below is a Liberty Bell with F.D.R. and Garner. Philadelphia, 1936. $60.

12
DEMOCRATIC (Kings County, New York Delegation) 2x6" blue ribbon with additional rwb ribbon holding a heavy brass piece featuring eagle, flag and seal of New York state. Philadelphia, 1936. $20.

13

14

15

13
REPUBLICAN "HONORARY ASSISTANT SERGEANT AT ARMS" $3\frac{3}{4}$ " tall brass with rwb ribbon. Cleveland, 1936. $25.

14
REPUBLICAN "DELEGATE" $1\frac{1}{2}$ x 5" brass with blue enamel accents and rwb fabric ribbons in its original box. Philadelphia, 1940. $40.

15
DEMOCRATIC "OFFICIAL" $1\frac{1}{2}$ x 5" badge of gold plastic meant to resemble brass with rwb color accents. "Assistant to Director" on the second bar. Chicago, 1944. $25.

16

17

18

16
DEMOCRATIC "HONORARY PAGE" 5" tall with medallion showing figures of William Penn, Philadelphia City Hall and the Liberty Bell. Philadelphia, 1948. $35.

17
REPUBLICAN "DELEGATE" badge $3\frac{3}{4}$ " tall with "Taft" brass tie tack. Chicago, 1952. $35.

18
DEMOCRATIC "ALTERNATE" $3\frac{3}{4}$ " tall brass badge. Chicago, 1956. $50.

19
DEMOCRATIC "ALTERNATE" $3\frac{3}{4}$" tall brass badge in original box. Los Angeles, 1960. $50.

20
REPUBLICAN "DELEGATE" $1\frac{1}{2}$ x 5" brass with dark blue ribbon. Brass hanger depicts Lincoln. Chicago, 1960. $40.

21
DEMOCRATIC "DELEGATE" 2x5" brass badge with rwb ribbons. Atlantic City, 1964. $25.

22
REPUBLICAN "PRESS" 4" brass badge with white ribbon. San Francisco, 1964. $20.

23
DEMOCRATIC "ALTERNATE" $4\frac{1}{2}$" brass badge with rwb fabric. Chicago, 1968. $25.

24
DEMOCRATIC "DELEGATE" 5" brass badge with rwb ribbons. Miami Beach, 1972. $20.

25
DEMOCRATIC "HONORED GUESTS" 4" gold colored badge with rwb ribbon. New York City, 1976. $15.

26
REPUBLICAN CONVENTION BUTTON. 3" bw/blue. Detroit, 1980. $8.

27
REPUBLICAN CONVENTION BUTTON. $2\frac{1}{4}$" multicolor. Dallas, 1984. $5.

28
DEMOCRATIC CONVENTION BUTTON. $3\frac{1}{2}$" multicolor. San Francisco, 1984. $5.

19 20 21 22 23 24 25 26 27 28

25. Ferrotype Portraits

The first ferrotypes appeared in time to document the historic election of 1860. The four-year-old Republican Party chose Abraham Lincoln to face Douglas, Bell, and Breckenridge representing three factions of a Democratic Party torn apart by the slavery issue. The photographic process used to produce ferrotypes used a japanned sheet of thin iron which was covered with a light-sensitive emulsion and then exposed, washed and varnished. Multiple identical images were produced on the small iron sheet and then the images were cut apart to make individual framed ferrotypes, also commonly called tintypes. The portraits were encased in rectangular brass frames or circular hollow frames which sometimes carried the candidate's name or a slogan. If the vice-presidential candidate was pictured on the reverse, the rim was drilled with a small hole so a ribbon could be used to attach the ferrotype to clothing. If only the front surface carried the photo, normally the reverse had a short stickpin soldered in place for fastening purposes. Particularly rare are jugate ferrotypes from 1860 and 1864 which command prices beginning at $2000. A jugate Lincoln/Johnson ferrotype in a very elaborate brass frame is valued around $20,000 while the matching McClellan/Pendleton is valued around $10,000. These are both exceptional rarities and more typical values fall within the $300 to $500 range. More common examples of Grant or Seymour ferrotypes from 1868 are priced around $200 to $300. Any scratches or missing flakes of emulsion quickly lower the value of ferrotypes. Cleaning should not be attempted because the emulsion is so fragile and easily damaged. Any prolonged exposure to sunlight can also damage the image. Ferrotypes largely gave way by 1880 to cardboard photo badges (see Section 23) but an infrequent item was produced as late as 1904. Together with ribbons, ferrotypes represent one of the most popular categories of nineteenth century campaign collectibles.

1

2

3

4

5

6

7

8

1
"ABRAHAM LINCOLN" 1" with brass rim and Hamlin reverse. 1860. $450.

2
"ABRAHAM LINCOLN" 1" with brass rim and Hamlin reverse. 1860. $450.

3
ABRAHAM LINCOLN" 1" with velvet covered rim and Hamlin reverse. 1860. $450.

4
"A. LINCOLN" 1" with brass rim and Johnson reverse. 1864. $600.

5
"A. LINCOLN" $\frac{3}{4}$" with brass rim and blank reverse. 1864. $800.

6
"A. LINCOLN" $\frac{3}{4}$" with brass rim and stickpin reverse. 1864. $400.

7
LINCOLN 1 $\frac{3}{8}$ x1 $\frac{5}{8}$" in brass shell frame with paper label on reverse reading "Abraham Lincoln, President of the United States." 1864. $650.

8
"STEPHEN A. DOUGLAS" 1 $\frac{7}{8}$" large silvered brass rim referred to as the *doughnut* style due to its rounded thickness. Herschel Johnson reverse. 1860. $2500.

9
"JOHN C. BRECKENRIDGE" 1" with brass rim and Lane reverse. 1860. $400.

10
"JOHN BELL" 1" with brass rim and Everett reverse. 1860. $300.

11
"JOHN BELL" 1" with brass rim and Everett reverse. 1860. $300.

12
McCLELLAN $\frac{3}{4}$ x 1" brass frame with blank reverse. 1864. $300.

13
"G.B. McCLELLAN" 1" with brass rim and Pendleton reverse. 1864. $1000.

14
"G.B. M'CLELLAN" 1" with brass rim and Pendleton reverse. 1864. $350.

15
"GRANT/COLFAX" 1 $\frac{1}{8}$ " brass shell frame with pin on reverse. 1868. $500.

16
"U.S. GRANT" 1" with brass rim and Colfax reverse. 1868. $300.

17
"GRANT" 1 $\frac{1}{8}$ " with brass rim and stickpin reverse. 1868. $175.

18
"GRANT" 1x1 $\frac{1}{4}$ " brass shell with pin on reverse. 1868. $250.

19
"GRANT" 1" with fabric rim and stickpin reverse. 1868. $200.

20
"GRANT/WILSON" 1x1" brass shell frame with pin on reverse. 1872. $1100.

9

10

11

12

13

14

15

16

17

18

19

20

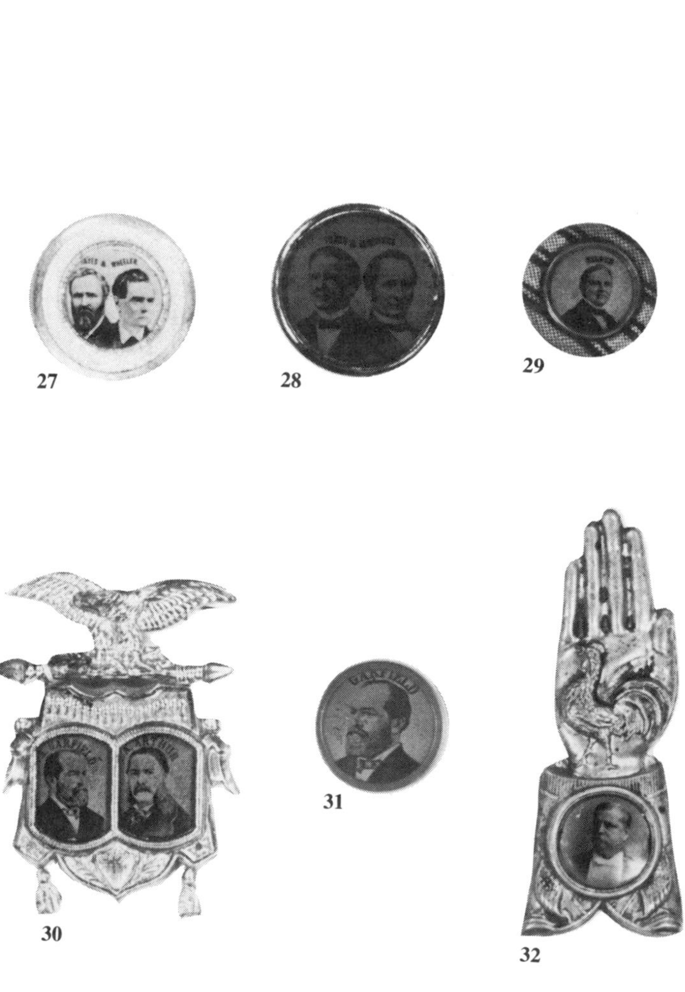

21
"GEN. U.S. GRANT" 1" brass rim dated 1872 with Wilson reverse. $300.

22
"SEYMOUR/BLAIR" 1 $\frac{1}{8}$ " brass shell frame with pin on reverse. 1868. $450.

23
"SEYMOUR/BLAIR" 1" with brass rim and pin on reverse. 1868. $450.

24
"H. SEYMOUR" 1" brass shell frame with pin on reverse. 1868. $175.

25
"GREELEY/BROWN" 1 $\frac{3}{8}$ " brass shell with brass shell portrait of Greeley on reverse. 1872. $1750.

26
GREELEY 1x1$\frac{1}{4}$ " brass shell with stickpin reverse. 1872. $950.

27
"HAYES & WHEELER" $\frac{7}{8}$ " with brass rim and stickpin reverse. 1876. $600.

28
"TILDEN & HENDRICKS" $\frac{7}{8}$ " with brass rim and stickpin reverse. 1876. $500.

29
"TILDEN" $\frac{5}{8}$ " with fabric rim and stickpin reverse. 1876. $250.

30
"J.A. GARFIELD/C.A. ARTHUR" 1$\frac{1}{4}$ x 1$\frac{3}{4}$ " brass shell with pin on reverse. 1880. $1000.

31
"GARFIELD" $\frac{5}{8}$ " with brass rim and stickpin reverse. 1880. $225.

32
HANCOCK $\frac{7}{8}$ x 2 $\frac{1}{4}$" tall brass shell pin with portrait. His name is implied by the rebus designs of a hand (Han) and rooster (cock). 1880. $2000.

26. Lapel Pins & Jewelry

Jewelry and lapel pins with a bar pin type fastener on the reverse are most common from the campaigns of 1940 and the post-World War II era. There are some nineteenth century examples including the beautiful sulphide brooches from 1836 and 1840 depicting Andrew Jackson, Martin Van Buren, and William Henry Harrison. Most frequently depicted is Harrison's log cabin symbol. Some log cabin brooches are done in brass and a few have hand-painted log cabin scenes under a glass cover. Brass examples are in the $400 range, hand-painted scenes approach $1000 and portrait examples can bring $3000 to $5000. More typical nineteenth century examples, in much lower price ranges, include bar pins spelling out the candidates' names, enameled pins with the candidates' initials, horseshoe-shaped pins, cuff links, and an assortment of watch chain charms. Most of the preceeding items are from the 1884-1888 era. Similar items occur in the early 1900s but a much larger volume of material, particularly women's jewelry, becomes available starting with the 1952 election. Earrings, bracelets, necklaces and circle pins were introduced. Many pieces are accented with rhinestones, cut glass stones or simulated pearls. Designs include the candidate's name or initials, portrait caricatures or some symbol related to the candidate's career. Among the best known of the latter are the shoe sole with worn hole issued as a tic-tac (around $25) to promote Adlai Stevenson in 1956 and the John F. Kennedy 'PT 109' boat pin from 1960 inspired by his World War II service. The original PT 109 item used in the campaign is a bar pin finished in brass or silver inscribed "Kennedy 60" (around $35). PT boats with tie clasp or tie-tac reverses and with other inscriptions such as "109" or "Kennedy" (around $20) were made after the election and probably in anticipation of his never-to-be 1964 campaign. Much of the twentieth century jewelry and lapel pins available are shunned by collectors so overall prices in the field are reasonable and interesting collections can be assembled on a modest budget.

1
"CLEVELAND" 3" long diecut brass pin. C. 1888. $40.

2
"CLEVELAND" 2½" brass bar pin designed like a banner. C. 1888. $35.

3
CLEVELAND/THURMAN 1¼" brass pin with rwb enamel. C. 1888. $60.

4
HARRISON/MORTON mate to item #3. C. 1888. $60.

5
"HARRISON" 2½" brass pin in the shape of a musical horn. C. 1888. $100.

6
"HARRISON" 2" long brass bar pin with diecut letters. C. 1888. $30.

7
"HARRISON" 2" long brass bar pin with rwb enamel. "1888." $60.

8
McKINLEY brass pin. "GOP" on elephant's red blanket. C. 1896. $130.

9
"McKINLEY/HOBART" enamel lapel stud with brass elephant head. 1896. $35.

10
"McKINLEY" brass hanger with rwb shield below. C. 1896. $15.

11
BRYAN 1½" tall oval sepia portrait in a brass frame with pin. C. 1896. $40.

12
BRYAN/ANTI-McKINLEY 1" pig charm with gold finish. Inside is a bw photo of McKinley. 1896. $200.

13
BRYAN/ANTI-McKINLEY 1" white metal pig. Lift tail to reveal McKinley photo. 1896. $200.

1 2 3 4 5 6 7 8 9 10 11 12 13

14
"ROOSEVELT/FAIRBANKS" $\frac{1}{2}$ x 1 $\frac{3}{4}$" brass pin designed like T.R.'s spectacles. 1904. $190.

15
ROOSEVELT 1" brass pin with his hat marked "T.R." 1912. $150.

16
"TAFT & SHERMAN" $\frac{3}{4}$" tall diecut brass forming his name. C. 1908. $15.

17
WILSON $\frac{3}{4}$" square enamel and silvered brass badge inscribed "Contributor/1912/ Pennsylvania/Wilson/ Marshall/ Cresswell/Barry." $35.

18
LA FOLLETTE/WHEELER 1" bronze. Progressive Party. 1924. $10.

19
"HOOVER/GOP" 1" gray and white enamel on brass pin. C. 1928. $20.

20
"HOOVER" 1" rwb enamel on brass pin. 1928. $10.

21
"HOOVER" silvered brass ring with rwb enamel top. "1928." $18.

22
"AL SMITH" matching item #21. $18.

23
SMITH 2x3" card holding a blue/brown enamel pin. 1928. $45.

24
"AL SMITH" 1$\frac{1}{4}$ x 1$\frac{1}{2}$"silvered brass pin. 1928. $35.

25
"SMITH & ROBINSON" 1" tall rwb enamel/brass pin. 1928. $90.

26
"AL" SMITH $\frac{5}{8}$" brass pin in the shape of Smith's brown derby hat. 1928. $15.

27
"VOTE FOR ROOSEVELT" 2$\frac{1}{2}$" tall leather donkey head pin. 1944. $12.

28
"LANDON X" 2$\frac{1}{2}$" long silvered brass tie bar with rwb enamel. 1936. $15.

29
"LANDON" $\frac{3}{4}$" brown and yellow enamel sunflower pin. 1936. $8.

30
"WILLKIE" 2x3$\frac{1}{2}$" rwb metal pin designed like ribbons. 1940. $35.

31
"WILLKIE" 1$\frac{1}{2}$ x 1$\frac{1}{2}$" gold/rwb pin. 1940. $20.

32
"DEWEY" $1\frac{1}{2}$ x $1\frac{1}{2}$ " brown plastic elephant pin. 1944. $15.

33
EISENHOWER/"I LIKE IKE" $2\frac{1}{4}$ " original card holds a diecut brass "Ike" tie tack. 1952. $5.

34
EISENHOWER. "IKE" $1\frac{3}{8}$ " diecut brass circle pin. 1952. $8.

35
EISENHOWER. "IKE" $1\frac{1}{4}$ x $1\frac{1}{2}$ " diecut metal pin finished in silver. 1952. $10.

36
EISENHOWER 2" long brass replica of a "Yale" key. Stamped on the shaft area is "First For Ike." From Yale University. 1952. $100.

37
STEVENSON. "ADLAI" $1\frac{1}{4}$ " long brass tie tack. 1952. $8.

38
"FOR PRESIDENT STEVENSON" 2" brass bar pin. 1952. $12.

39
STEVENSON 1" sterling silver shoe tie tack. 1952. $25.

40
"KENNEDY 60" $1\frac{3}{4}$ " long brass pin with black lettering. $35.

41
KENNEDY 2" long silvered brass tie clip with bw flashing disk showing portrait plus slogan "The Man for the 60's." 1960. $25.

42
"SEN. KENNEDY" $1\frac{5}{8}$ " round brass tie clip with inset white plastic disk that has gold caricature of J.F.K. 1960. $40.

43
KENNEDY $\frac{3}{4}$ " tall rocking chair metal pin with gold finish made in anticipation of the 1964 campaign. $25.

44
"NIXON" brass charm bracelet on 2x$7\frac{1}{2}$" original card. 1960. $10.

45
"REPUBLICANS FOR JOHNSON" $1\frac{1}{2}$ x 2" gold finish metal pin. 1964. $15.

32

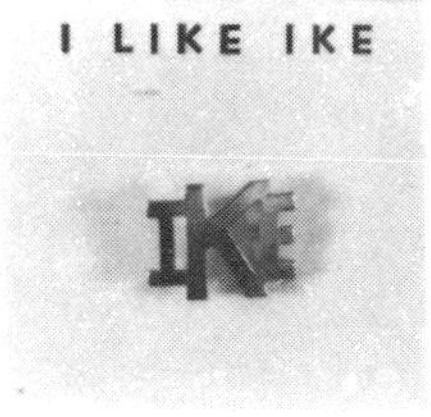

33

34

35 36 37

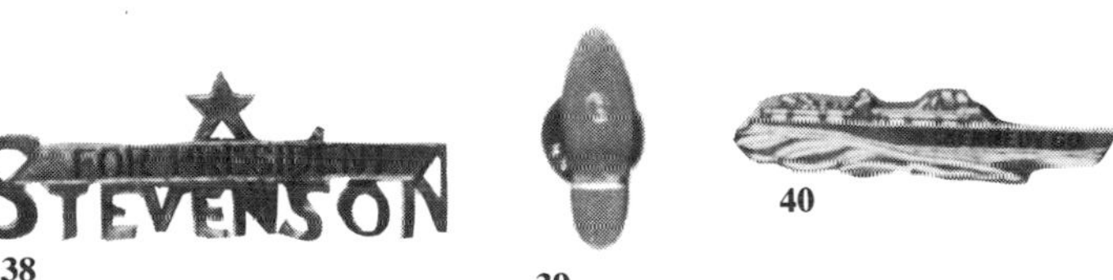

38 39 40

41 42 43

44

45

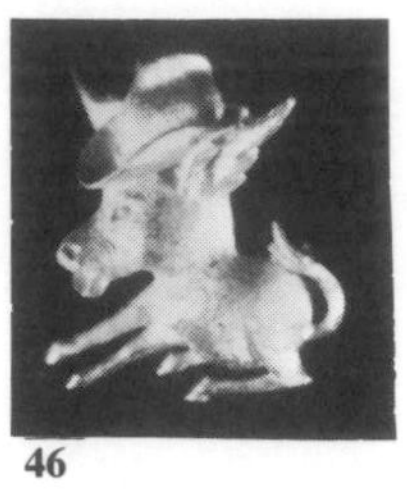
46

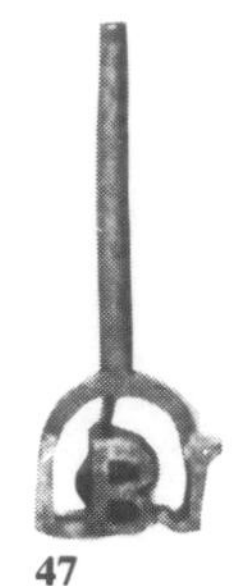
47

48

49

50

51

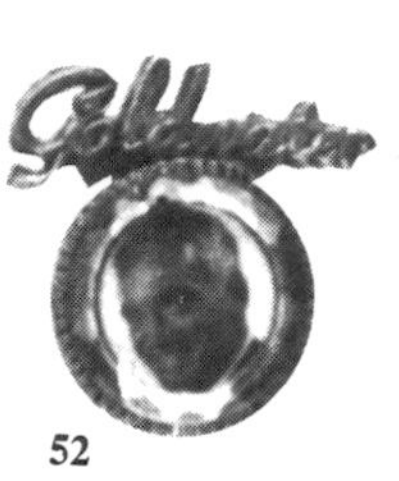

52

53

54

55

56

46
JOHNSON $1\frac{1}{2}$ x 2" high relief brass pin depicting donkey wearing western hat. 1964. $8.

47
JOHNSON 2" long silver colored metal branding iron pin with initials "L.B.J." 1964. $20.

48
JOHNSON 1" brass pin shaped like Texas with raised initials "L.B.J." 1964. $10.

49
JOHNSON 3" diameter brass bangle bracelet holding 1" diecut brass charm with initials "L.B.J." 1964. $12.

50
JOHNSON 3x3" white on dark blue original card holds a brass hat tie clip with "L.B.J." in black lettering. 1964. $15.

51
"GOLDWATER 1964" brass hanger designed like a bow holding a $1\frac{3}{4}$" dark wood disk which has a brass portrait in the center. 1964. $20.

52
"GOLDWATER" metal pin $1\frac{1}{2}$" tall with bright gold finish surrounding a thick glass insert that has faceted edges covering a bw photo. 1964. $25.

53
"GOLDWATER IN '64" brass figural pin 2" tall with textured cactus and bw photo image. 1964. $15.

54
"GOLDWATER" brass bracelet of linked bw beads spelling out his name. Jug is meant to hold 'Gold-water.' 1964. $40.

55
"GOLDWATER IN '64" black metal glasses pin $1\frac{3}{4}$ x $2\frac{1}{8}$" with bw portrait flasher. $50.

56
"GOLDWATER IN '64" $2\frac{1}{4}$" tall tin star with gold finish and black lettering. $6.

57
GOLDWATER 2x2" original bw card holding small brass letter "G" clutch pin. 1964. $5.

58
GOLDWATER $2x2\frac{1}{4}$" bw original card holding small full-dimensioned brass elephant pin with tiny inset red glass eyes and black plastic spectacles. 1964. $8.

59
NIXON pair of matched $\frac{7}{8}$" rwb brass cuff links on original $2\frac{1}{2}$ x 3" card with matching $2\frac{1}{4}$" long brass tie clip. 1968. SET $25.

60
NIXON silver colored metal chain necklace holding $3\frac{1}{2}$" molded white metal figure. 1968. $12.

61
NIXON $2\frac{1}{2}$ x 4" die-cut ivory colored plastic elephant pin with gold colored glitter pieces, most mounted in small metallic green circles. 1968. $8.

62
"NIXON" die-cut textured brass elephant pin $1\frac{1}{2}$ x $1\frac{3}{4}$" with small blue inset glass eye and blue accent enamel on his name. 1968. $8.

63
"NIXON" metal pin 2" tall with gold finish. Elephant has red/white sash across its back and small red accent eyes. 1968. $20.

64
HUMPHREY 2" blue/green/white plastic disk earrings. 1968. $15.

65
HUMPHREY $\frac{7}{8}$" diameter cuff link pair, $1\frac{1}{2}$" long tie clip and 1" charm on bracelet. All are bright brass and each features "H.H.H." initials in raised letters. 1968. EACH $5.

57

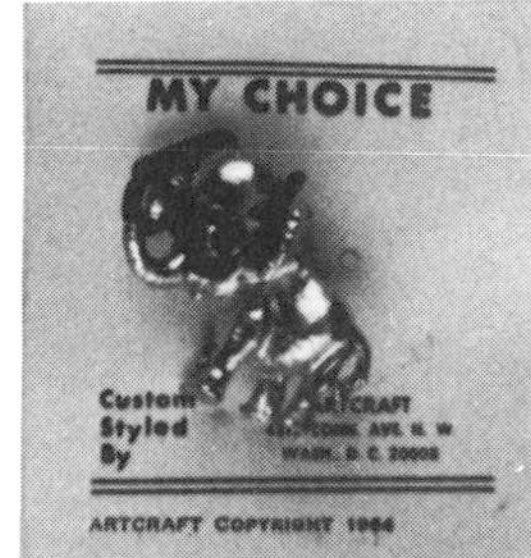

58

59

60

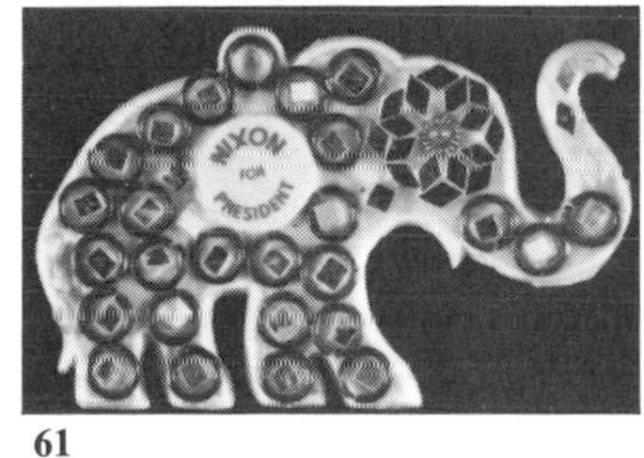

61

62

63

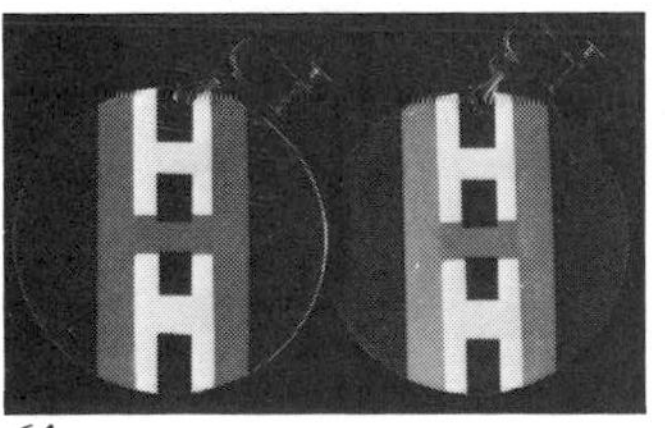
64

65

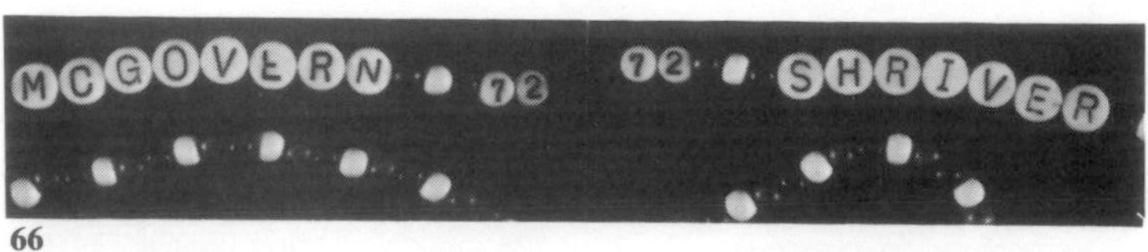

66

67

68

69

70

71

72

73

74

75

76

66
McGOVERN/SHRIVER '72" necklace consisting of rwb plastic beads threaded on elastic string. 1972. $10.

67
McGOVERN silver colored metal chain necklace holding 3 $\frac{1}{2}$ " molded white metal figure. 1972. $12.

68
"McGOVERN '72" metal 1" tie tack with brass finish. $5.

69
CARTER 1" rwb enameled brass pin with silvertone photo. Clutch pin is on reverse. Green/white original card. 1976. $5.

70
"CARTER 4 PRESIDENT" 3 $\frac{1}{2}$ " long molded ceramic peanut in tan with inscription in black. Yellow fabric cord. 1976. $12.

71
"FORD" diecut $\frac{1}{2}$ x 2" burnished brass name pin. 1976. $6.

72
"FORD" brass pin 1 $\frac{1}{4}$ x 1 $\frac{3}{8}$ " with enameled rwb brass pendant in shape of automobile. 1976. $10.

73
"REAGAN" enameled brass pin 1 $\frac{1}{4}$ " tall depicting Reagan in western outfit with clutch pin reverse. 1980. $15.

74
"REAGAN/BUSH '84" oval brass 1" pin with rwb enameled inscription and clutch pin reverse. $6.

75
"MONDALE" 1" rwb enameled brass flag with clutch pin reverse. 1984. $5.

76
"MONDALE/FERRARO/AFT" rwb $\frac{7}{8}$ " enameled brass with clutch pin reverse. 1984. $5.

27. Lapel Studs

Lapel studs exist in great profusion from the 1880 to 1900 campaigns. The front surface with the image or inscription is usually made of brass, copper, white metal or, starting in 1896, most often celluloid. The O'Hara Company of Waltham, Massachusetts, most known for their pocket watch dials, made a number of all-porcelain studs in 1896. The back of a stud is designed with a short peg or shaft that has a round cap on the end to slip through the buttonhole of a lapel. Most lapel studs are $\frac{1}{2}$" to 1" in diameter. A few are shaped like hats, flags, shields, and, occasionally die-cut in the image of the candidate. Hundreds of varieties exist for political candidates and several hundred designs were produced around 1896 to advertise bicycles. Collector demand for lapel studs is not great so even attractive and uncommon examples often fall within a price range of $15 to $35.

1
CLEVELAND $\frac{3}{4}$" bw. 1888. $35.

2
CLEVELAND $\frac{3}{4}$" bw. 1888. $30.

3
CLEVELAND $\frac{3}{4}$" white enamel/brass. 1888. $25.

4
CLEVELAND 1" tall brass. 1888. $40.

5
CLEVELAND $\frac{3}{4}$" brass drum. 1888. $50.

6
CLEVELAND $\frac{3}{4}$" rwb. 1892. $35.

7
CLEVELAND $\frac{3}{4}$" gold/blue fabric. 1892. $30.

8
HARRISON 1" bw celluloid. 1888. $50.

9
HARRISON $\frac{3}{4}$" bw celluloid. 1888. $30.

10
HARRISON $\frac{3}{4}$" bw celluloid. 1888. $30.

11
HARRISON $\frac{3}{4}$" rwb. 1888. $25.

12
HARRISON $\frac{3}{4}$" rwb/black. 1888. $25.

13
HARRISON $\frac{1}{2}$" brass/rwb. 1888. $30.

14
HARRISON $\frac{7}{8}$" brass/rwb. 1888. $35.

15
HARRISON $\frac{3}{4}$" brass hat. 1888. $30.

16
HARRISON $\frac{3}{4}$" rwb fabric. 1888. $20.

17
HARRISON $\frac{5}{8}$" brass/blue enamel. 1888. $5.

18
HARRISON $\frac{5}{8}$" brass. 1892. $35.

19
McKINLEY/HOBART $\frac{7}{8}$" bw/rwb. 1896. $35.

20
McKINLEY/HOBART $\frac{7}{8}$" bw/rwb. 1896. $20.

1

2

3

4

5

6

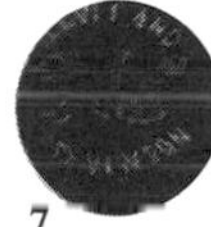
7

8

9

10

11

12

13

14

15

16

17

18

19

20

21

22

23

24

25

26

27

28

29

30

31

32

33

34

35

36

37

38

39

21
McKINLEY/HOBART $\frac{7}{8}$" sepia/rwb. 1896. $25.

22
McKINLEY/HOBART $\frac{3}{4}$" sepia. 1896. $20.

23
McKINLEY/HOBART $\frac{3}{4}$" sepia. 1896. $20.

24
McKINLEY brass gold bug with bw paper photo on original card. 1896. $300.

25
McKINLEY $\frac{7}{8}$" bw. 1896. $75.

26
McKINLEY $\frac{7}{8}$" bw/rwb. 1896. $12.

27
McKINLEY $\frac{7}{8}$" sepia/rwb. 1896. $30.

28
McKINLEY $\frac{7}{8}$" bw with black celluloid rim. 1896. $20.

29
McKINLEY $\frac{3}{4}$" bw. 1896. $15.

30
McKINLEY $\frac{3}{4}$" rwb/gold fabric. 1896. $20.

31
McKINLEY $\frac{7}{8}$" long brass replica of Napoleon's hat. 1896. $20.

32
McKINLEY $\frac{3}{4}$" colorful porcelain showing gold bug by O'Hara Watch Dial Co. 1896. $125.

33
McKINLEY $\frac{7}{8}$" bw/red. 1896. $25.

34
McKINLEY $\frac{7}{8}$" bw/gold. 1896. $25.

35
BRYAN $\frac{7}{8}$" bw/rwb. 1896. $15.

36
ROOSEVELT $\frac{1}{2}$" blue/white. 1904. $10.

37
ROOSEVELT $\frac{1}{2}$" brass 'Bull Moose' on original card. 1912. $35.

38
COX 1" white metal. 1920. $25.

39
COX $\frac{7}{8}$" white metal. 1920. $20.

28. Mechanicals

Mechanical lapel devices are among the most desired small political collectibles. The term mechanical is loosely applied to any item with a moving part; but, when applied to lapel devices, the term usually refers to brass or silvered brass shell badges that use a tiny spring to produce some action when released. Such devices were most popular in 1896 but examples are known from 1892, 1900, and 1904 as well. A few other lapel devices with moving parts, usually operated manually without the aid of a spring, were used before 1892 and after 1904. The most famous and widely distributed mechanical device is the "gold bug" or "silver bug" from 1896. Designed like a beetle, a small tab is pushed down, causing a pair of wings to fly out from under the body displaying paper photos of McKinley and Hobart on gold bugs or Bryan and Sewell on silver bugs. Because of their popularity at the time, gold bugs are not scarce but collector popularity has put working examples in the \$200 to \$300 range. Silver bugs are less common and examples still working and with the silver finish largely intact normally exceed \$300. A silver bug variety that pictures Bryan on one wing with the inscription "16/1" on the opposite wing brings around \$450. Mechanicals can be pricey, but they are so novel and fascinating that it may be worth stretching the collecting budget to acquire a few examples.

1
BLAINE NOSE-THUMBER brass $1\frac{1}{2}$" tall. 1884. \$275.

2
CLEVELAND 1" rwb litho shield that covers and slides down to reveal sepia portrait. Stickpin reverse. 1888. \$200.

3
HARRISON matches item #2. 1888. \$200.

4
HARRISON "Presidential Chair/Who Shall Occupy It?" 2" tall silvered brass with paper photo. Shown with seat closed and open. 1888. \$300.

5
McKINLEY/HOBART GOLD BUG $1\frac{1}{4}$" tall brass pin with paper photos on wings that open and close. 1896. \$200.

6
McKINLEY/HOBART $\frac{3}{4}$" brass pin with paper photos under elephant's "GOP" blanket. 1896. \$175.

7
McKINLEY/HOBART $1\frac{5}{8}$" brass eagle pin holding silver bug in beak. Paper photos on wings that open and close. 1896. \$600.

8
McKINLEY/HOBART rwb brass flag with paper photos, shown open. 1896. \$250.

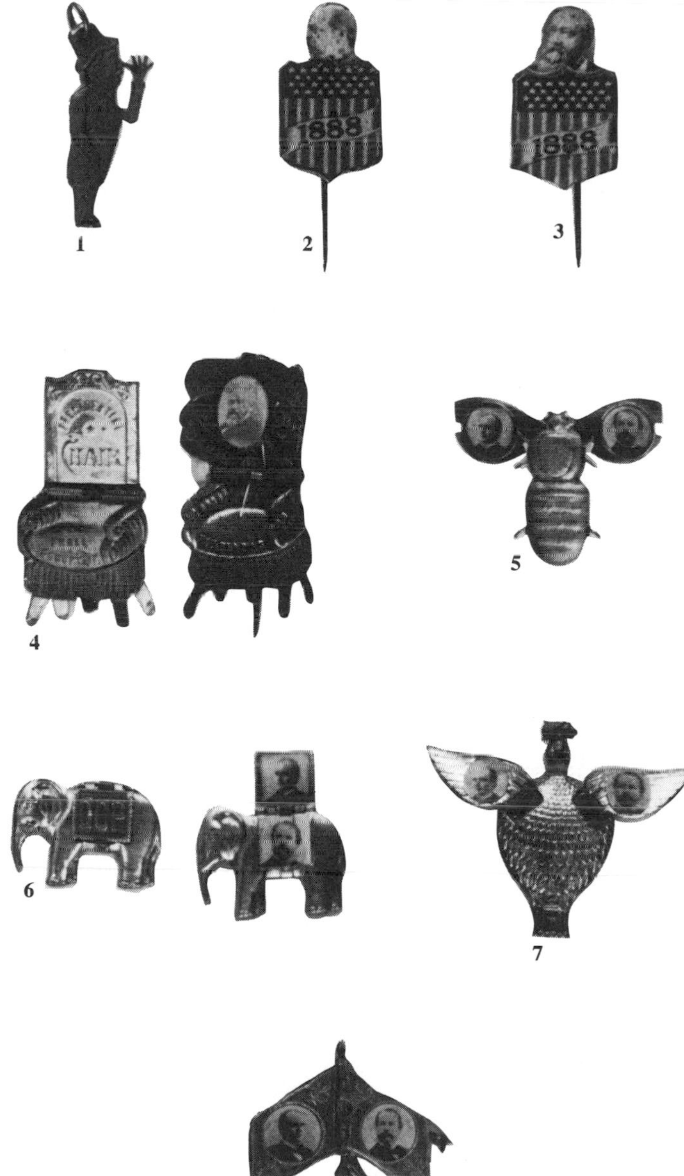

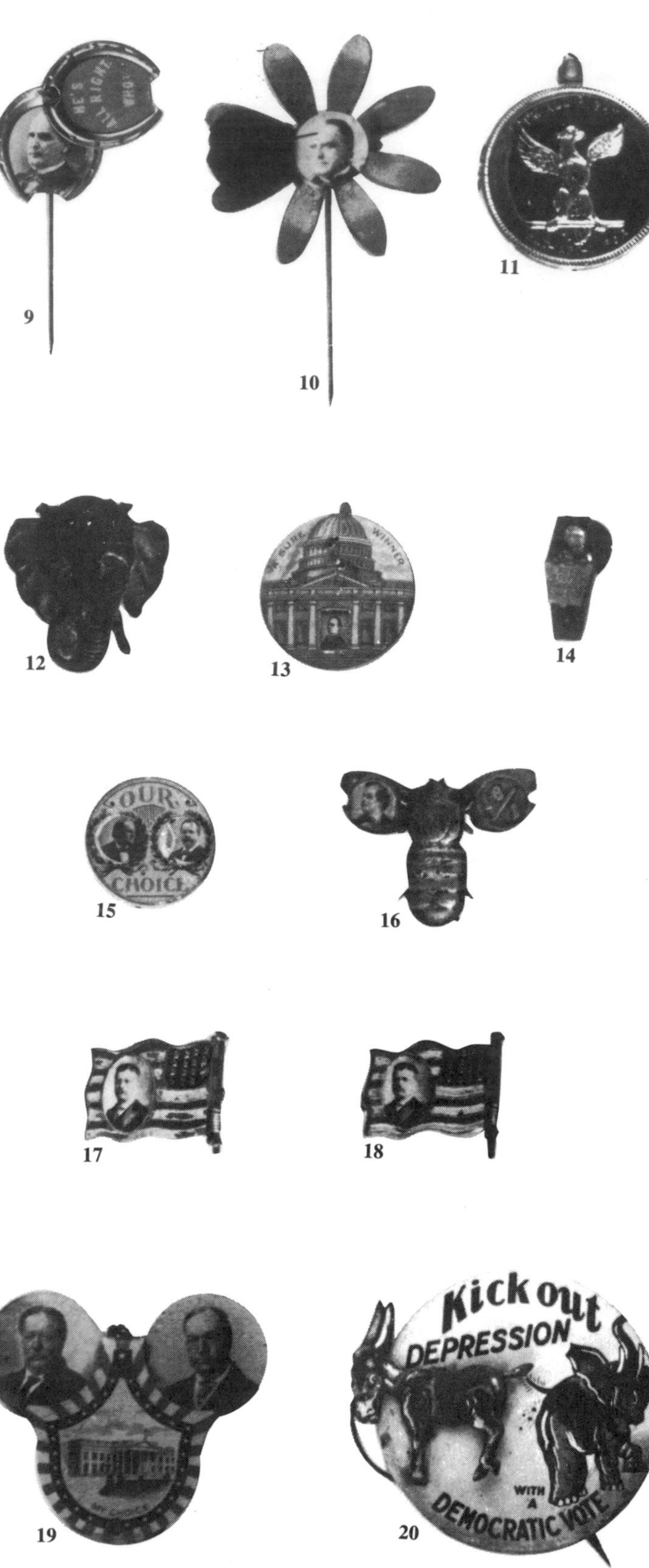

9
McKINLEY "He's All Right" brass stickpin 2" tall with paper label and sepia photo. Shown open. 1896. $200.

10
McKINLEY DAISY STICKPIN 2" yellow painted brass petals with bw paper photo under center cover. Shown open. 1896. $625.

11
McKINLEY/ANTI-BRYAN $1\frac{1}{2}$" mechanical disk with slide that changes eagle's image and slogans. 1896. $50.

12
McKINLEY "GOP" ELEPHANT HEAD $1\frac{3}{8}$" brass pin with paper labels inside hinged cover that show woman's undergarment with a padlock and inscription "(Locked) For Protection." 1896. $200.

13
McKINLEY/BRYAN $1\frac{1}{4}$" litho tin pin inscribed "A Sure Winner." Plunger at top positions one of the candidates in the Capitol doorway. 1896. $500.

14
ANTI-BRYAN COFFIN LAPEL STUD 1" silvered brass with hinged lid inscribed "Billy Bryan Nov. 3 '96." Lid opens to reveal Bryan in coffin with inside lid inscribed "Free Silver Knocked Him Out." 1896. $500.

15
McKINLEY/BRYAN "Our Choice" colorful 1" litho lapel stud with movable cover to show Bryan/Sewall or McKinley/Hobart. 1896. $350.

16
BRYAN SILVER BUG $1\frac{1}{4}$" tall silvered brass pin with paper photo and inscription "16/1" on wings that open and close. 1896. $450.

17
ROOSEVELT 1x$1\frac{1}{8}$" rwb brass flag pin with sepia paper photo plus inside paper label reading "Be Your Own Boss..." 1904. $300.

18
ROOSEVELT same as item #17 but reads "Bust the Trust/or the Trust Will Bust You." 1904. $300.

19
TAFT/SHERMAN "My Choice" rwb $2\frac{1}{2}$" litho tin pin with bw portraits that pop up from behind shield. 1908. $650.

20
ROOSEVELT $2\frac{1}{2}$" brown/beige litho pin with string fastened to movable donkey who kicks the elephant. 1932. $60.

29. Ribbons

Ribbons have been issued by the thousands for campaigns and candidates over the past 160 years but certainly not in equal quantities for all candidates. Candidate W. H. Harrison, the first to make extensive use of the ribbon, was also among the most prolific, with more than a hundred variations known for his campaign. Silk, the time-honored fabric for ribbons from the early years, has been replaced by synthetic fabrics since World War II years. Silks are inherently susceptible to weave splits, edge fray and ink fades; nevertheless, a remarkable number of examples have survived. Synthetic fabric can be expected to have longevity but hardly any modern examples can begin to capture the grace, graphics, messages or typography of the nineteenth century classics. Early ribbons came with frequent embellishments such as decorative fabric rosettes. Examples from the 1880s through 1904 often have metal fringe on the bottom edge. Ribbons from the earliest to modern times have been issued for campaign, inaugural, commemorative or memorium purposes. The earliest examples are usually in printed or embossed format and served the dual purpose of a bookmark. Woven designs became popular in the latter third of the nineteenth century and continued in vogue until the 1920s. Ribbon values range from low to high depending upon the age and candidate. Lewis Cass ribbons from 1848 and Franklin Pierce ribbons from 1852 are particularly rare. Campaign ribbons are documented in an excellent reference by Sullivan and Fischer titled *American Political Ribbons and Ribbon Badges* (see bibliography).

1
HARRISON 3x6" long bw. 1840. $250.

2
HARRISON 3x7" long bw. 1840. $250.

3
POLK/DALLAS $3\frac{1}{2}$ x $8\frac{1}{2}$" long bw. 1844. $1200.

4
POLK 3x7" long bw. 1844. $1000.

5
FREMONT $2\frac{1}{2}$ x $6\frac{1}{2}$" long blue/pink. 1856. $300.

6
GRANT $7\frac{1}{2}$" long bw. 1868. $200.

7
GRANT 1x$4\frac{1}{2}$" long bw/rwb. C. 1868. $150.

8
HAYES $1\frac{1}{2}$ x $5\frac{1}{2}$" long bw. 1876. $300.

9
TILDEN/HENDRICKS 2x4" long bw. 1876. $175.

1

2

3

4

5

6

7

8

9

10

11

12

13

14

15

16

17

18

19

20

21

10
GARFIELD/ARTHUR $3\frac{1}{2}$ x 8" long rwb/brown with sepia paper photos. 1880. $300.

11
GARFIELD/ARTHUR $1\frac{1}{4}$ x $2\frac{1}{2}$" long rwb/bw on linen-like paper. 1880. $200.

12
GARFIELD 2x6 $\frac{1}{2}$" long black/gray. 1880. $100.

13
GARFIELD 2x7" long black/blue. 1880. $125.

14
GARFIELD memorial $1\frac{3}{4}$ x $4\frac{1}{2}$" long bw. 1881. $25.

15
CLEVELAND $1\frac{1}{2}$ x $3\frac{1}{2}$" long rwb/bw. 1892. $100.

16
CLEVELAND $2\frac{1}{2}$ x 8" long rwb/gold with sepia paper photo. 1888. $100.

17
CLEVELAND 5" long red celluloid ribbon shaped bookmark with paper photo. 1892. $75.

18
BLAINE/LOGAN 2x6" long bw. 1884. $200.

19
BLAINE $2\frac{1}{2}$ x 9" long bw. 1884. $60.

20
BLAINE/LOGAN $1\frac{3}{4}$ x $3\frac{1}{2}$" long red/gold depicting pine cone. 1884. $50.

21
HARRISON/REID $2\frac{1}{4}$ x7" long bw. 1892. $75.

22
HARRISON 2x7" long bw. 1892. $125.

23
HARRISON/REID 2x6" long bw/rwb. 1892. $125.

24
HARRISON/REID 5" long blue celluloid ribbon shaped bookmark with paper photos. 1892. $125.

25
McKINLEY/HOBART $2\frac{1}{2}$x7" long black/yellow. 1896. $150.

26
McKINLEY 2x7" long black/blue. 1896. $40.

27
McKINLEY 3x7" long black/pink. 1890. $75.

28
McKINLEY $3\frac{1}{2}$x8" long white/blue. 1896. $40.

29
McKINLEY/ROOSEVELT 2x7" long blue/white. 1900. $70.

30
BRYAN $5\frac{1}{4}$" long black/gold. 1908. $65.

31
BRYAN 2x4" long rwb. 1908. $60.

32
BRYAN 5" long bw. 1908. $40.

33
ROOSEVELT 3x7" long blue/white. 1900. $200.

34
ROOSEVELT 2x8" long black/blue. 1900. $35.

22

23

24

25

26

27

28

29

30

31

32

33

34

35

36

37

38

39

40

41

42

43

44

45

46

35
ROOSEVELT $2\frac{1}{2}$ x8" long white/blue. 1912. $175.

36
ROOSEVELT $1\frac{1}{2}$ x $4\frac{1}{2}$ " long rwb. 1912. $35.

37
TAFT/SHERMAN 3x9" long multicolor. 1908. $125.

38
TAFT 2x7" long bw/rwb. 1908. $85.

39
WILSON 3x7" long bw. 1912. $75.

40
COOLIDGE $1\frac{1}{2}$ x4" long blue/gold. 1924. $70.

41
DEWEY/WARREN 2x6" long black/ silvery white. 1948. $20.

42
EISENHOWER/NIXON $2\frac{1}{4}$ x6" long rwb. 1956. $20.

43
KENNEDY $2\frac{1}{2}$ x9" long purple/white. 1956. $250.

44
NIXON $1\frac{1}{2}$ x6" long rwb. 1960. $20.

45
NIXON 2x6" long silver/black. 1968. $10.

46
FORD/DOLE AND CARTER/ MONDALE 2x9" matched pair rwb/gold. 1976. EACH $8.

30. Ribbon Badges

Ribbon badges differ from ribbons, which are fabric strips, by having an added element, usually a medal, celluloid sheet or celluloid button mounted on the fabric or suspended below it. From 1880 through 1920 ribbons and ribbon badges were used concurrently, but then the ribbon badge became the dominant form. As with ribbons, a wide range of prices apply. Convention badges are a type of ribbon badge (see Section 24).

1
HARRISON $2\frac{1}{4}$ x $5\frac{3}{4}$ " long rwb/yellow/ brown with tin disk at center. 1888. $150.

2
HARRISON $2\frac{1}{2}$ x8" long bw/purple with portrait on celluloid sheet. 1892. $100.

3
McKINLEY/HOBART $8\frac{1}{2}$ " long rwb/ silver with bw celluloid. 1896. $125.

4
McKINLEY/HOBART $8\frac{1}{2}$ " long rwb/ gold with sepia celluloid. 1897. $90.

5
McKINLEY/ROOSEVELT $2\frac{3}{4}$ x9" long rwb/green with full color celluloid. 1900. $125.

6
BRYAN tin frame with blue ribbon, sepia cardboard photo and white metal bell. 1908. $60.

7
ROOSEVELT 3x$9\frac{1}{2}$ " long multicolor with sepia celluloid photo. 1904. $200.

8
ROOSEVELT/FAIRBANKS 7" long blue/gold with sepia celluloid. 1904. $150.

9
HARDING 2x5" overall with $1\frac{3}{4}$ " yellow fabric button and yellow ribbon. Commemorates women's right to vote in 1920 election. 1920. $300.

10
COX 5" long bw celluloid in white metal frame with blue ribbon. 1920. $600 or $650 with card.

11
SMITH $2\frac{1}{2}$ " bw button suspended from rwb flag and brass hanger. 1928. $600.

1

2

3

4

5

6

7

8

9

10

11

31. Stickpins

Stickpins feature a long vertical pin about 2" in length. Typical examples start around 1880 and numerous examples are known through 1916. After that, stickpins were less frequently issued and were largely gone by the 1930s. Most stickpins feature display areas of embossed brass, prior to 1896, and then celluloid became the usual medium, usually in a 1" oval format. The majority of stickpins sell between $25 and $75 but the Hughes campaign issued several stickpins with celluloid attachments in a flag shape. These are quite colorful and rare, with values around $1000 for a single portrait and $1500 for jugates.

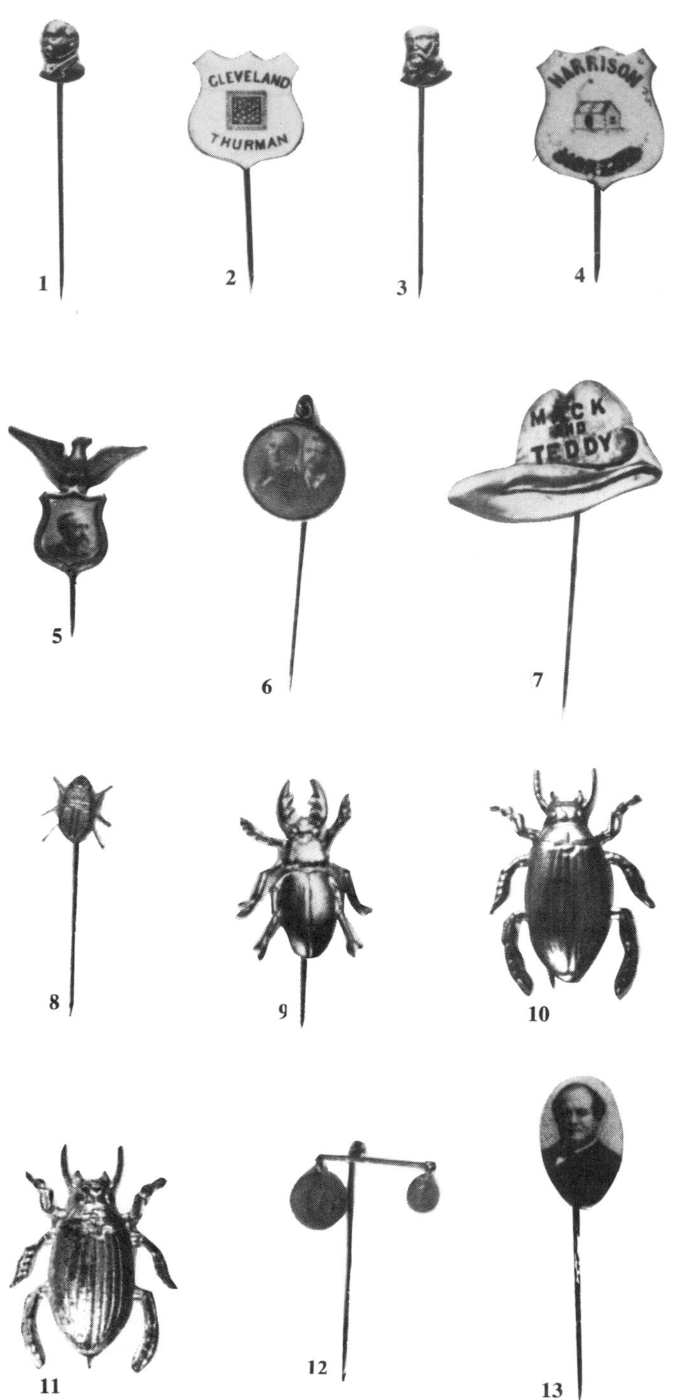

1
CLEVELAND $2\frac{1}{4}$" long brass. 1888. $35.

2
"CLEVELAND/THURMAN" $1\frac{3}{4}$" long bw/red porcelain on brass. 1888. $175.

3
HARRISON $2\frac{1}{4}$" long brass. 1888. $25.

4
"HARRISON/MORTON" 2" long bw porcelain on brass. 1888. $175.

5
HARRISON $1\frac{1}{2}$" tall brass shell with cardboard photo. 1888. $100.

6
McKINLEY/ROOSEVELT $2\frac{1}{4}$" long brass stickpin with bw photo on front and Indian head penny on reverse. 1900. $100.

7
"MACK AND TEDDY" $2\frac{3}{4}$" long brass depicting Rough Rider hat. 1900. $75.

8
McKINLEY $1\frac{3}{4}$" long brass shell gold bug. 1896. $35.

9
McKINLEY $1\frac{1}{2}$" long brass shell gold bug. 1896. $30.

10
McKINLEY $1\frac{3}{4}$" long brass shell gold bug. 1896. $100.

11
BRYAN $1\frac{3}{4}$" long silvered brass shell silver bug. 1896. $120.

12
BRYAN $1\frac{3}{4}$" long brass with miniature "16/1" scale. 1896. $100.

13
BRYAN 1" tall multicolor oval celluloid on stickpin. 1908. $75.

14
ROOSEVELT/FAIRBANKS $1\frac{1}{4}$ " sepia celluloid on stickpin depicts T.R.'s spectacles and lunch pail with slogan "Let Well Enough Alone." 1904. $750.

15
ROOSEVELT 3x$3\frac{1}{2}$ " original card with brass "Fac-simile of the Signature of our Next President." 1904. $100.

16
ROOSEVELT $1\frac{1}{2}$ " long with sepia celluloid. 1904. $30.

17
ROOSEVELT $1\frac{5}{8}$ " long with sepia celluloid. 1904. $30.

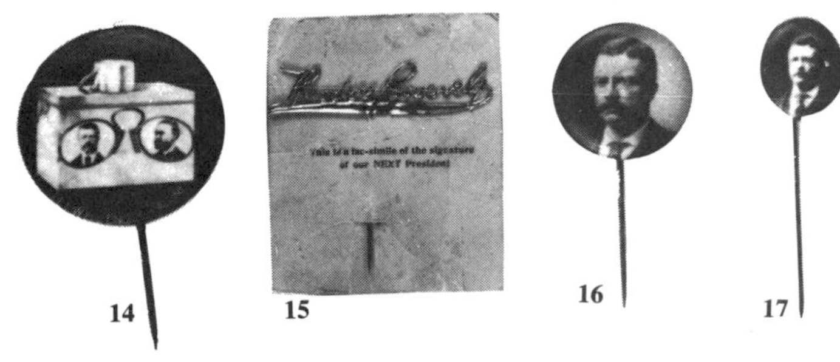

14 15 16 17

18
"T.R." $2\frac{1}{8}$ " embossed brass shell depicting his 'Big Stick.' 1904. $60.

19
PARKER $1\frac{1}{2}$ " long brass with sepia paper photo. 1904. $40.

20
TAFT $1\frac{1}{4}$ " tall white metal bust. 1908. $25.

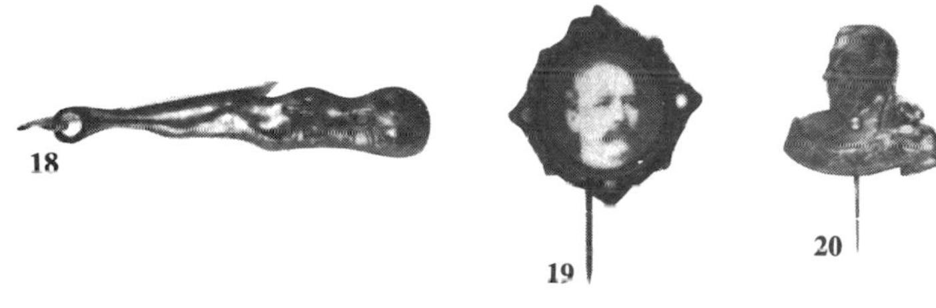

18 19 20

21
TAFT $2\frac{1}{4}$ " long brass with bw paper photo. 1908. $60.

22
TAFT $1\frac{3}{4}$ " tall with sepia celluloid. 1908. $20.

23
HARDING 3" long silvered brass with gray/white photo. 1920. $60.

24
COX $\frac{3}{4}$ " tall with white/blue celluloid. 1920. $60.

25
COX $\frac{3}{4}$ " tall with white/red celluloid. 1920. $60.

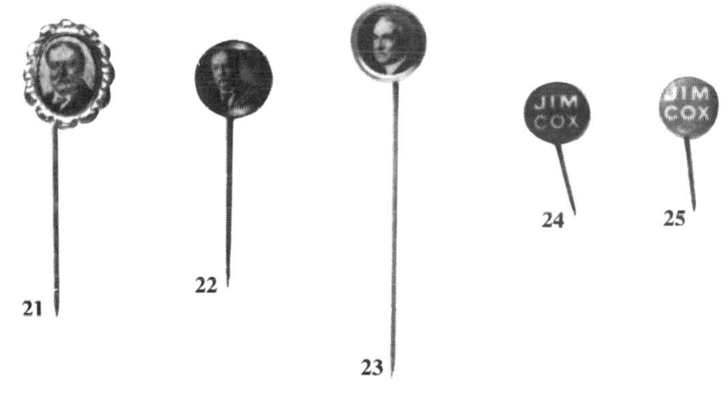

21 22 23 24 25

26
ROOSEVELT $1\frac{3}{4}$ " tall rwb fabric miniature flag. 1936. $12.

27
GEORGE BUSH 2x3" original box holding enamel/brass stickpin inscribed "Vice-President of the United States." C. 1985. $15.

26

27

32. Tabs

Tabs are flat metal pieces, usually lithographed tin, with an extended segment on the top edge which is folded back for attachment to clothing, usually a pocket edge. Most tabs are rectangular but some are die-cut in shapes representing flags, elephants, donkeys, and similar symbolic motifs. The earliest tab, of silvered brass, is from Coolidge's 1924 campaign and brass tabs were used for Hoover and Smith in 1928. The F.D.R. and Willkie 1940 campaigns utilized paper tabs covered with metallic foil. Tabs represent the most inexpensive lapel device give-away an organization can purchase and they are common for all campaigns from 1928 to present. The majority are in the $1 to $5 range.

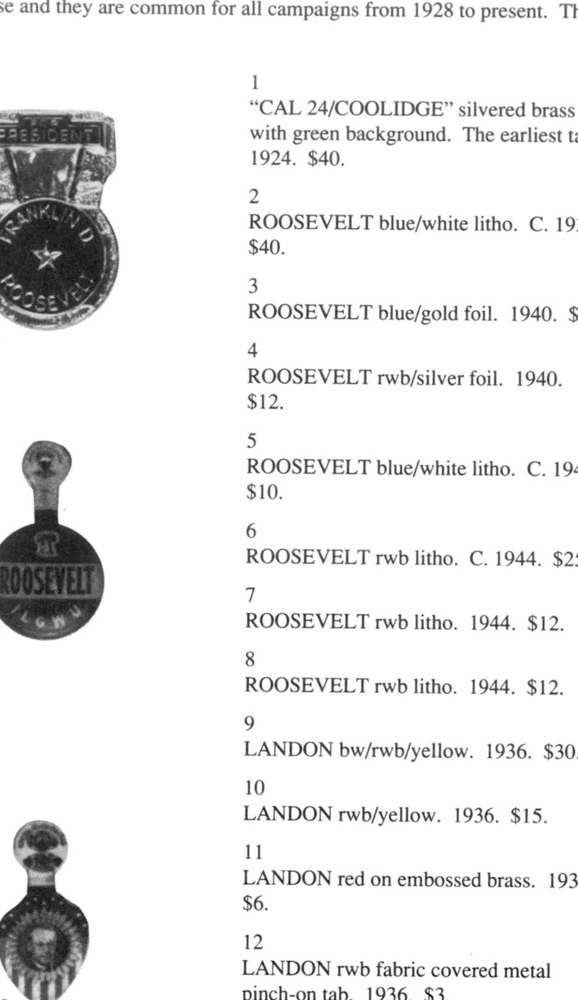

1
"CAL 24/COOLIDGE" silvered brass with green background. The earliest tab. 1924. $40.

2
ROOSEVELT blue/white litho. C. 1936. $40.

3
ROOSEVELT blue/gold foil. 1940. $8.

4
ROOSEVELT rwb/silver foil. 1940. $12.

5
ROOSEVELT blue/white litho. C. 1940. $10.

6
ROOSEVELT rwb litho. C. 1944. $25.

7
ROOSEVELT rwb litho. 1944. $12.

8
ROOSEVELT rwb litho. 1944. $12.

9
LANDON bw/rwb/yellow. 1936. $30.

10
LANDON rwb/yellow. 1936. $15.

11
LANDON red on embossed brass. 1936. $6.

12
LANDON rwb fabric covered metal pinch-on tab. 1936. $3.

13
WILLKIE rwb. 1940. $5.

14
WILLKIE rwb. 1940. $12.

15
DEWEY large rwb litho. C. 1948. $40.

16
DEWEY rwb litho. 1948. $8.

17
TRUMAN blue/white litho. 1948. $20.

18
TRUMAN rwb litho. 1948. $20.

19
TRUMAN rwb litho. 1948. $65.

20
EISENHOWER blue/white litho. C. 1954. $75.

21
EISENHOWER rwb litho. C. 1956. $2.

22
EISENHOWER rwb litho. C. 1956. $2.

23
EISENHOWER rwb litho. C. 1956. $2.

24
EISENHOWER rwb litho. C. 1956. $2.

25
EISENHOWER blue/white litho. 1956. $4.

26
STEVENSON rwb litho. 1956. $5.

27
STEVENSON blue/yellow litho. 1956. $6.

13

14

15

16

17

18

19

20

21

22

23

24

25

26

27

28

29

30

31

32

33

34

35

36

37

38

39

40

41

42

28
KENNEDY red/white litho. 1960. $35.

29
KENNEDY blue/white litho. 1960. $4.

30
KENNEDY rwb litho. 1960. $5.

31
KENNEDY rwb litho. 1960. $5.

32
KENNEDY rwb litho. 1960. $5.

33
KENNEDY blue/white litho. 1960. $25.

34
KENNEDY blue/white. 1960. $15.

35
NIXON blue/white. 1960. $10.

36
NIXON rwb litho. 1960. $5.

37
JOHNSON bw/rwb. 1964. $1.

38
WALLACE rwb litho. 1968. $2.

39
NIXON black/purple/orange. 1972. $5.

40
McGOVERN blue/white litho. One of the few items issued before Eagleton left ticket. 1972. $6.

41
McGOVERN red/white litho. 1972. $10.

42
McGOVERN blue/white litho. 1972. $10.

33. License Plates & Automotive Accessories

Automobiles quickly became vehicles for promoting candidates. Window decals were used in 1920 and at least two 1924 Coolidge license plates are known. License plates are still issued in recent times for use in states where a front plate is not required. Steel or tin license plate attachments were issued for most candidates until automotive streamlining removed license plate brackets from bumpers in favor of standard-sized recesses at car front and rear. This development also gave birth to the widespread use of bumper stickers, political and others. License plate attachments often were an embossed steel or tin rectangle with the candidate's name. Variations include circular attachments, some with reflective glass as part of the design. Other auto accessories include radiator hood mounts, some with receptacles for holding a set of small flags. In the years when spare tires were carried externally on the passenger vehicles, tire covers of canvas or oilcloth were issued with a political printed message. Window stickers and decals also have given way to the bumper sticker in recent years.

1
COOLIDGE 2.5" diameter bw tin litho in silvered metal holder for attachment to car hood. 1924. $350.

2
"HOOVER" silver finished cast aluminum license plate 5x12". C. 1928. $100.

3
"HOOVER" red and white license plate attachment 12" long. C. 1928. $40.

4
"HOOVER" black painted metal/glass reflective car sign. 2.25x2.5x10" long. C. 1928. $175.

5
" 'AL' SMITH FOR PRESIDENT" flat tin oval 4x6" rwb license plate. 1928. $50.

6
SMITH matches item #4. 1928. $175.

7
SMITH 3x10" rwb license plate with pictures of New York skyline on left and U.S. Capitol on right. "From The Sidewalks Of New York To The White House." 1928. $110.

8
SMITH 2.5x10" blue/white litho tin license. 1928. $80.

9
ROOSEVELT matches items #4 and #6. 1932. $175.

1

2

3

4

5

6

7

8

9

10

11

12

13

14

15

16

17

18

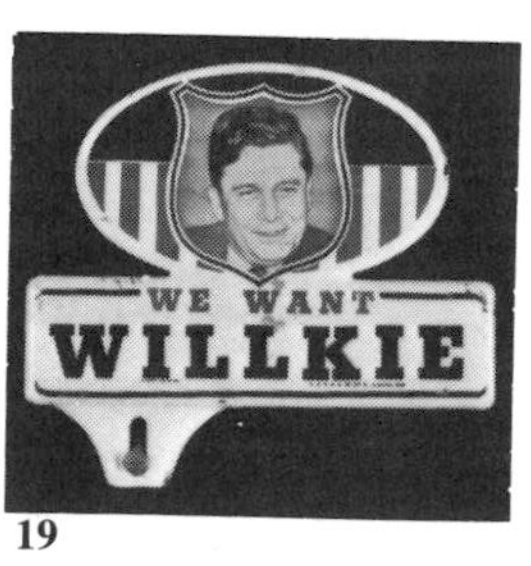

19

10
"ROOSEVELT/GARNER" blue metal license 4x5.5" which has reflective red background behind the blue/white image of the Capitol and the candidates' names. C. 1932. $50.

11
"ROOSEVELT" diecut tin 7x8" which is covered with .25" diameter depressions so that the gold colored donkey and the name will reflect headlights. C. 1936. $85.

12
ROOSEVELT 4.5x11.5" tin plate in rwb inscribed "Forward With Roosevelt 'No Retreat'." C. 1936. $125.

13
"RISE WITH ROOSEVELT" dark blue car attachment with the lettering in white and red. 4.5x12". 1932. $75.

14
ROOSEVELT 3.5" diameter with red reflective background and the slogan "Roosevelt For President" in blue and white. C. 1930s. $30.

15
"RE-ELECT ROOSEVELT" rwb 3x5" license plate. C. 1940. $40.

16
"LANDON AND KNOX" brown/yellow metal car attachment with embossed sunflower petals. 4.5x6.75". 1936. $40.

17
"LANDON/KNOX" blue metal plate with celluloid insert on yellow reflective background with inscription in blue/white. 4x5". 1936. $50.

18
LANDON 6x9" dark blue metal plate with raised white lettering. 1936. $30.

19
"WE WANT WILLKIE" diecut metal with bw portrait and rwb design. 6x6". 1940. $125.

20
WILLKIE 6x8.5" rwb/bw litho tin diecut plate. 1940. $65.

21
"WE WANT WILLKIE" rwb litho tin plate. 4". 1940. $30.

22
"DEWEY/BRICKER" wood fiberboard in rwb. 6x7". 1944. $125.

23
"DEWEY-BRICKER" yellow/blue 12" long fiberboard license plate covered with tiny reflective plastic beads. 1944. $35.

24
"I LIKE IKE" heavy metal license plate in white with raised letters in black. 6x12". C. 1952. $25.

25
EISENHOWER 4x10" heavy metal plate finished in dark red and white. C. 1952. $30.

26
EISENHOWER 12" long blue and white license plate with inscription "Give IKE A Republican Congress In 1954." $35.

27
STEVENSON 3.5x7.5" dark blue bumper sticker with figure of a man in white. "Adlai-Estes" is in day-glo red. 1956. $12.

28
"STEVENSON" metal license plate in white with raised letters in dark blue. 4x12". C. 1956. $40.

29
"KENNEDY FOR PRESIDENT" 4x17.5" bw/rwb bumper sticker. 1960. $8.

30
KENNEDY 4x7" orange/black sticker designed like a license plate. 1960. $30.

31
NIXON 4x7" blue/day-glo orange sticker designed like a license plate. 1960. $15.

20

21

22

23

24

25

26

27

28

29

30

31

32

33

34

35

36

37

38

39

40

41

42

43

32
"LBJ 464" miniature 2x4" yellow on black tin license plate. Also inscribed "California." 1964. $12.

33
"GOLDWATER" red on white 6x12" metal license plate. 1964. $10.

34
"GOLDWATER" metal plate 4x12" in yellow with raised letters in blue and slogan "Victory In '64." $20.

35
GOLDWATER 3.75x11.5" black/orange bumper sticker. 1964. $5.

36
"NIXON/AGNEW" rwb metal car plate. 5x12". C. 1968. $25.

37
"NIXON NOW" plastic form 4x4.5x20" long with rwb sticker for placing on top of a car. 1972. $15.

38
"WALLACE FOR PRESIDENT" bw/fleshtone/pink license plate. 6x12". 1968. $12.

39
"1972 DEMOCRATIC NATIONAL CONVENTION/MIAMI BEACH" rwb plastic license. 6x11". $15.

40
"McGOVERN-EAGLETON UNITE AMERICA" rwb 6x11" plastic license plate. Probably an original McGovern/Eagleton item as it matches item #39. 1972. $30.

41
CARTER 6x12" white plastic with rwb/green design. 1976. $20.

42
REAGAN/CARTER campaign novelty set. Flat diecut white plastic figures on a thin wire and rubber suction cup that can be mounted to a dashboard or other object. 1980. EACH $12.

43
"BUSH/QUAYLE 88" rwb bumper sticker. 3.5x9.5". $2.

34. Medalets & Medals

Medalets and medals are coin-like medallic pieces struck to promote or commemorate people and events. Issues under $1\frac{3}{4}$" in diameter are known as medalets and those $1\frac{3}{4}$" or larger are referred to as medals. Within the political collectibles hobby, medalets are frequently called tokens, although the more exacting definition of a token is an issue used as a substitute for money. There are a few political issues from the Civil War era and from the financial depression of the 1830s that can properly be referred to as tokens.Medalets and medals are most often struck from white metal, copper, brass, or bronze. Medalets frequently have a rim hole as made, for fastening to clothing, and this does not detract from the value. Worn surfaces, dents, nicks, and scratches do decrease the object's value. Many nineteenth century medalets and medals were struck in very small quantities and are undervalued considering their beauty and scarcity. Escalating prices in other areas, particularly early celluloid buttons, is beginning to generate increased collector interest in medallic issues.Inauguration commemoratives are known as early as the George Washington to John Adams era. Campaign issues blossomed in 1840 and continued with numerous varieties of high quality throughout the rest of the century. Medallic issues slacked after 1904 and revived with the presidency of Franklin D. Roosevelt. Medallic issues are still struck for campaigns and inaugurations. Official inauguration medals in recent years are usually issued in limited but ample numbers. Early 1900s inauguration pieces were issued in very limited numbers to satisfy only a selected few party faithfuls. As a result, scarcity commands top dollar for these issues.

1
WASHINGTON 1" brass with reverse slogan "Success to the United States." 1792. $300.

2
JACKSON 1" brass. 1824. $70.

3
HARRISON $1\frac{3}{4}$" white metal depicting Bunker Hill monument. 1840. $140.

4
HARRISON 1" brass with log cabin reverse. 1840. $25.

5
HENRY CLAY $1\frac{3}{8}$" white metal. 1844. $150.

6
TAYLOR 1" brass. 1848. $30.

7
CASS $1\frac{5}{8}$" white metal. 1848. $500.

8
VAN BUREN $1\frac{1}{8}$" U.S. copper penny counterstamped "Vote the Land Free." 1848. $150.

9
PIERCE $1\frac{5}{8}$" white metal. 1852. $300.

10
SCOTT $1\frac{3}{16}$" brass. 1852. $35.

11
BUCHANAN $1\frac{1}{8}$" brass. 1856. $35.

12
FILLMORE $1\frac{3}{8}$" white metal. 1856. $90.

13  14  15

16  17  18  19

20  21  22

23  24  25

26

27

28

29

13
FREMONT 2 $\frac{3}{8}$" white metal. The largest 1856 medal depicting the first Republican candidate. $400.

14
FREMONT $\frac{7}{8}$" brass. 1856. $30.

15
LINCOLN 1$\frac{1}{2}$" white metal. 1860. $200.

16
LINCOLN 1$\frac{1}{4}$" white metal. 1860. $125.

17
LINCOLN 1 $\frac{1}{8}$" copper with reverse depicting the "Rail Splitter of the West." 1860. $65.

18
LINCOLN 1 $\frac{3}{8}$" white metal. 1864. $125.

19
LINCOLN $\frac{3}{4}$" German silver. 1864. $100.

20
BELL 1 $\frac{1}{8}$" brass. 1860. $50.

21
McCLELLAN 1 $\frac{3}{8}$" white metal. 1864. $50.

22
McCLELLAN 1 $\frac{3}{16}$" brass. 1864. $60.

23
GRANT 1 $\frac{1}{4}$" white metal. 1868. $55.

24
GRANT 1" white metal with brass shield hanger. 1872. $75.

25
SEYMOUR 1 $\frac{1}{8}$" brass. 1868. $50.

26
GREELEY $\frac{15}{16}$" brass. 1872. $35.

27
TILDEN 1 $\frac{1}{4}$" silver. 1876. $90.

28
GARFIELD 1" brass. 1880. $20.

29
HANCOCK 1" brass. 1880. $20.

30
CLEVELAND 3" wood with brass ring at top. 1884. $140.

31
CLEVELAND 1" brass. 1884. $25.

32
CLEVELAND 1 $\frac{3}{4}$ " aluminum. 1892. $40.

33
BLAINE 1 $\frac{1}{4}$ " white metal. 1884. $50.

34
BLAINE 1 $\frac{1}{8}$ " white metal. 1884. $35.

35
HARRISON 1" brass with brass hanger. 1888. $35.

36
HARRISON 1 $\frac{1}{2}$ " white metal. 1888. $50.

37
HARRISON 1 $\frac{3}{4}$ " aluminum. 1892. $40.

38
McKINLEY/ANTI-BRYAN 3 $\frac{3}{8}$ " white metal satirical medal with Liberty on obverse and eagle on reverse inscribed "United States of America 16 to 1 NIT." 1896. $35.

39
TAFT 3" bronze Philadelphia Mint medal for Taft's 1909 inauguration. $75.

40
HOOVER 3" silvered brass metal by the sculptor C. Devreese. C. 1930. $50.

41
EISENHOWER 2 $\frac{3}{4}$ " bronze 1957 official inaugural medal by Medallic Art Co. 21,705 were issued. $15.

42
NIXON 2 $\frac{3}{4}$ " bronze 1969 official inaugural medal by Medallic Art Co. in original box. $12.

43
NIXON 2 $\frac{3}{4}$ " bronze 1973 official inaugural medal by Franklin Mint. $20.

30 31 32 33 34 35 36 37 38 39 40 41 42 43

35. Metal Trays

Metal trays are another rather limited area of political collecting. Earlier and later examples are known, but most of the highly desired trays were produced in a 12-year period ending with the 1908 campaign. As a result, McKinley, Bryan, Roosevelt, Parker and Taft are pictured almost to the total absence of others before and after. These trays are lithographed metal and generally quite beautiful. Typical sizes are the serving tray and smaller coaster tray. During the same era, the newly produced metal aluminum was used for making small trays to hold pins or other small objects. The images and inscriptions are usually done in black ink on the bare silver-colored metal. These trays, being small and much less graphically appealing, are valued at a fraction of what full color lithographed trays are worth.

1

2

3

4

5

6

7

8

1
McKINLEY/ROOSEVELT 3x5" rwb aluminum pin tray with raised scalloped edge. C. 1900. $25.

2
"W. McKINLEY" 13x16" multicolor lithographed tin serving tray w/1" high raised rim. C. 1900. $125.

3
McKINLEY 3.5x5" thin aluminum pin tray with raised edge surrounding brown portrait and inscription "Our Next President." 1896. $15.

4
GARFIELD/LINCOLN/McKINLEY 3x5" aluminum pin tray with black on silver portraits and inscription "Our Three Martyred Presidents." C. 1901. $20.

5
ROOSEVELT 3x5" rwb pin tray with inscription "Souvenir Eastern Maine State Fair." 1902. $25.

6
TAFT/SHERMAN 4.25" multicolor lithographed tin pin tray with names of Republican presidential candidates from 1856 to 1908 printed around raised rim. 1908. $80.

7
TAFT 3x5" aluminum pin tray with black and silver photo and inscription "Souvenir Savanna, Ill." C. 1910. $25.

8
KENNEDY 8" multicolor metal memorial tray featuring the famous quote "Ask Not What Your Country Can Do For You/Ask What You Can Do For Your Country." 1963. $20

36. Mourning Items

Since George Washington's death in 1799, numerous objects have been issued to mark the passing of a current or former president. Presidents dying in office are eulogized by the greatest number of items; so a wide variety of objects exist for W. H. Harrison, Lincoln, Garfield, McKinley, Franklin Roosevelt and Kennedy. In the nineteenth century, ceramic pieces, medallic issues, and ribbons are the most common forms, while in the twentieth century buttons, medallic issues and all forms of paper predominate. Mourning items are not avidly collected, with the exception of objects related to the Founding Fathers since any material associated with these earliest presidents is rare.

1
JACKSON 9.5x13.5" tinted bw print by N. Currier with caption "We Mourn Our Loss." C. 1845. $85.

2
HARRISON 3x6.5" bw silk ribbon inscribed "In Memory of Departed Worth." 1841. $125.

3
HARRISON 2.25x7" bw silk ribbon inscribed "Our Nation Mourns A Hero Gone." 1841. $85.

4
LINCOLN 13x20" "Funeral of Abraham Lincoln" Philadelphia Inquirer newspaper from Thursday, April 20, 1865 showing his funeral car and coffin. $100.

5
LINCOLN bw portrait surrounded by purple oval on 2x10" woven silk ribbon by T. Stevens. C. 1865. $225.

6
DOUGLAS 3x7" fabric ribbon with facsimile signature, birth date, and death date. C. 1861. $150.

7
GRANT 2.5" square by .5" deep gray/ blue tin box by Sommers Brothers holds 2.5" white metal medal. 1885. $95.

8
GRANT 2.25x7" bw ribbon with black crepe rosette. Inscribed "Obsequies/ Cleveland/ Veterans." 1885. $25.

9
"U.S. GRANT" 24x36" bw/blue banner. C. 1885. $225.

10
"GARFIELD" 9.5" tall bisque bust. C. 1881. $150.

1 2 3 4 5 6 7

8

9

10

11

12

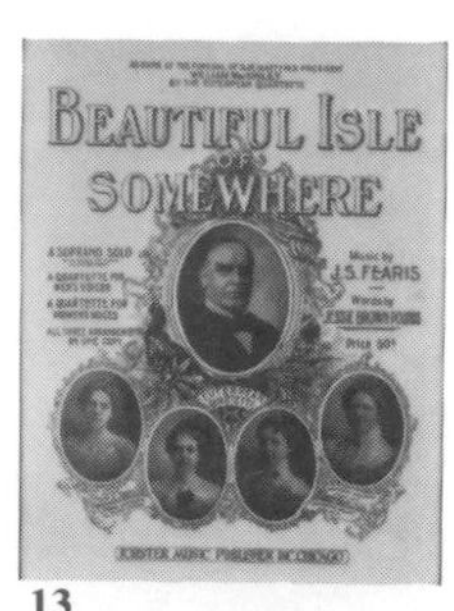

13

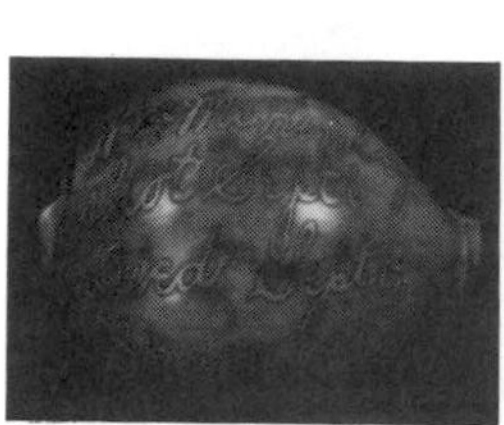

14

15

16

17

18

19

20

21

22

23

24

25

11
"GARFIELD'S FUNERAL MARCH" 6 page sheet music with bold black cover. 9.5x12.5". 1881. $12.

12
"McKINLEY'S MEMORIAL MARCH" 6 page sheet music with bw cover. 11x13.5". 1901. $10.

13
McKINLEY 6 page sheet music with bw cover. 9x12". 1901. $13.

14
"WM. McKINLEY" 2.5" long seashell etched with dates of shooting and death. 1901. $30.

15
LINCOLN/GARFIELD/McKINLEY 9.5" white china calendar plate with full color portraits and rwb flags. Captioned "Drink Bonnie Rye/Every Swallow Makes A Friend." 1912. $30.

16
THEODORE ROOSEVELT 10x13" bronze plaque by James Earle Fraser. 1920. $150.

17
FRANKLIN ROOSEVELT 11x14" full color memorial poster. 1945. $25.

18
"ADLAI STEVENSON" 8x10" memorial comic book by Dell with front color picture and bw portraits on back. 1966. $10.

19
KENNEDY complete issue of "The New York Times-Saturday, Nov. 23, 1963" that followed his assassination. $25.

20
KENNEDY 8x10" full color memorial comic book. 1964. $15.

21
KENNEDY 5.5" tall clear glass with blue/white portrait and famous quote "Ask Not..." C. 1963. $20.

22
KENNEDY 7" diameter bw celluloid memorial button. 1963. $12.

23
KENNEDY 20x36" woven tapestry with blue fringe at bottom. C. 1964. $25.

24
"JOHN-JOHN/CAROLINE" pair of 6" tall colored china figures by "Inarco." 1964. EACH $40.

25
JACKIE in mourning clothing 3x4x6" tall colored china planter by "Inarco" Japan. 1964. $40.

37. Novelties (Miscellaneous)

Novelties include probably hundreds of random campaign objects but few produced in sufficient quantity to form a comprehensive collection based on similarities between the objects. Examples are thread boxes, needle cases, sewing kits, trinket boxes, collar boxes, pillboxes, hair brushes, mechanical pop-up "eggs," change purses, key purses, bottle openers, beverage cans, bookends, razors, knives, doorstops, stereoscope picture cards, phonograph records, shaving mugs, food boxes or similar containers.

1
WASHINGTON 2.5" tall dark maroon on white china mug. C. 1815. $1250.

2
"JOHN ADAMS M.4. 1797" leather bridal rosette, 3" diameter, used on a horse that pulled Adams' carriage in the inaugural procession. $1035.

3
"THOMAS JEFFERSON" steel engraving from a period book. C. 1801. $125.

4
MADISON 24x33" brown/yellow fabric picturing Washington/Jefferson/Madison with slogan "Liberty and Independence Our Country's Pride & Boast." C. 1812. $3000.

5
"MUNROE" (MONROE) 2.5" tall blue and white mug. C. 1817. $5000.

6
"JOHN Q. ADAMS" hexagonally-shaped sewing box with "People's Choice" motto on lid and bw portrait under glass inside the lid. 1824. $1500.

7
ANTI-VAN BUREN 3x5.5" metamorphic card with colorful image of Van Buren holding either "A BEAUTIFUL GOBLET OF WHITEHOUSE CHAMPAGNE" or "AN UGLY MUG OF LOG-CABIN HARD CIDER." 1840. $175.

8
POLK 10x14" blue/yellow/pink hand-colored print with portraits of Presidents Washington through Polk by N. Currier. 1844. $150

1

2

3

4

5

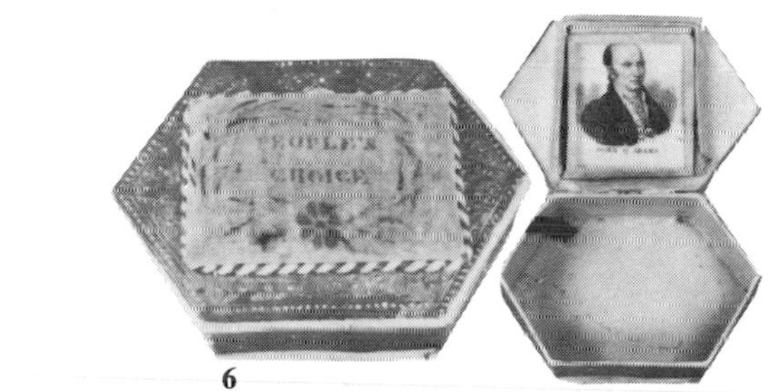

6

7

8

9

10

11

12

13

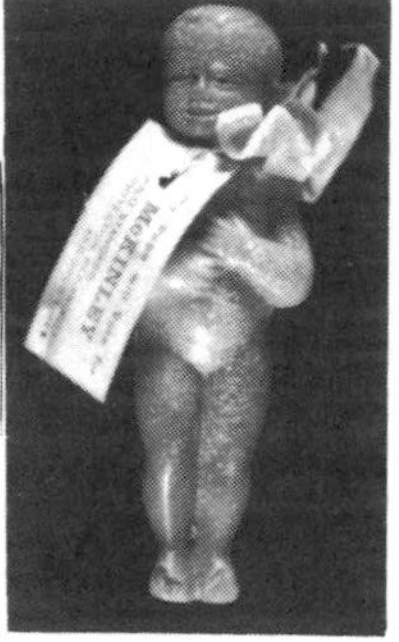

14

15

16

9
LINCOLN photograph on 4x5" translucent white glass sheet known as a 'lithopane'. C. 1864. $1000.

10
"ABRAHAM LINCOLN" print by Kellogg about 10x14". 1860. $300.

11
"ABRAHAM LINCOLN/ANDREW JOHNSON" print by Currier & Ives about 10x14". 1864. $1000.

12
McCLELLAN tin type photo with hand-tinted gold buttons and bars on his uniform. Mounted in a sixth plate case. C. 1864. $500.

13
McKINLEY 4.5" long naked baby molded in light tan soap with original tag and box reading "My Papa Will Vote For McKinley..." 1896. $100.

14
McKINLEY 12x18" bw/blue parade flag with slogan "Patriotism, Protection & Prosperity." 1896. $200.

15
BRYAN 1.25x3.25x5" tall black cardboard box with bw/gold/red label reading "My Choice Whiskey/Bryan For President." Inside is a clear glass whiskey flask. C. 1896. $150.

16
ROOSEVELT/JOHNSON 4x7.5 green/white certificate awarded for a $1 Progressive Party contribution in 1912. $100

17
TAFT 2.5x2 3/4" tall diecut aluminum bookmark in the shape of a teddy bear with portraits of Taft on the front and Sherman on the back. C. 1908. $125.

18
"HOOVER" hot pad with blue/white cover and brown asbestos underneath. 5x5.5". C. 1928. $50.

19
"HOOVER/CURTIS" 1.25x4x2.5" tall beige celluloid elephants with red and black detailing. C. 1928. $150.

20
HOOVER/CURTIS 3x5" rwb needle book. C. 1928. $20.

21
"HOOVER FOR PRESIDENT" flat litho tin 8" stove pipe cover in white/dark blue. 1928. $40.

22
"SMITH FOR PRESIDENT" matches item #21. 1928. $40.

23
"AL SMITH" cardboard sign in bw/rwb. 9.5". C. 1928. $150.

24
"AL SMITH" colorful 16x19" cardboard sign with inscription "You Know Him By His Hat." Easel on reverse. 1928. $200.

25
SMITH 4.5x6" celluloid sign with rwb border surrounding bw portrait. 1928. $150.

26
ROOSEVELT/LANDON 2x3" with six moveable bw celluloid sheets showing the 1936 candidates. $125

17

18

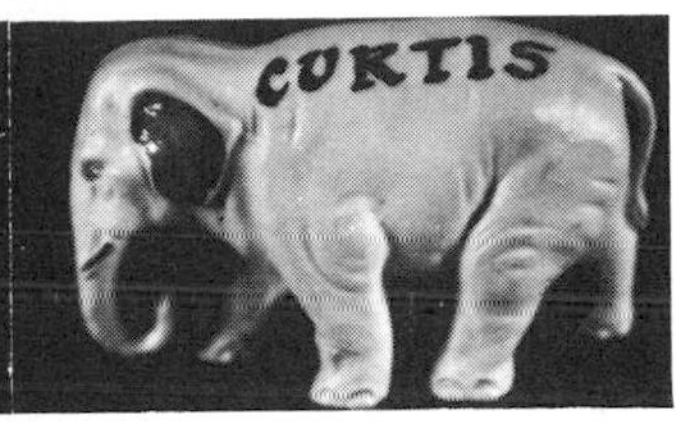

19

20

21

22

23

24

25

26

27

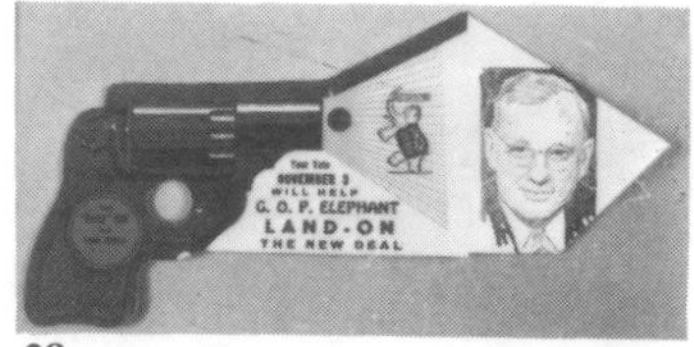

28

29

30

31

Chicago Daily Tribune

DEWEY DEFEATS TRUMAN

G.O.P. Sweep Indicated in State; Boyle Leads in City

32

33

34

35

Look

LINCOLN'S LAST DAYS

NIXON FIT TO BE PRESIDENT?

36

John Fitzgerald Kennedy

United States Senate

Massachusetts

37

27
ROOSEVELT 5x8" colorful cardboard 'bang' gun marked "Vote The Straight Ticket." 1936. $100.

28
LANDON similar to item #27. Inscribed "Land-On The New Deal." 1936. $80.

29
LANDON 3.5x5.5" mechanical card with pro-Landon slogans and face with moveable lips. 1936. $40.

30
WILLKIE 15x17" blue cloth flag with white lettering attached to a 3 foot wood stick. 1940. $75.

31
DEWEY 2.75" diameter by .625" deep blue/white celluloid cover on brass compact. C. 1944. $50.

32
"DEWEY DEFEATS TRUMAN" complete issue of the "Chicago Daily Tribune" newspaper from Wednesday, Nov. 3, 1948. One of America's most famous newspaper headlines. $700.

33
TRUMAN/DEWEY 4x8" rwb cardboard folder with a push or pull tab to select either a Truman or Dewey image. 1948. $100.

34
TRUMAN 4" tall composition/cork bottle stopper in full color. C. 1950. $50.

35
EISENHOWER from same series as item #34. $40.

36
"IS NIXON FIT TO BE PRESIDENT? Exclusive Copies of his Income Tax Returns." Issue of *Look* magazine for Feb. 24, 1953. $12.

37
KENNEDY 1.75x3.75" stiff white card inscribed "John Fitzgerald Kennedy/ United States Senate/Massachusetts" with small gold embossed eagle at upper left corner. 1950s. $75

38
KENNEDY 4" tall colored composition/cork bottle stopper. C. 1961. $60.

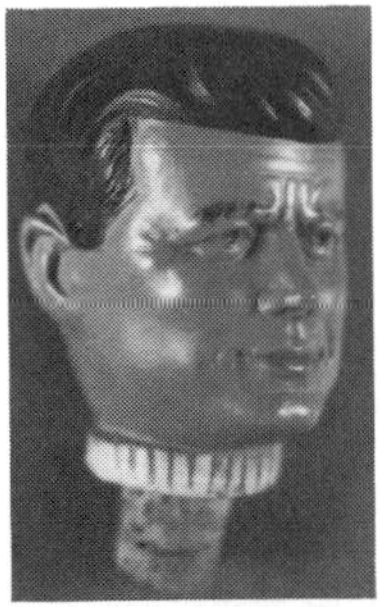

38

39
KENNEDY/NIXON pair of 3x6" rwb "Good Humor Ice Cream" bags for covering "Presidential Bars" for a meeting or party. 1960. J.F.K. $30. R.M.N. $10.

39

40
ANTI-JOHNSON 4x6" bw cardboard doorknob hanger. C. 1964. $10.

40

41
"GOLD WATER" green/white cardboard carrying wrapper holds complete set of six white/gold/green metallic tin cans that once held "Gold Water" soda. 1964. $90.

41

42
"GOLD WATER" same as #41 but a single 5" tall can. 1964. $12.

42

43
"GOLD WATER/A COLOGNE FOR AMERICANS" gold box 2x4" with a glass bottle of cologne. 1964. $30.

43

44
"NIXON'S THE ONE" cardboard fund raiser record with excerpts from the 1968 acceptance speech. 7x7". $12.

44

45
NIXON 1.5" brass/rwb plastic keychain disk with knife blades. C. 1972. $15.

45

46
McGOVERN/EAGLETON 5x8" "Campaign Products Catalog" from Votes Unlimited Corp. with bw/purple cover. 1972. $40.

46

47
ANTI-McGOVERN 7x10x1" box containing satirical "give-away" objects issued by Fun Factory Productions. 1972. $25.

47

48
CARTER "THE PREZ" plastic fishing lure in rwb box with clear plastic slip cover. 2.25" long. C. late 1970s. $15.

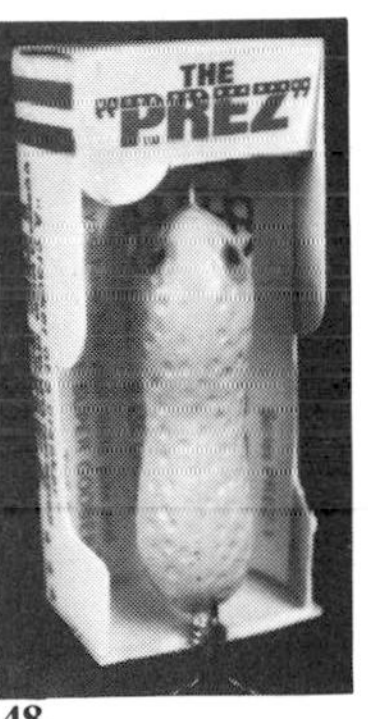

48

49
GEORGE BUSH actual golf ball by "Wilson" with .5" diameter full color decal depicting Vice-Presidential Seal. Original blue box has gold facsimile signature. C. mid-1980s. $75.

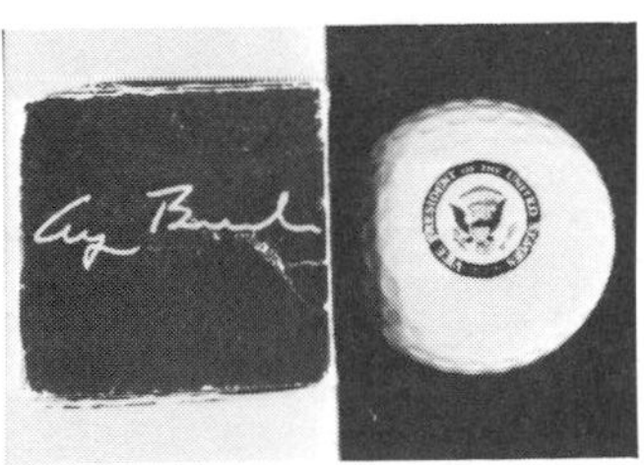

49

50
"ABC NEWS ELECTION NIGHT" full color 3x4"tag laminated in clear plastic. Tag has black background with illustrations of Bush and Dukakis pinback buttons. Nov. 8, 1988. $15.

50

38. Paperweights

Paperweights are a recurring artifact of political history although there are no known examples for many nineteenth century campaigns. By their nature, paperweights are normally of iron, lead or heavy glass. Paperweights are known for many twentieth century campaigns and date back to Millard Fillmore. The most popular use occurred between 1896 and 1904; these weights were made from heavy glass domes or rectangles with pictures applied to the underneath surface so they could be seen through the glass.

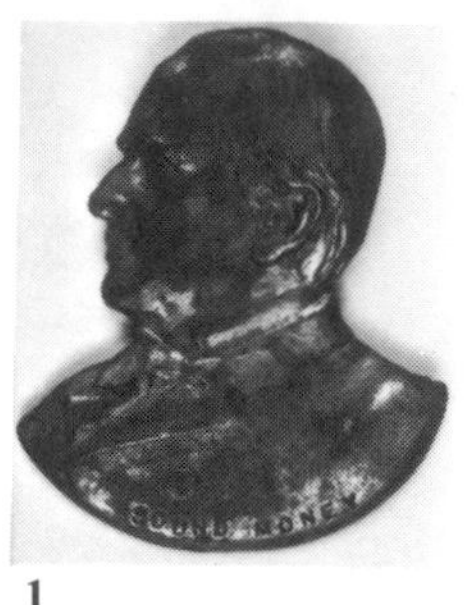

1

2

3

4

5

6

7

1
McKINLEY "SOUND MONEY" 4x4" lead bust with brass finish. The image is slightly raised and the inscription is along the bottom edge. C. 1896. $35.

2
McKINLEY 3.5" tall silvered white metal bust similar to a cane head but with a 2.25" edge inscribed "Protection-Prosperity." Bottom edge of bust is inscribed "Hon. Wm. McKinley-Our Next President." C. 1896. $100.

3
McKINLEY 2.5x4x1" deep clear glass with sepia photo inscribed "Pres. McKinley, Wife and Home/Canton, O." Marked on reverse "Sent Glass & Nov. Co." 1896. $30.

4
THEODORE ROOSEVELT 3x3x1" thick clear glass with sepia photo inscribed "G.A.R. Washington, D.C., October 6-11, 1902/President Theo Roosevelt." $75.

5
ROOSEVELT BEARS 3x3" clear glass depicting Roosevelt bears in gold. C. 1908. $80.

6
"TAFT" 2.5x5x3" tall figural weight designed like a steamroller with inscription on the bottom "The Grid Iron Club Dec. 12, 1908 Willard Hotel, Washington D.C." $250.

7
ROOSEVELT "A NEW DEAL" 2x3" silvered metal with flat reverse and front high relief portrait. Reverse has a 1932 copyright and letters standing for "National Democratic Committee." $40.

39. Parade Canes, Lanterns & Torches

Parade canes and torches are believed by many to be the most representative artifacts of campaign excitement in the middle 1800s through the turn of the next century. A major parade could easily attract thousands of spectators, with related oratory and rallies lasting up to three days. Parades were commonly of the torchlight variety with great clatter added by sirens, horns, ratchet noisemakers, whistles, drums and other musical instruments. Parade canes and swagger sticks exist for most successful presidential candidates from U.S. Grant through the Wilson campaign of 1912. Most examples feature a life-like bust handle of brass, silver or pewter with a few examples in tin or lead. Non-portrait canes usually serve a dual purpose of noisemaker or torch carrier. Torches and lanterns are a fascinating collecting area with a surprising number still in existence. Torchlights were designed for an open flame and lanterns for an enclosed flame. Torches are generally of the metal canister type, with the exceptions of several clever figural designs or function designs such as hat torches. Lanterns exist in many design forms, either basically tin or glass or a combination of the two. In an era when function obviously overruled safety, lantern examples are also known in wood and paper.

1
LINCOLN/EAGLE TORCH 2.5x9x12.5" tall brass colored tin torch supported by a wire loop with fitting for carrying pole. Eagle image is two-sided and serves as the fuel reservoir. Similar designs date to Harrison's inaugural parade in 1841 although this example is c. 1860. $1250.

2
"GRANT/WILSON" paper and cardboard lantern 7.5" diameter by 12" tall with design in dark blue and light purple with stars above and below the names inscribed around the center. There is a tin holder on the inside for a candle. 1872. $300.

3
"SEYMOUR/BLAIR" 7.5" diameter by 12" tall cardboard and paper lantern in beige but most of its surface is covered with purple and dark blue designs. 1868. $300.

4
"GREELEY AND BROWN" 7.5" diameter by 12" tall cardboard and paper lantern in beige with designs in fuschia and blue with a pair of clasped hands depicted above the names. 1872. $300.

5
CAMPAIGN PARADE TORCH 4x5x9" tall that swivels on the metal frame when fitted on a wooden pole. C. 1888. $50.

6
CAMPAIGN PARADE TORCH in brass, only 4" tall with two wires for mounting atop a parade helmet. C. 1880s. $50.

7
HARRISON 'BEAVER-HAT' parade torch made of tin finished in black. There is a brass holder for the wick. 6.5x6.5x10.5" tall. 1888. $350.

8
"HARRISON AND MORTON/ PROTECTION" wood cane 35" long covered with rwb paper and bw labor symbol of an arm and hand holding a hammer. 1888. $150.

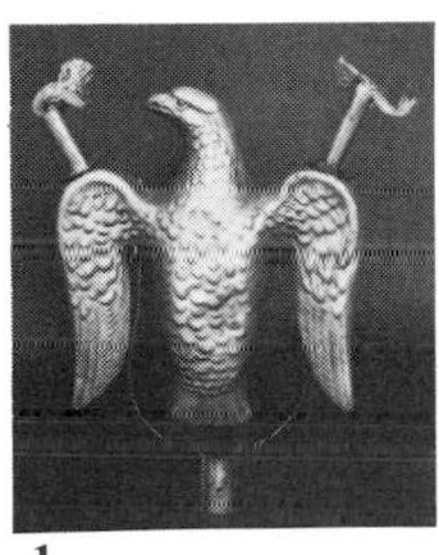
1

2

3

4

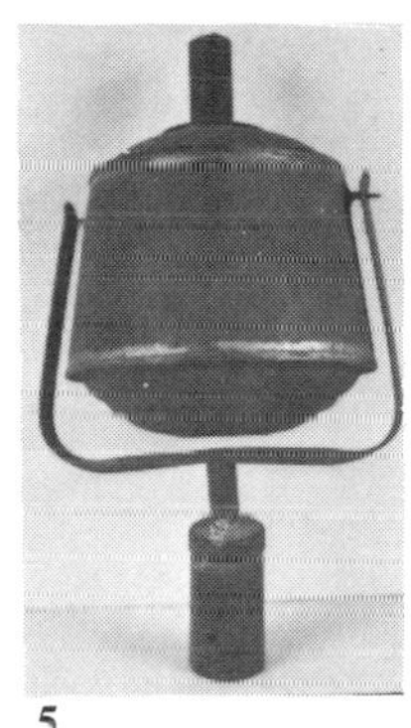
5

6

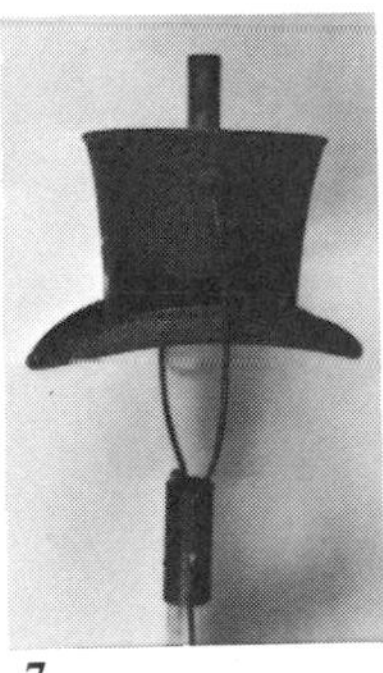
7

8

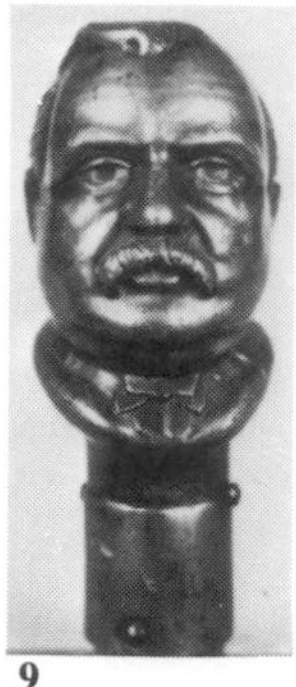

9

10

9
CLEVELAND walking stick 36" tall which has white metal bust of Cleveland as the handle. C. 1888. $200.

10
"McKINLEY AND ROOSEVELT" lunch bucket type lantern 10" tall of painted black tin with handle and removable lid. A 3x4" hole is cut into each side and covered with fine wire screen. When lit from the inside, the light shows through the papers behind the screens to reveal the messages. 1900. $700.

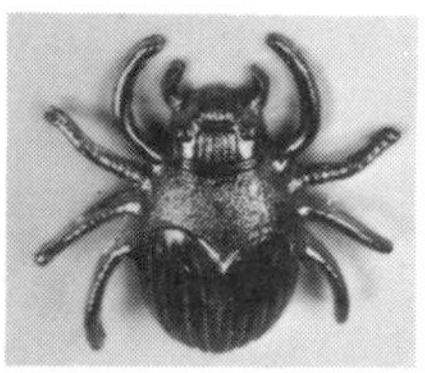

11

12

11
McKINLEY 3.5" long by 3" wide horse saddle blanket gold bug pin. White metal with a gold finish. C. 1896. $125.

12
McKINLEY 4.5" long tin horn with inscription "Patriotism/Protection/ Prosperity." C. 1896. $75.

13

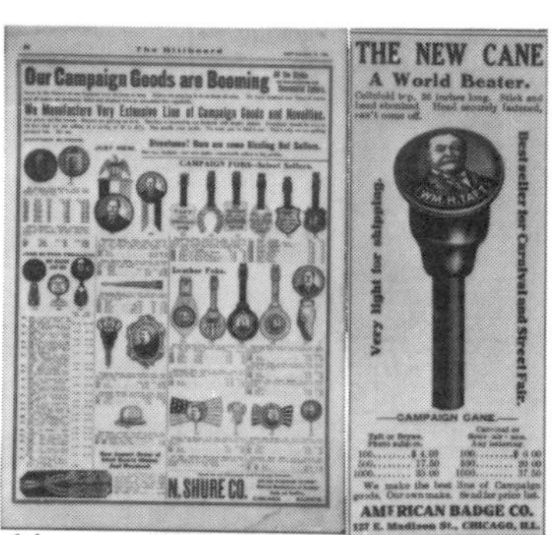
Our Campaign Goods are Booming

We Manufacture Very Extensive Line of Campaign Goods and Novelties.

CAMPAIGN FOBS

N. SHURE CO.

THE NEW CANE
A World Beater.

Very light for shipping.

Best seller for Carnival and Street Fair.

—CAMPAIGN CANE—

We make the best line of Campaign goods. Our own make. Send for price list.

AMERICAN BADGE CO.
127 E. Madison St., CHICAGO, ILL.

14

13
"ROOSEVELT/FAIRBANKS" wood noisemaker. A 4.5" handle holds a 1.5x1.5x8.5" wood bar that swings around. A wood slat is snapped by a gear-like wheel creating a very loud sound. 1904. $150.

14
TAFT/BRYAN CAMPAIGN GOODS. Complete issue of "The Billboard-America's Leading Amusement Weekly" magazine from Sept. 19, 1908. Back cover shows items available from the "N. Sure Co., Chicago." Inside page includes an ad for the Taft "Campaign Cane" by the "American Badge Co." 10x14". 56 pages. $30.

15

16

15
"ROOSEVELT/CENTURY OF PROGRESS" finely detailed cane head with 2.75" tall bust of F.D.R. in white metal with dark bronze finish. C. 1933. $35.

16
"CROW FOR THE DEMOCRATS" cardboard canister 2.5x9.5" tall with dark red metal end caps and brightly colored three-dimensional tin rooster riveted on top. Side of canister has heavy wire crank that turns to produce a rooster-like crowing sound. Probably c. 1930s. $200.

VOTE STRAIGHT
DEMOCRATIC
November 2, 1948

17

17
TRUMAN rwb cardboard horn with donkey design around all sides. "Vote Straight Democratic November 2, 1948." $35.

40. Pennants

Pennants, traditionally felt fabric, sometimes paper, are known for practically all presidential candidates from 1896 to the present. The most desirable versions picture the candidate(s), followed by those issued for specific conventions or inaugurations.

1
WILSON 22" long with full color portrait and slogan "Governor Woodrow Wilson Our Next President." 1912. $40.

2
WILSON INAUGURATION 7x17" dark purple felt with tin support bar crimped onto the top edge. Glued inside a gold design is a paper shield 3x4" in rwb with bw picture of Wilson and inscription "March 4th Inauguration/1913 Washingt'n D.C." $40.

3
"CALVIN COOLIDGE" with name in white letters on blue felt 10x25." Portrait is in fleshtone with red and blue accents plus there is a rwb circle around portrait and below is a bw scroll with yellow outlining. 1924. $100.

4
"COOLIDGE-DAWES" white lettering on blue felt 11x29". Pennant is for "Official Car" taking part in the "Lincoln Tour 1924." $75.

5
"KEEP COOL-IDGE" cut-out beige felt letters on black felt background 7.5x26." 1924. $30.

6
"HARRY TRUMAN FOR PRESIDENT" white on bright red felt pennant 8.5x25" with four small streamers. 1948. $35.

7
DEWEY white/dark maroon pennant 4.5x12" with four felt streamers. 1948. $15.

8
EISENHOWER dark blue felt 8.5x24" with image in bright yellow. Jugate pictures with slogan "Your Best Bet In 52 For A Winning Team." $15.

9
"EISENHOWER-NIXON INAUGURATION" dark brown felt 11x29" with lettering in white plus illustration of Ike and the Capitol in white with some blue, yellow and green shading. 1953. $20.

10
"DWIGHT D. EISENHOWER" rwb felt 17" long. "Inauguration Jan-20-1953." $20.

1 2 3 4 5 6 7 8 9 10

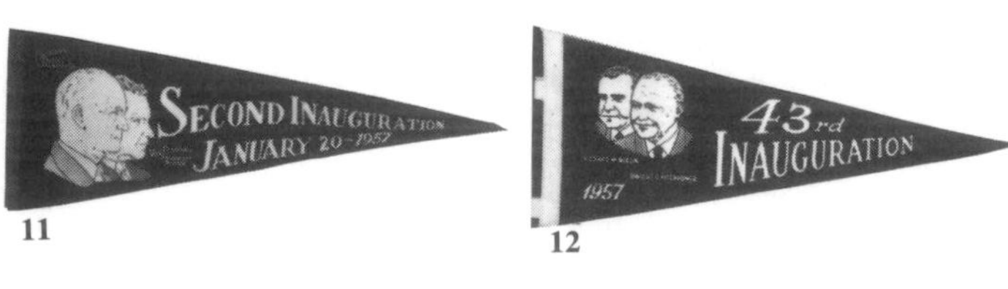

11 12

13

14

15

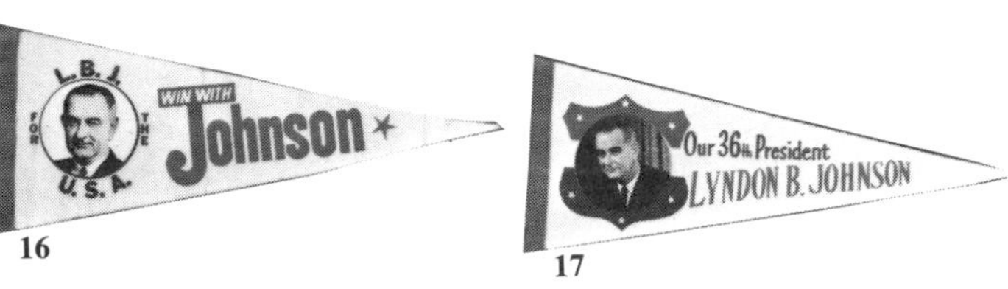

16 17

18

19

20

11
EISENHOWER INAUGURATION dark blue felt 11x30"with inscription and image in white/ gray/pink. Inscribed "Second Inauguration January 20, 1957" along with candidates' names. $15.

12
EISENHOWER AND NIXON black felt 5x12" with bright yellow streamers and full color portraits. 1957. $15.

13
KENNEDY/JOHNSON 10" long thin plastic in blue/white/day-glo pink. Piece has identical design on each side. 1960. $20.

14
"KENNEDY/JOHNSON" rwb felt 30" long. 1960. $30.

15
"OUR 35th PRESIDENT JOHN F. KENNEDY" rwb on white felt 11x30" with a large full color paper photo. 1960. $15.

16
"WIN WITH JOHNSON" rwb on white felt 11x30" with 5.5" bw paper photo. 1964. $12.

17
"OUR 36th PRESIDENT LYNDON B. JOHNSON" rwb felt 18" long with full color paper portrait of L.B.J. 1964. $10.

18
"NIXON'S THE ONE" white felt 17" long with color scenes of Washington landmarks plus full color 3.5" cardboard portrait. 1968. $10.

19
HUMPHREY 30" long rwb felt. "Unite With Humphrey." 1968. $10.

20
"STAND UP FOR AMERICA-GEORGE WALLACE" rwb felt 28" long. 1968. $8.

41. Pens & Pencils

Pens and pencils are among the most consistent campaign souvenirs of the twentieth century. Variations include fountain pens, ballpoint pens, mechanical pencils and traditional lead pencils. Surprisingly few examples of pencil clips exist. Since the late 1960s, presidents have used pen and pencil sets, attractively boxed and inscribed with their name and the Presidential Seal, as souvenir gifts for White House visitors.

1
CLEVELAND/STEVENSON 3" litho tin pencil. Mounted on the tube is a 1" long metal slide in rwb/gold. 1892. $225.

2
McKINLEY 9" pink wood lead pencil capped by 1.25x2x2" tall tin head of McKinley in realistic colors. C. 1900. $300.

3
HUGHES bw ink blotter. Depicts Washington and Lincoln with slogans about tyranny and slavery plus Hughes and slogan "Who Will Blot Out The Past Four Years In 1917." $45.

4
ROOSEVELT 7" rwb wood pencil with inscription "President Roosevelt Needs Kramer In Congress..." On one end where the eraser should be is the inscription "Uncle Sam Needs the Brass and Rubber that Used to Be Here." 1944. $20.

5
"ROOSEVELT & GARNER 1936" jugate 4" bullet pencil. A celluloid wrap-around has the portraits in black on rwb shield and star background. $250.

6
"LANDON & KNOX 1936" jugate bullet pencil. This item matches item #5. $250.

7
"WILLKIE" rwb 5" long mechanical pencil. 1940. $50.

8
CAMPAIGN MECHANICAL PENCILS 3.5" long matched pair of pencils from 1940. On one is a blue portrait of F.D.R. with slogan in red "Roosevelt and Humanity." The other has a black portrait of Willkie with slogan "Win With Willkie." Backgrounds have a white pearlized finish. EACH $35.

9
"DON'T GAMBLE, ELECT WILLKIE" 3" tall by 2.5" diameter, thick leather container which is apparently a dice cup but which would also serve as a pencil holder. 1940. $45.

10
EISENHOWER 5" long bw plastic ball point pen inscribed "For the Love of Ike-Vote Republican." C. 1952. $15.

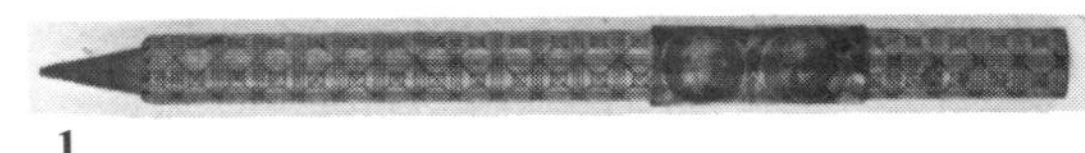
1

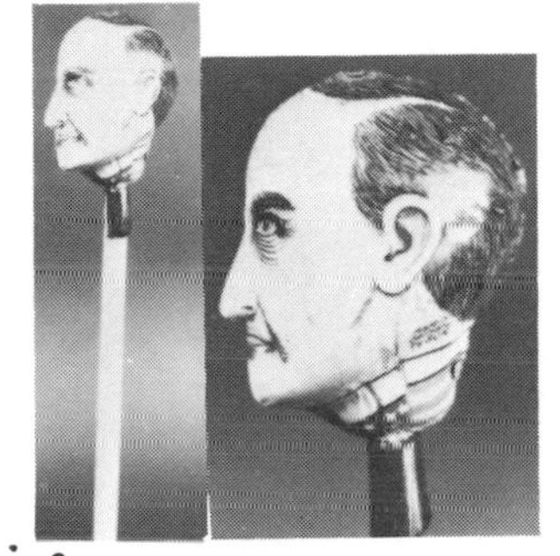
2

3

4

5

6

7

8

9

10

11

11
STEVENSON 5.5" long dark blue and white plastic mechanical pencil with slogan in red and blue "Win With Adlai Stevenson/Stevenson For President." At top of pencil under clear plastic is a bw photo. C. 1952. $20.

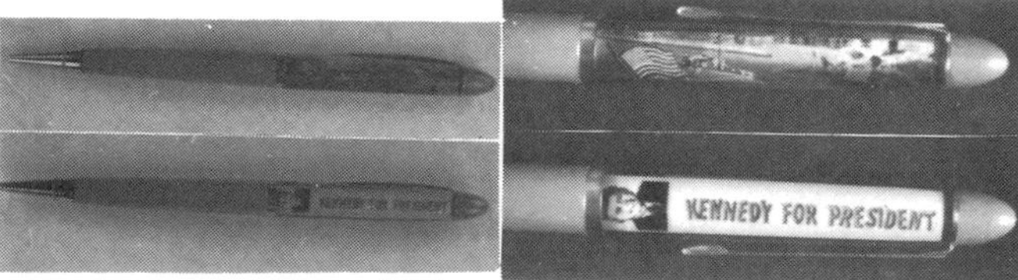

12

12
"KENNEDY FOR PRESIDENT" mechanical pencil 5.5" long with a portrait on one side. Opposite side features a die-cut figure of PT-109 that floats in a liquid with city skyline in the background. 1960. $25.

13

13
NIXON/LODGE jugate mechanical pencil with 'floating' pictures of the two candidates plus several slogans and an illustration of the Republican elephant. 1960. $15.

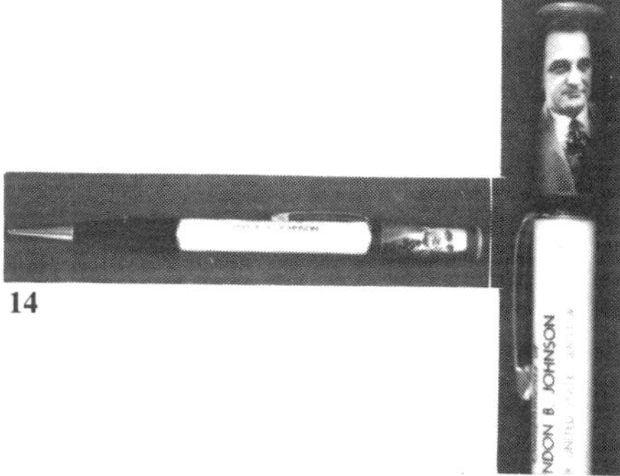
14

14
JOHNSON 5.75" rwb mechanical pencil with inscription "Compliments of Lyndon B. Johnson Your United States Senator" in red and blue letters on white. On the top under plastic is a bw photo of L.B.J. along with his facsimile signature. C. 1952. $50.

15

15
JOHNSON/GOLDWATER felt covers that slip over wooden pencils. One cover features an "LBJ" Texan hat, another features a "LBJ" die-cut of the United States and the other two depict a donkey and an elephant, each with moveable plastic eye. 1964. EACH $5.

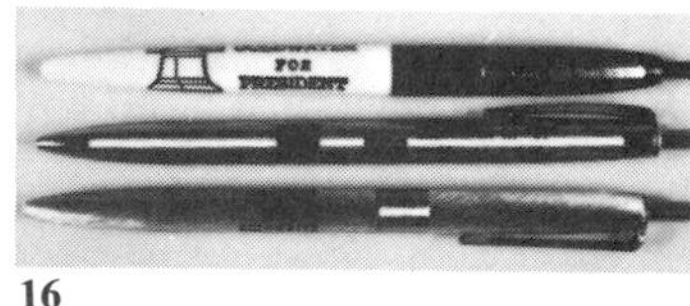

16

16
GOLDWATER 5" long campaign pens. One is blue and white plastic with a black image of the Liberty Bell and a slogan. The other two pens are brass with black inscriptions. 1964. EACH $10.

17

17
CARTER/FORD wood pencils each 7". The Carter/Mondale inscription is green on white and the Ford/Dole inscription is blue on white. 1976. EACH $3.

18

18
CARTER-MONDALE/FORD-DOLE 5.25" plastic ballpoint pens. Carter/Mondale is green/white and Ford/Dole is blue/white. 1976. EACH $4.

42. *Pocket Mirrors*

Pocket mirrors are an offshoot of the celluloid campaign revolution of 1896. All pre-World War II examples are scarce and, compared to buttons, very few designs exist. Mirrors are generally a larger size than most pinback buttons and have a typical diameter of slightly more than two inches. In recent years, rectangular mirrors are also produced. Mirrors continue to be issued to a small degree in campaigns of the present.

1
"GEN. W.H. HARRISON" bw engraving under glass with $2\frac{5}{8}$" pewter rim and brass edge ring. 1840. $3000.

2
TAYLOR $2\frac{5}{8}$" pewter case with inside mirror. Imported from France. 1848. $500.

3
"McKINLEY MONUMENT/CANTON, OHIO" $2\frac{3}{4}$" tinted sepia. C. early 1900s. $40.

4
PARKER $1\frac{1}{4}$" celluloid disk under brass edge with rope design. On the top is a metal loop for hanging from a brass chain. C. 1904. $150.

5
TAFT $2\frac{1}{16}$" color portrait with inscription "Oh My! The Souvenir Popcorn, Made By National Candy Co." C. 1908. $300.

6
TAFT 3" oval multicolor portrait with gold letters "Bonnie Brier Chocolates." C. 1908. $300.

7
TAFT $2\frac{1}{4}$" bw with inscription "IT'S UP TO THE MAN ON THE OTHER SIDE TO PUT THIS TRIED & SAFE MAN AT THE HEAD OF THE GOVERN-MENT." C. 1908. $400.

8
WILSON $2\frac{1}{2}$" with bw portraits of Wilson and allied leaders from World War I surrounded by full color national flags on a gold background. C. 1918. $125.

1 2 3 4 5 6

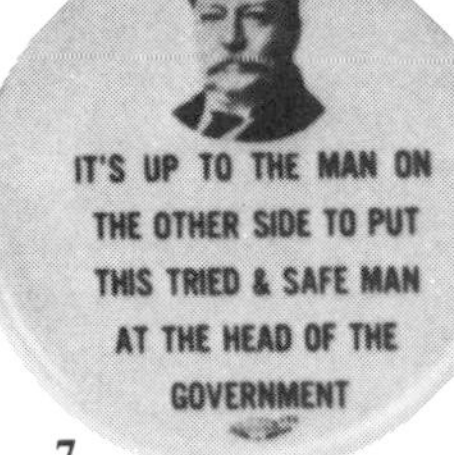

7

8

9

10

11

12

The NEW DEAL
is spending $15,000.00
Every Minute, Night and Day
TURN THIS OVER AND SEE
WHO PAYS THE BILL
VOTE FOR
LANDON and KNOX
AND END THIS EXTRAVAGANCE

13

14

15

16

9
HOOVER $2\frac{1}{8}$" bw trigate with inscription "The lady on the other side is requested to vote for Hoover/Keene/ Larson." 1928. $350.

10
"HOOVER/CURTIS" bw $2\frac{1}{8}$" jugate with inscription "Hoover for President/ Field for Senator/Turner for Governor." 1932. $450.

11
"IT'S AN ELEPHANT'S JOB" bw $2\frac{1}{4}$" with cartoon picture of the GOP elephant pushing a truck labeled "U.S. and Company" out of the mud. C. 1936. $125.

12
"DEMOCRATIC TICKET/ VERMILLION COUNTY" 2x3" black on pink paper with portrait of Roosevelt. 1936. $100.

13
"LANDON AND KNOX" brown/beige 2x$2\frac{3}{4}$" paper with inscription "The NEW DEAL...Vote For Landon and Knox and End This Extravagance." 1936. $50.

14
EISENHOWER $2\frac{1}{8}$" rwb with slogan "I'm For Ike." C. 1952. $20.

15
"FORD/DOLE" bw/blue 2" jugate. 1976. $8.

16
"PRESIDENT FORD '76" bw/blue 2" with single photo. $5.

43. Postcards

Postcards, as opposed to advertising trade cards, are intended for mailing. The vast majority are privately published cards with a postcard design printed on the back. Many examples were issued for early 1900s campaigns in particular and those from this era are considered to be the epitome of design creativity and striking color. Mechanical cards (those with a moving part or attachment) and political cartoon or satire cards are quite desired by collectors. Cards are normally stiff paper, frequently embossed, with a few examples also in leather, wood or fabric.

1
BRYAN "The Bottom is Out of the Full Dinner Pail" bw/rwb. 1908. $35.

2
BRYAN "The Man Who Made Lincoln Famous" bw/rwb. 1908. $20.

3
BRYAN/KERN "Our Choice" bw/rwb/gold. 1908. $25.

4
"THE WASHINGTON-BRYAN COMBINATION PICTURE" bw/rwb three-fold card comparing Bryan to Washington. 1908. $30.

5
"HON. WM. J. BRYAN" sepia depiction from the "Sepia Campaign Series." 1908. $15.

6
BRYAN "Next Occupant of the White House" multicolor. 1908. $12.

7
BRYAN "Two of America's Great Essentials (Bryan and Corn) To Peace and Prosperity" multicolor. 1908. $40.

8
"GIVE US ROOSEVELT OR GIVE US TAFT" bw/rwb. 1908. $25.

9
TAFT "Our Presidents/Past/Present/Future" bw/gray/dark brown. 1908. $25.

1

2

3

4

5

6

7

8

9

10

11

12

13

14

15

16

17

19

18

20

10
"TAFT & SHERMAN/A Winning Pair" bw/rwb/gold. 1908. $20.

11
TAFT/SHERMAN "Our Next President and Vice-President" multicolor. 1908. $15.

12
TAFT/SHERMAN "The Nation's Choice" bw/rwb/gold. 1908. $20.

13
"TAFT FOR PRESIDENT/Prosperity For All" bw/rwb. 1908. $20.

14
TAFT "For President of the U.S.A./Wm. H. Taft of Ohio" bw/rwb. 1908. $25.

15
"HON. WM. H. TAFT" sepia photo from the "Sepia Campaign Series." 1908. $15.

16
"TAFT" multicolor with fabric outfit and brass buttons. 1908. $45.

17
UNCLE SAM in rwb wearing campaign buttons for both Taft and Bryan. This salesman's style card is titled "Which?" 1908. $35.

18
"HELLO BILL!" multicolor "Billy Possum" in Uncle Sam style rwb costume complete with top hat. 1908. $40.

19
TAFT MECHANICAL featuring bw/yellow elephant which has a rope tail. The rope is pulled and bw portrait of Taft slides out to the left. 1908. $50.

20
TAFT/ANTI-BRYAN "Back to the Farm!/3 Strikes and Out" bw. 1908. $40.

21
ROOSEVELT "Teddy in Africa" multicolor. T.R. and baboon shake hands and bare their teeth. 1909. $40.

22
"T.R./COMING HOME/GLAD TIDINGS" multicolor. Uncle Sam, Taft and "GOP" elephant dance on the dock as T.R. arrives. 1910. $40.

23
ROOSEVELT "Dee-Lighted" multicolor. 1905. $20.

24
"FOR PRESIDENT/WOODROW WILSON" brown/white. 1916. $12.

25
HARDING "AMERICA FIRST" with rwb flag, eagle and Capitol design. Also shows Coolidge and Boies Penrose. 1920. $40.

26
COOLIDGE bw captioned "President Calvin Coolidge And Vice-President Charles G. Dawes." C. 1924. $20.

27
"HON. ALFRED M. LANDON" bw. 1936. $15.

28
WILLKIE bw opposition card to F.D.R.'s third term using the character later adopted as *MAD* magazine's "What, Me Worry" boy. 1940. $30.

29
"DEWEY-WARREN The Way Ahead" bw. 1948. $12.

30
EISENHOWER/NIXON "Vote for Your Future/Vote Republican" multicolor. 1956. $10.

31
"VOTE FOR JOHN F. KENNEDY" multicolor. 1960. $10.

32
NIXON 5x7" multicolor of Nixon at piano with his family and David Eisenhower. 1968. $5.

33
MONDALE/REAGAN "Pull for Your Candidate" bw/rwb mechanical. An insert moves to show either one in the White House. 1984. $15

21

22

23

24

25

26

27

28

29

30

31

32

33

44. Posters & Banners

Posters and banners are basic tools of all campaigns since the mid-19th century. Posters range from primitive hand-drawn-and-lettered paper to the frequently bland cardboard duplicates printed by the thousands in modern times. In between, particularly in the early 1900s, are some of the finest examples of political graphic art. Cloth banners are still a mainstay of current campaigns, rallies and conventions although again visual excitement has waned greatly in recent years. The finest banners in terms of art and message are from the 1800s and the early part of the 1900s. Examples of these are practically non-existent except as museum holdings. Huge street banners or headquarters banners are particularly rare, although smaller banners from more recent years surface from time to time. The smallest banner versions, designed for hanging in a household window, became popular in 1940 and those picturing Franklin Roosevelt or Wendell Willkie are quite attractive but not particularly scarce.

1

2

3

4

5

6

7

8

REPUBLICAN CANDIDATES

Election Tuesday, November 2, 1920

9

1
BUCHANAN 9.25x24" paper titled "Who Is James Buchanan?" with bw portrait. 1856. $350.

2
"GARFIELD & ARTHUR" black on beige paper 11.5x18" for a campaign rally. 1880. $100.

3
BLAINE/LOGAN 22.5x28" bw paper poster titled "The Republican Candidates For 1884." 1884. $300.

4
CLEVELAND 20x28" bw/yellow paper poster put out in 1884 to recall the 'stolen' election in 1876. $300.

5
McKINLEY/ANTI-BRYAN 20.5x27.5" multicolor paper poster showing Uncle Sam reluctantly paying wages with silver dollars worth only 53¢. 1896. $750.

6
"ROOSEVELT AND JOHNSON" 19x25" bw paper poster. 1912. $125.

7
"FOR PRESIDENT CHARLES E. HUGHES" 16x21" paper poster with sepiatone portrait. 1916. $30.

8
HARDING/COOLIDGE 16x21" multicolor paper poster with sepia portraits. 1920. $65.

9
HARDING/COOLIDGE 11x14" bw cardboard poster with portraits of Pennsylvania candidates. 1920. $85.

10
"WARREN G. HARDING" 12x18" brown/white paper poster. 1920. $75.

11
"JAMES M. COX" 11x17" bw paper poster. 1920. $200.

12
"CALVIN COOLIDGE" 9x12" sepia paper poster. 1924. $35.

13
"PRESIDENT HOOVER" 39x60" bw/blue/bright orange fabric banner. 1932. $250.

14
SMITH 3x4.5' canvas banner in rwb with a large bw illustration. 1928. $400.

15
"FORWARD WITH ROOSEVELT" bw cardboard 12x16". 1936. $60.

16
ROOSEVELT 8x11" blue/white paper window poster. 1936. $70.

17
ROOSEVELT 11x14" rwb cardboard window poster showing Truman and other Missouri candidates. 1940. $150.

18
ROOSEVELT 9x12" rwb fabric banner with bright yellow fringe below. 1940. $45.

19
ROOSEVELT 9x11.5" rwb fabric with metal bar at top. C. 1940. $25.

20
ROOSEVELT 6.5x7" rwb fabric banner with gold cord hanger. 1940. $25.

10

11

12

13

14

15

16

17

18

19

20

21

22

23

24

25

26

27

28

29

30

31

21
"LANDON AND KNOX FOR US" 14x21" rwb paper poster. 1936. $50.

22
"LANDON FOR PRESIDENT" 11x16" brown/white paper poster. 1936. $25.

23
WILLKIE 9x11.5" rwb fabric banner. Matches item #19. 1940. $25.

24
"WORK WITH WILLKIE" 13x19" rwb paper poster. 1940. $75.

25
EISENHOWER 14x20" rwb cardboard poster. 1956. $25.

26
EISENHOWER 12x17" bw paper poster. C. 1956. $25.

27
STEVENSON 8.5x22" red/white/purple cardboard poster. 1956. $75.

28
KENNEDY 13.5x21" paper poster with bw portraits on light pink background and tan, black and gray lettering. 1960. $125.

29
KENNEDY/JOHNSON 14x20" rwb paper poster. 1960. $65.

30
KENNEDY 13x21" bw/rwb paper poster. 1960. $40.

31
KENNEDY 8.5x11" bw paper poster for a personal appearance in Springfield, Mass. the day before the 1960 election. $50.

32
NIXON 11x14" cardboard with bw portrait and black/red lettering. 1950. $200.

33
NIXON/LODGE 14x22" bw/yellow paper poster. 1960. $35.

34
"JOHNSON/HUMPHREY FOR THE U.S.A." bw/rwb 13x21" paper poster. 1964. $15.

35
"JOHNSON/HUMPHREY FOR THE U.S.A." bw/rwb 13x21" paper poster. Similar to item #34. 1964. $12.

36
"GOLDWATER AND MILLER" rwb 14x22" cardboard poster. 1964. $25.

37
"VOTE HUMPHREY/MUSKIE" 20x26" bw paper poster. 1968. $10.

38
HUMPHREY 21x28" blue/white/orange cardboard poster. 1968. $15.

39
AGNEW 19x30" bw paper poster with red letters. 1968. $40.

40
"PRESIDENT NIXON/NOW MORE THAN EVER" multicolor 22x34" paper poster. 1972. $30.

41
McGOVERN 14x20" multicolor paper poster. 1972. $15.

42
McGOVERN 21x28" multicolor cardboard poster. 1972. $15.

32

33

34

JOHNSON
HUMPHREY
FOR THE
USA

35

36

37

WE'RE COMING
BACK!
STUDENT COALITION
for
HUMPHREY
MUSKIE

38

For Vice President
SPIRO T. AGNEW

39

40

41

42

43

44

45

46

47

48

49

50

51

MONDALE
FOR
PRESIDENT

52

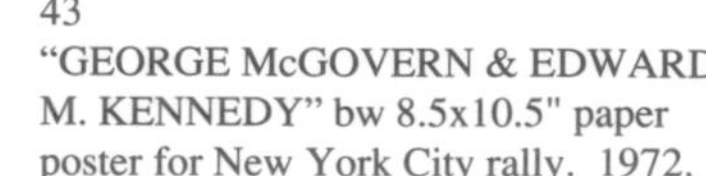

43
"GEORGE McGOVERN & EDWARD M. KENNEDY" bw 8.5x10.5" paper poster for New York City rally. 1972. $30.

44
"McGOVERN" rwb 14x22" poster. 1972. $8.

45
"VOTE FOR JIMMY CARTER" green/white 14x22" cardboard poster. 1976. $8.

46
CARTER bw/green 13x20" cardboard inscribed "Re-Elect Carter/Mondale/Keep Them Working For You." 1980. $10.

47
"FORD FOR V.P." red/white 14x22" paper poster. 1960. $60.

48
"PRESIDENT FORD '76" multicolor 18x25" paper poster. $8.

49
"FORD/DOLE NEIGHBORHOOD HEADQUARTERS" rwb 16x22" cardboard poster. 1976. $5.

50
"ANDERSON" bw/red 11x17" paper poster. 1980. $5.

51
"REAGAN-BUSH '84" multicolor 16x22" paper poster. $12.

52
"MONDALE FOR PRESIDENT" white on blue 17x22" paper poster. 1984. $5.

45. Sheet Music & Songbooks

Sheet music and songbooks are collected generally for the color or graphic quality of the cover rather than the memorable quality of the actual music. Songbooks are also frequently called *songsters* and examples are known from as early as the 1844 campaign of James K. Polk. Predictably, most music is for rousing marches or campaign tunes. Times of national stress, particularly war or economics, generated a fair share of political music. This collectible has faded almost to non-existence in recent times, replaced occasionally with phonograph records that contain excerpts of the candidate's most inspirational speeches.

1
JACKSON. "President Jackson's Inauguration March For The Piano Forte" 10x13" with cover and detail pictured. 1828. $60.

2
LINCOLN. "The Republican Campaign Songster No. 1" published by "American Publishing House/Cincinnati O." with Lincoln 1860 bw portrait on title page. Photo example is missing its cover. 4x5.5". 48 pages. $100.

3
"HAIL, BRAVE GARFIELD" bw/blue 10.5x14" cover. 1880. $35.

4
"CLEVELAND'S MARCH TO VICTORY" bw 10x14" cover. C. 1888. $25.

5
ROOSEVELT AND PARKER. "The New Campaign March And Two Step" showing both candidates on red/green cover. About 10x14". 1904. $35.

6
"GET ON THE RAFT WITH TAFT" bw/pink 10.5x13.5" cover. 1908. $20.

7
"TAFT'S GRAND MARCH AND 2 STEP" bw 10.5x13.5" cover. C. 1908. $20.

8
ROOSEVELT. "We're Ready For Teddy Again" gray/white 11x13.5" with flesh colored tinting. 1912. $25.

9
WILSON. "I Think We've Got Another Washington And Wilson Is His Name." Cover is 10.5x13.5" in blue/white/orange/brown. 1915. $15.

10
WILSON. "Never Swap Horses When You're Crossing A Stream." Cover is 10.5x13.5" in orange/white/blue. 1916. $25.

11
"WILSON MARCH" rwb/brown 10x13.5". 1912. $25.

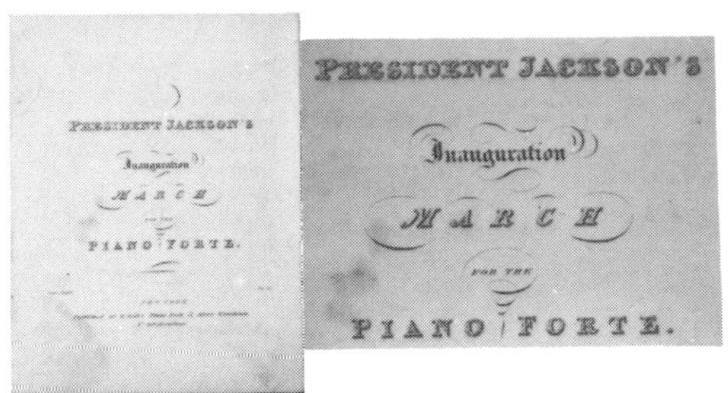

1

2

3

4

5

6

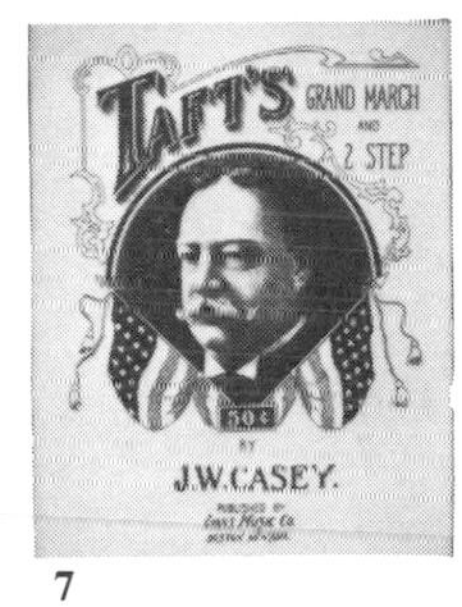

7

8

9

10

11

12

13

14

15

16

17

18

19

20

21

22

23

12
"WILSON'S INAUGURAL MARCH" rwb 11x14" cover. 1913. $30.

13
"PRESIDENT HARDING MARCH" brown/white 9x12" cover. C. 1920. $20.

14
HARDING/COOLIDGE. "America First-Republican Campaign Songbook" 20 pages, 6x8", with jugate portraits in black on tan cover. 1920. $50.

15
COX. "The Tie That Binds Or Jimmy Is The Man For Us." Bw sheet music 5.5x8.5" with Governor Cox's record of legislation on back cover. 1920. $100.

16
COOLIDGE/DAWES. "Songs of 1924 Republican Campaign in Ohio" 12 pages, 4x9", with bw jugate pictures on front cover. $25.

17
"COOLIDGE AND DAWES For the Nation's Cause" browntone 9x12" sheet music. 1924. $20.

18
"KEEP COOL AND KEEP COOLIDGE" bw/brown 9x12" cover. 1924. $25.

19
"KEEP COOL-IDGE" bw 9x12" cover. 1924. $25.

20
"PRESIDENT HOOVER MARCH" bw 9x12" cover. C. 1929. $20.

21
AL SMITH. "The Sidewalks of New York" brown/white 9x12" cover. 1928. $20.

22
SMITH. "He's Our 'Al' " bw 9x12" cover. 1928. $20.

23
"WE'LL ALL GO VOTING FOR AL" SMITH bw 9x12" cover. Music by Irving Berlin. 1924. $30.

24
"ROW, ROW, ROW WITH ROOSEVELT" rwb 9x12" cover. 1932. $30.

25
"ON WITH ROOSEVELT" bw/rwb 9x12" cover. 1936. $20.

26
"WIN WITH ROOSEVELT" rwb 9x12" cover. 1940. $30.

27
"OUR LANDON" rwb 9x12" cover. 1936. $20.

28
LANDON. "Happy Landin' With Landon" rwb 9x12" cover. 1936. $20.

29
EISENHOWER. "Out Of The Wilderness With Ike" rwb 9x12" cover. 1952. $20.

30
"I LIKE IKE" rwb 9x12" cover. Music is by Irving Berlin. 1952. $10.

31
"MARCH ON WITH ADLAI & JOHN" bw 6x10" cover. 1952. $40.

32
"BELIEVE IN STEVENSON" blue/white 9x12" cover. 1956. $15.

33
"SING ALONG WITH JACK" bw/red 9x12" booklet with 16 pages of "Hit Songs from the New Frontier." 1963. $25.

34
NIXON. "We're Voting For Nixon To Keep The Country Strong" blue/white 9x12" cover. 1960. $15.

35
"HELLO JIMMY" rwb 9x12" cover. 1976. $5.

24

25

26

27

28

29

30

31

32

33

34

35

46. Tickets

Admission tickets to political events exist in great variety. Many are rather plain and designed much like a theater ticket, but those issued to national convention delegates can be quite elaborate featuring fine engraving and portraits of the political parties' greatest heroes. Tickets to inauguration events also feature quality printing on high-grade paper often with the new president's portrait. Among the most historically significant tickets are those issued for the impeachment of President Andrew Johnson in 1868. As the proceedings lasted a number of days, tickets for different dates were printed on cardboard sheets of various colors. The ticket for March 31, 1868, was reproduced in 1974 on blue cardboard stock. The bottom margin is marked "REPRODUCTION JULY 1974" but this edge can be easily trimmed off. Original 1868 tickets have a thin plain border around all four sides surrounding the border design printed on both the ticket and the stub. The vast majority of tickets are priced at $15 or less, although a complete (ticket and stub) 1868 Impeachment ticket can exceed $200.

1

2

3

4

5

6

7

8

9

1
"DEMOCRATIC CONVENTION" black on light blue stiff cardboard 2.5x3.75" with illustration of Andrew Jackson wearing eyeglasses. Worcester, Mass. 9/15/1859. $50.

2
ANDREW JOHNSON U.S. SENATE IMPEACHMENT 3x3.5" ticket stub for the 5/4/1868 session with card in dark green with black lettering. Tickets for other dates were on different colored cards. $200.

3
HAYES/TILDEN 1876 ELECTION. 3x5" stiff white admission ticket to the "Gallery of House of Representatives" for the 2/17/1877 "Counting the Vote for President and Vice-President." $200.

4
ROOSEVELT 3x6" bw/green "Special Guest" ticket to the 1936 Democratic convention. $10.

5
LANDON 2x5" ticket with illustration designed like a .875" bw button surrounded by yellow sunflower. Ticket for Illinois reception dated 10/9/1936. $20.

6
"DEWEY-BRICKER RALLY" green stiff cardboard ticket 2x6" with inscriptions and jugate portraits in black from Madison Square Garden 11/4/1944. $12.

7
EISENHOWER/NIXON 3x5.5" bw/pink cardboard inaugural ticket with silver star border. 1/20/1953. $30.

8
NIXON 3.5x5" rwb ticket stub from a "Salute to the President Dinner" held in Chicago 11/9/1971. $8.

9
"RONALD REAGAN RALLY" bw Cincinnati convention hall ticket 2.5x4" dated 10/27/1967. $15.

47. Tobacco Related Items

The variety of tobacco related campaign items has dramatically decreased in recent years as use of tobacco became less socially acceptable. Previous years provided a fascinating array of campaign and candidate items, mostly geared to the male voter even after the 19th Amendment of 1920 granted nationwide suffrage to women. Snuff boxes are known from the 1820s and are probably the earliest campaign associated tobacco memorabilia. Other items in succession include cigar boxes, cigar vest cases, match safes, matchboxes and portrait pipes. Twentieth century items include novelty cigarette cases or dispensers, cigarette lighters, glass cigar box lids in tin frames, cigarette packs, matchbooks and even bubble gum cigars.

1
"HENRY CLAY" clay pipe 1x2.5 tall without stem. C. 1844. $200.

2
GREELEY 5x6" cast iron match holder. Originals are riveted together; reproductions are held together by heavy wire with "LB 77/3" on the reverse. A Grant original exists but may also have been reproduced. 1872. $250.

3
McKINLEY 2.5x4.5" thin silver ashtray with raised fluted edge and large high-relief silver bug at center with an actual brass (gold-colored) nail impaled in its back. 1896. $250.

4
"FOR PRESIDENT" (BRYAN) 1.5x3" silvered brass matchsafe. 1896. $150.

5
"BRYAN & SEWALL-16 TO 1" wooden cigar box about 2x5x8" long. 1896. $75.

6
BRYAN 2x2.25" clay pipe without stem. C. 1908. $75.

7
ROOSEVELT "SQUARE DEAL" wood cigar box 2.5x5.5x9" long with bw paper label copyrighted 1904 on inside lid. $75.

8
"T.R. JUNIOR" cigar box 5x5x9" with multicolor labels. C. 1912. $85.

9
"JUDGE TAFT" cigar box 4x5.5x8" long with blue/white label inside the lid plus a glass and metal cover. C. 1908. $45.

10
"WOODROW WILSON" brown/beige/gold/blue embossed label 4.5" square for the end panel of a cigar box. C. 1916. $20.

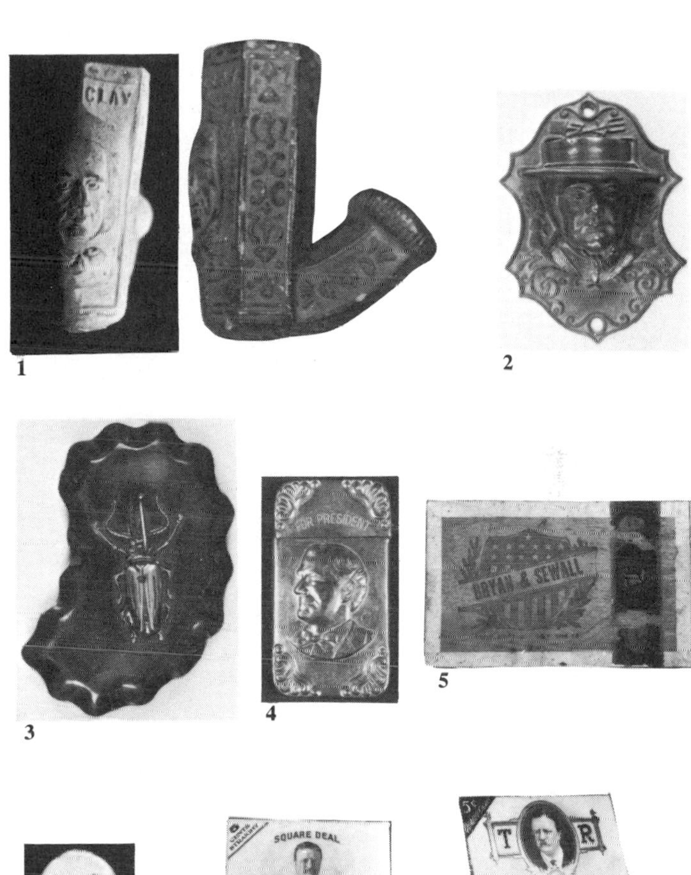

1 2 3 4 5 6 7 8

9

10

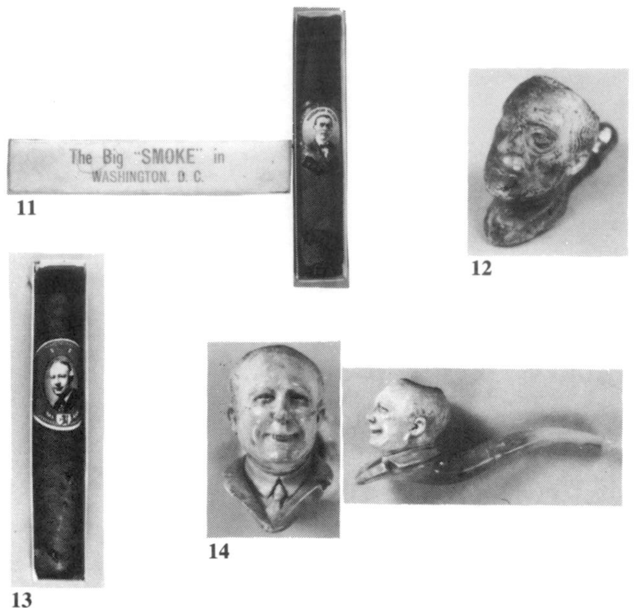

11 12 13 14

15

16

17

18

19

11
WOODROW WILSON "The Big 'Smoke' in Washington, D. C." 10 " cardboard box holding jumbo cigar with multicolor embossed paper label. C. 1912. $50.

12
WOODROW WILSON 2.5x3" long pipe without stem. Beige meerschaum-like material. C. 1912. $75.

13
AL SMITH 8.5" long jumbo cigar with bw/gold/red/green paper label picturing Smith. 1928. $40.

14
AL SMITH 2x3" long carved portrait pipe with 2" yellow celluloid stem. 1928. $200.

15
AL SMITH 1.5x5.5x8.5" long wooden box with Smith's name in black on dark brown wooden lid. Inside lid label is sepia portrait surrounded by gold frame and floral design with buildings to left and right. C. 1928. $40.

16
"PRESIDENTS-ROOSEVELT AND GARNER" 6x8x3" deep, white wooden cigar box with jugate paper label on inside of lid. C. 1932. $85.

17
ROOSEVELT 3x3.5x1.5" thick hinged metal case with black celluloid covering and multicolor portrait on lid. C. 1936. $100.

18
WILLKIE 1.5x2" rwb match pack with die-cut cardboard fold-out Willkie head and depictions of voters on the match sticks. 1940. $30.

19
STEVENSON 4.5x8.5x3" deep cardboard box which held bubble gum cigars. Inside lid has bw/red design with portrait and inscription "I Like Adlai." C. 1952. $25.

20
"I LIKE IKE" cigarette pack 2.25x3x.75" thick in rwb. C. 1952.
$25.

21
"KENNEDY AND JOHNSON 1960" jumbo cigar 10" long with cellophane wrapper plus a bw/red/green/gold paper band. $55.

22
JOHNSON/HUMPHREY 1.5x2" tall bw/ rwb jugate match pack. 1964. $3.

23
"JOHNSON FOR PRESIDENT" blue/ white matchbook 1.5x2" with inscription on the other side "U.S.A. Likes L.B.J." 1964. $3.

24
"GOLDWATER FOR PRESIDENT" blue/white matchbook 1.5x2". 1964. $3.

25
"NIXON" stiff cardboard cigarette box 3x3.5x.75" deep with rwb lid and inscription "Campaign '72." $20.

26
McGOVERN matching item to #25. $30.

27
"NIXON'S THE ONE!" red/white 1.5x2" match pack. C. 1972. $2.

28
"CARTER/MONDALE" bw/blue litho tin 5.5" ashtray from Iowa. C. 1976.
$15.

29
FORD 5.5x5.5" bw china inauguration souvenir ashtray. 1974. $10.

30
DUKAKIS 6" long bubble gum cigar with red/gold/black/white paper label and cellophane cover slogan "The Duke In '88". $2.

20

21

22

23

24

25

26

27

28

29

30

48. Toys, Games, Paper Dolls & Puzzles

Toys, games, paper dolls and puzzles date politically from the 1880s, with only a few rare earlier examples. Small novelty games or block puzzles exist for Benjamin Harrison, William McKinley, William H. Taft and Al Smith. A few clever toy-related items were issued depicting Theodore Roosevelt mostly after he became President. Card games are known as early as President Grover Cleveland and continue through the Reagan years. Figural campaign dolls, rather than commemorative dolls, for presidents are quite rare although a plastic set issued for the Johnson-Goldwater campaign may still be frequently found. Paper doll books and satirical coloring books are mostly an innovation from the 1960s.

1

2

3

4

5

6

7

1
CLEVELAND/HARRISON CHECKERS SET in 4.5x5x9" long hinged box with brass closure and paper covers simulating brown alligator skin. There are inside compartments for storing the checkers plus multicolor jugate labels inside the hinged lids. 1888. $350.

2
BLAINE/HARRISON "Blocks Of Five" boxed wooden puzzle 4x4x.5" deep with white/ blue/orange label. Lid slides off and wood letters are moved to spell out "Blaine" or "Harrison." Puzzle's theme relates to Harrison replacing Blaine as the dominant Republican leader. 1888. $150.

3
HARRISON/CLEVELAND multicolor bisque figures, each wrapped in rwb bisque flag. Figures can be positioned on wood bar about 6" long so that the scale is tipped in favor of one or the other. 1888. $1200.

4
"McKINLEY" three-dimensional 2.5" tall cast iron cap bomb with nickel plated finish. Back is incised with number "603514" while the front bears his facsimile signature. C. 1896. $300.

5
ROOSEVELT puzzle with political verse urging support in 1912. Diecut cardboard figure of Teddy's head measuring 5x8" (photo example is missing a corner). For his glasses there are two metal disks with celluloid covers each with a large steel ball inside. Object is to place the balls in the center of the containers. 1912. $350.

6
"ROOSEVELT AT SAN JUAN" multicolor heavy cardboard box about 4x5" that holds a card game. 1899. $150.

7
ROOSEVELT 5x6" multicolor cardboard puzzle with moving wheel titled "You Now See Seven Men And Seven Lions/ Which Black Man Turns Into A Yellow Lion." 1909. $150.

8
"PLAYING POSSUM WITH TAFT" multicolor box and jigsaw puzzle 8x14". 1909. $125.

9
TAFT POLITICAL PALM PUZZLE with front depicting a black man with five white balls to line up as teeth. Reverse has black and orange paper label inscribed "Solve Your Political Puzzle By Voting Full Republican Ticket-Election November 3, 1908." $150.

10
HOOVER/ROOSEVELT 4x5" bw cardboard box holds small wooden blocks of assorted sizes and various captions. Object is to move either the Roosevelt block or the Hoover block into the corner of the box designated as the White House. 1932. $50.

11
ROOSEVELT/GARNER 8x10" rwb inauguration jigsaw puzzle. 1933. $35.

12
ROOSEVELT/GARNER 11x13.5" inaugural jigsaw puzzle with brown and white picture of the Capitol and jugate portraits above. C. 1932. $35.

13
ANTI-KENNEDY "New Frontier/The Game Nobody Can Win." Game comes in large tan/black/red paper envelope measuring 11x20". Game is satirical in nature and modeled after the principles of the game of Monopoly. 1962. $40.

14
"THE KENNEDYS" 10x19x1.5" deep multicolor box depicting the Kennedy family-Mt. Rushmore style. The elaborate satirical game was designed by Harrison and Winter who were both Harvard graduates involved with the Harvard Lampoon. Distributed by Transogram, 1962. $35.

15
"P.T. BOAT 109" boxed game 10x19x1.5" deep by Ideal Toy Co. with 2 plastic boats to assemble. 1963. $35.

8

9

The Presidential Puzzle
MAY THE BEST MAN WIN

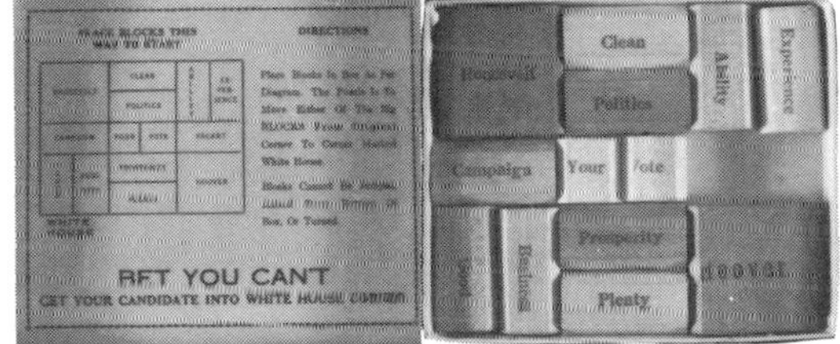

10

11

12

13

14

15

16

17

18

19

20

21

22

23

24

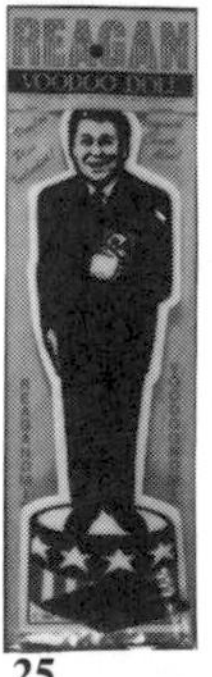

25

26

27

16
"BLUFF/THE EXCITING NEW PARTY GAME" multicolor cardboard box 6.5x9x3" deep holding a game by Saalfield Publishing. Lid has cartoon pictures of Kennedy in his rocking chair playing the game with Khrushchev. 1963. $50.

17
JOHN F. KENNEDY 10x11x2" deep multicolor box holding plastic model kit made by Aurora. 1965. $50.

18
JACKIE & CAROLINE 10x14" box holding die-cut cardboard stand-up paper dolls with clothing. C. 1962. $35.

19
"JOHNSON" dark blue fabric hand puppet 10" long designed like a donkey. 1964. $8.

20
"WHITE HOUSE PAPER DOLLS" by Saalfield with punch-out figures of Pat, Julie and Tricia plus 6 pages of cut-outs. 8x12". 1969. $20.

21
"STICK DICK" fiberboard 11.5" square dart board with bw/rwb silkscreen design of Nixon giving the "V" sign. Board comes with pair of brass/yellow plastic darts. C. 1972. $25.

22
ANTI-AGNEW 16x16" blue/white fiberboard dart board inscribed "Et Tu, Spiro!" C. 1972. $30.

23
"JIMMY THE WALKING PEANUT" multicolor plastic windup toy with key in 2.5x2.5x5" tall box. C. 1980. $25.

24
REAGAN "FIRST FAMILY" paper doll and cut-out book published by Dell. 9x12". 1981. $15.

25
"REAGAN VOO-DOO DOLL" flat Styrofoam cut-out 4x13". Includes 3 long "Voo-Doo Pins." Satirical item issued for the 1984 campaign. $20.

26
"REAGANOMICS" rwb boxed board game 10x20x1.5" deep. Object of the game is to become the first player to balance the budget. 1981. $12.

27
"REAGAN-BUSH" miniature 5.5" long white plastic football inscribed on one side "New York Republicans" and on the other side "Win One For The Gipper/ Reagan-Bush." 1984. $12.

49. Watch Fobs

Once an essential accessory for the man who carried a pocket watch, the watch fob is all but forgotten today. A leather strap joined the watch and fob and the fob was pulled to remove the watch from the safety of a vest pocket. Most fobs are made of brass or white metal frequently with a nickel-plated surface. There are also all celluloid fobs and fobs with a metal, leather or fibre board backing surrounding an inset celluloid disk at the center. Still another style used four segmented metal sections joined to the fob. This eliminated the leather strap and a small clasp on one end fastened to the pocket watch. The political watch fob became popular in 1904 and over one-hundred varieties appeared for Taft and Bryan in 1908. The number of designs rapidly diminished throughout the 1920s. Of note are 1920 jugate watch fobs for Harding/Coolidge and Cox/Roosevelt. Jugate items for these candidates are particularly scarce but a small hoard of these 1920 fobs with matching designs was discovered in the 1980s. The Harding variety in brass and the Cox variety in silvered brass are normally offered in excellent condition with much original luster at prices between \$100 and \$200 each. These are the least expensive non-paper jugate items for the 1920 candidates.

1
"HARRISON & MORTON" brass jugate. "1888." \$50.

2
"WILLIAM J. BRYAN" $1\frac{1}{4}$" bw celluloid on leather. C. 1908. \$50.

3
"BRYAN/KERN" brass. "Washington." "1908." \$25.

4
"BRYAN/KERN" rwb enamel on brass. 1908. \$40.

5
"BRYAN" $2\frac{1}{8}$" tall white metal fob in the shape of a rooster. "1908." \$100.

6
"KEY TO THE WHITE HOUSE/ BRYAN" die-cut brass. "1908." \$50.

7
"ROOSEVELT" $1\frac{1}{4}$" celluloid in bw/ rwb riveted to a $1\frac{3}{4}$" black fiberboard watch fob. 1904. \$125.

8
"ROOSEVELT AND FAIRBANKS" shield shaped brass. 1904. \$25.

9
"ROOSEVELT/FAIRBANKS" brass. "Washington 1904." \$20.

1

2

3

4

5

6

7

8

9

10
"ROOSEVELT AND FAIRBANKS" brass elephant. 1904. $100.

11
"ROOSEVELT/FAIRBANKS" rwb lettering on silvered brass. "1904." $20.

12
ROOSEVELT copper with very high relief detailed portrait. C. 1904. $25.

13
"ROOSEVELT/JOHNSON" silvered brass showing Bull Moose. "1912." $200.

14
"ROOSEVELT & JOHNSON" embossed brass with large raised letter "R" at center. "1912." $200.

15
ROOSEVELT white metal showing moose with "Progressive" above. 1912. $100.

16
TAFT/SHERMAN $1\frac{1}{4}$" bw celluloid on leather. 1908. $550.

17
TAFT bw/rwb/gold $1\frac{1}{4}$" celluloid on fiberboard. 1908. $150.

18
"W.H. TAFT" diecut brass with raised portrait. 1908. $25.

19
"W.H. TAFT" brass designed and textured like a pine cone. Detailed bust of Taft at center. 1908. $60.

20
"TAFT" white metal with dark silver finish designed as an oppossum holding its tail. "1908." Matches item #5. $100.

21
"TAFT AND SHERMAN" brass shield with black lettering which also includes "Washington 1908." $25.

22
"WOODROW WILSON" bw/blue/yellow $1\frac{3}{4}$" celluloid with mirror on reverse. 1912. $400.

23
"WOODROW WILSON" bw $1\frac{3}{4}$" celluloid with mirror on reverse. "1912." $200.

24
"WOODROW WILSON" bw $\frac{7}{8}$" celluloid on leather. 1912. $80.

25
"WILSON & MARSHALL" embossed brass that matches item #14. "1912." $125.

26
WILSON brass fob designed like a lock with inscription "Lock to White House 1912." A small metal disk riveted at center swings to either side to reveal the word "Wilson." $50.

27
"WILSON" brass with copper finish depicting Wilson and scales with a quill pen out-weighing a sword. C. 1912. $25.

28
WILSON rwb enamel/brass with $\frac{7}{8}$" bw/rwb/gold celluloid insert. 1912. $150.

29
WILSON $1\frac{3}{4}$" bw on fiberboard. C. 1916. $75.

22 23 24 25 26 27 28 29

30

31

32

33

34

35

36

37

38

39

40

30
"CHARLES E. HUGHES" bw $1\frac{3}{4}$" celluloid. 1916. $150.

31
HARDING brass shell with embossed portrait. "1920." $85.

32
HARDING/COOLIDGE "Our Choice" brass with slightly raised portraits under inscription "E Pluribus Unum." 1920. $125.

33
COX/ROOSEVELT "Our Choice" silvered brass with design matching item #32. 1920. $155.

34
"JAMES M. COX" silvered brass with raised portrait at center. 1920. $250.

35
"CALVIN COOLIDGE" bw $\frac{7}{8}$" celluloid on embossed silvered brass. 1924. $80.

36
"HERBERT CLARK HOOVER" bw $\frac{7}{8}$" celluloid on embossed silvered brass. 1928. $60.

37
"AL SMITH" bw $\frac{7}{8}$" celluloid on embossed silvered brass. 1928. $60.

38
"ROOSEVELT" bw $\frac{7}{8}$" celluloid on silvered brass. 1932. $50.

39
"KENNEDY/WELSH" dark blue enamel paint on brass. Indiana state convention. 1962. $30.

40
"CARTER" white metal with bronze finish. 1976. $5.

50. Window Stickers & Decals

Once a window sticker or decal is used, it is probably too late for collectors. Nevertheless, a surprising number of these items survived campaigns in unused condition. Recent campaign stickers are frequently available in large unused quantities, as are bumper stickers. Stickers and decals are mostly from the 1920s and later campaigns.

1
"COOLIDGE AND DAWES" rwb paper window sticker 4.5x12". 1924. $15.

2
HOOVER 4" diameter pair of rwb paper stickers. Oval is gummed on the front while the circle is gummed on the back. 1932. EACH $12.

3
"HOOVER AND CURTIS" rwb 5x7" gummed paper with slogan. 1932. $25.

4
" 'AL' SMITH FOR PRESIDENT/NOV. 6" blue/white paper sign 4x18". 1928. $30.

5
ROOSEVELT/GARNER 5.5x5.5" rwb jugate sticker. 1932. $35.

6
"WIN WITH WILLKIE" rwb 3x4" window decal. 1940. $10.

7
"WILLKIE" rwb 5" paper sticker. 1940. $12.

8
"WE WANT WILLKIE" rwb 4" paper sticker showing the Capitol dome. 1940. $5.

9
"PUT IT ON WILLKIE!" rwb 5x6" paper sticker showing an Uncle Sam-style hat. 1940. $8

1

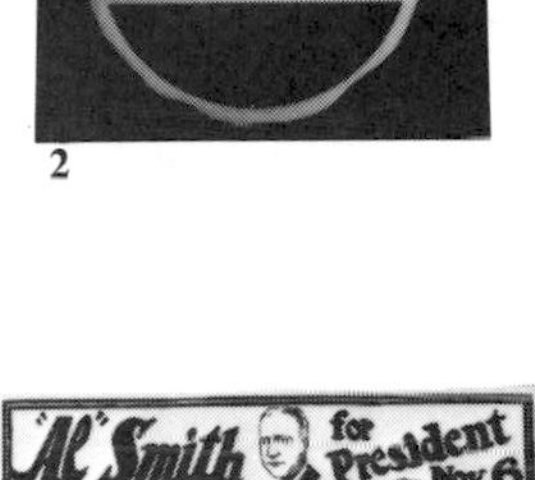

2

3

4

5

6

7

8

9

10

11

12

13

KENNEDY
FOR U.S. SENATOR

14

15

16

17

18

LBJ

19

20

10
"WILLKIE/THE HOPE OF AMERICA" die-cut 3.5x6" foil sticker in silver/blue/red. 1940. $20.

11
TRUMAN 4x5.5" bw portrait window sticker with 2 gum strips on the blank reverse. 1948. $25.

12
TRUMAN 1.5x7" blue and cream window sticker. Sticker is gummed on the front and meant to be placed on a car windshield. 1948. $15.

13
TRUMAN – "VOTE DEMOCRATIC" yellow on black 4" square paper window sticker. 1948. $12.

14
KENNEDY 3.5x10" rwb paper window sticker. 1952. $60.

15
"KENNEDY FOR PRESIDENT" die-cut 6x6" bw/rwb paper sticker. 1960. $18.

16
"KENNEDY FOR PRESIDENT" die-cut bw/rwb 5x6" window sticker. 1960. $12.

17
"NATIONAL NIXON-LODGE CLUB" rwb 4x9" paper oval window sticker. 1960. $12.

18
"NIXON" yellow/blue die-cut 7" paper sticker in the shape of California. C. 1960. $8.

19
JOHNSON 3.5x7.5" western "LBJ" hat in yellow/black with peel-off backing. 1964. $3.

20
"GOLDWATER '64" bw/gold 3x3" paper sticker. $5.

APPENDIX

I. Presidential Candidates
1789-1988

Election of 1789	Party	Electoral	Popular
George Washington	None	69	n/r
John Adams	None	34	n/r
John Jay	None	9	n/r
Robert H. Harrison	None	6	n/r
John Rutledge	None	6	n/r
John Hancock	None	4	n/r
George Clinton	None	3	n/r
Samuel Huntington	None	2	n/r
John Milton	None	2	n/r
James Armstrong	None	1	n/r
Edward Teifair	None	1	n/r
Benjamin Lincoln	None	1	n/r
Not voted		12	

Election of 1792	Party	Electoral	Popular
George Washington	Federalist	132	n/r
John Adams	Federalist	77	n/r
George Clinton	Anti-Federalist	50	n/r
Thomas Jefferson	Anti-Federalist	4	n/r
Aaron Burr	Anti-Federalist	1	n/r

Election of 1796	Party	Electoral	Popular
John Adams	Federalist	71	n/r
Thomas Jefferson	Democratic-Republican	68	n/r
Thomas Pinckney	Federalist	59	n/r
Aaron Burr	Democratic-Republican	30	n/r
Samuel Adams	Democratic-Republican	15	n/r
Oliver Ellsworth	Federalist	11	n/r
George Clinton	Democratic-Republican	7	n/r
John Jay	Federalist	5	n/r
James Iredell	Federalist	3	n/r
Samuel Johnston	Federalist	2	n/r
George Washington	Federalist	2	n/r
John Henry	Federalist	2	n/r
Charles Cotesworth Pinckney	Federalist	1	n/r

n/r - vote not recorded

Election of 1800	Party	Electoral	Popular
Thomas Jefferson	Democratic-Republican	73	n/r
Aaron Burr	Democratic-Republican	73	n/r
John Adams	Federalist	65	n/r
Charles Cotesworth Pinckney	Federalist	64	n/r
John Jay	Federalist	1	n/r

Election of 1804	Party	Electoral	Popular
Thomas Jefferson	Democratic-Republican	162	n/r
Charles Cotesworth Pinckney	Federalist	14	n/r

Election of 1808	Party	Electoral	Popular
James Madison	Democratic-Republican	122	n/r
Charles Cotesworth Pinckney	Federalist	47	n/r
George Clinton	Democratic-Republican	6	n/r
Not voted		1	

Election of 1812	Party	Electoral	Popular
James Madison	Democratic-Republican	128	n/r
DeWitt Clinton	Federalist	89	n/r
Not voted		1	

Election of 1816	Party	Electoral	Popular
James Monroe	Democratic-Republican	183	n/r
Rufus King	Federalist	34	n/r
Not voted		1	

Election of 1820	Party	Electoral	Popular
James Monroe	Democratic-Republican	231	n/r
John Quincy Adams	Democratic-Republican	1	n/r

n/r - vote not recorded

Election of 1824	Party	Electoral	Popular
John Quincy Adams	Democratic-Republican	84	108,740
Andrew Jackson	Democratic-Republican	99	153,544
William Harris Crawford	Democratic-Republican	41	47,136
Henry Clay	Democratic-Republican	37	46,618

Election of 1828	Party	Electoral	Popular
Andrew Jackson	Democrat	178	647,286
John Quincy Adams	National Republican	83	508,064

Election of 1832	Party	Electoral	Popular
Andrew Jackson	Democrat	219	687,502
Henry Clay	National Republican	49	530,189
John Floyd	Independent Democrats	11	n/r
William Wirt	Anti-Masonic	7	101,051
Not voted		2	

Election of 1836	Party	Electoral	Popular
Martin Van Buren	Democrat	170	762,678
William Henry Harrison	Anti-Masonic/Whig	73	549,508
Hugh Lawson White	Whig	26	145,352
Daniel Webster	Whig	14	41,287
Willie Person Mangum	Independent/Whig	11	n/r

Election of 1840	Party	Electoral	Popular
William Henry Harrison	Whig	234	1,275,016
Martin Van Buren	Democrat	60	1,129,102
James G. Birney	Liberty (Prohibition)	0	7,069

Election of 1844	Party	Electoral	Popular
James Knox Polk	Democrat	170	1,337,243
Henry Clay	Whig	105	1,299,062
James G. Birney	Liberty (Prohibition)	0	62,300

n/r - vote not recorded

Election of 1848	Party	Electoral	Popular
Zachary Taylor	Whig	163	1,360,099
Lewis Cass	Democrat	127	1,220,544
Martin Van Buren	Free Soil (Democrat)	0	291,263
Gerrit Smith	National Liberty/Liberty League	0	2,733

Election of 1852	Party	Electoral	Popular
Franklin Pierce	Democrat	254	1,601,474
Winfield Scott	Whig	42	1,386,580
John Parker Hale	Free Soil (Democrat)	0	155,285
Daniel Webster	Whig	0	7,407
Broome	American	0	2,666
George Michael Troop	Southern Rights	0	2,300
Gerrit Smith	National Liberty	0	72

Election of 1856	Party	Electoral	Popular
James Buchanan	Democrat	174	1,838,169
John C. Fremont	Republican	114	1,341,264
Millard Fillmore	American (Know Nothing) Whig	8	874,534
Gerrit Smith	Land Reform	0	484

Election of 1860	Party	Electoral	Popular
Abraham Lincoln	Republican	180	1,866,452
John Cabell Breckinridge	Southern Democrat	72	847,953
John Bell	Constitutional Union	39	590,631
Stephen Douglas	Democrat	12	1,375,157

Election of 1864	Party	Electoral	Popular
Abraham Lincoln	Republican	180	2,213,665
George Brinton McClellan	Democrat	21	1,805,237
Not voted (states of the Confederacy)			81

Election of 1868	Party	Electoral	Popular
Ulysses S. Grant	Republican	214	3,012,833
Horatio Seymour	Democrat	80	2,703,249
Not voted (unreconstructed states of MS, TX, VA)		26	

n/r - vote not recorded

Election of 1872	Party	Electoral	Popular
Ulysses S. Grant	Republican	286	3,597,132
Horace Greeley	Democrat/Liberal Republican	66*	2,834,125
Thomas A. Hendricks	Independent Democrat	42	0
B. Gratz Brown	Democrat	18	0
Charles Jones Jenkins	Democrat	2	0
David Davis	Democrat	1	0
Charles O'Conor	"Straight-Out" Democrat	0	29,489
James Black	National Prohibition	0	5,608
Victoria Claflin Woodhull	People's Party (Equal Rights)	0	n/r
William Slocum Goresbeck	Independent Liberal Republican	0	n/r
Not counted		17	

Election of 1876	Party	Electoral	Popular
Rutherford B. Hayes	Republican	185	4,036,298
Samuel Jones Tilden	Democrat	184	4,300,590
Peter Cooper	National Independent (Greenback)	0	81,737
Green Clay Smith	Prohibition	0	9,522
James B. Walker	American National	0	2,508

Election of 1880	Party	Electoral	Popular
James A. Garfield	Republican	214	4,454,416
Winfield Scott Hancock	Democrat	155	4,444,952
James Baird Weaver	Greenback Labor	0	308,578
Neal Dow	Prohibition	0	10,305
John Wolcott Phelps	American/Anti-Masonic	0	1,045

Election of 1884	Party	Electoral	Popular
(Stephen) Grover Cleveland	Democrat	219	4,874,986
James G. Blaine	Republican	182	4,851,981
Benjamin F. Butler	National Greenback/Anti-Monopoly	0	175,370
John Pierce St. John	Prohibition	0	150,369
Belva Ann (Bennett) Lockwood	Equal Rights	0	4,149
Peter Dinwiddie Wigginton	American	0	n/r
Samuel Clark Pomeroy	American Prohibition National	0	n/r

*Votes scattered after Greeley's death, which occured before the Electoral College met.
n/r—votes not recorded

Election of 1888	Party	Electoral	Popular
Benjamin Harrison	Republican	233	5,444,337
(Stephen) Grover Cleveland	Democrat	168	5,540,309
Clinton Bowen Fisk	Prohibition	0	249,506
Alson Jenness Streeter	Union Labor	0	146,935
Robert Hall Cowdrey	United Labor	0	2,818
James Langon Curtis	American	0	1,600
Belva Ann (Bennett) Lockwood	Equal Rights	0	n/r
Albert Redstone	Industrial Reform	0	n/r

Election of 1892	Party	Electoral	Popular
(Stephen) Grover Cleveland	Democrat	277	5,556,918
Benjamin Harrison	Republican	145	5,176,108
James Baird Weaver	People's (Populist)	22	1,041,028
John Bidwell	Prohibition	0	264,133
Simon Wing	Socialist-Labor	0	21,164

Election of 1896	Party	Electoral	Popular
William McKinley	Republican	271	7,104,779
William Jennings Bryan	Democrat/People's (Populist)	176	6,502,925
John McAuley Palmer	National Democrat	0	133,148
Joshua Levering	Prohibition	0	132,007
Charles H. Matchett	Socialist-Labor	0	36,274
Charles Eugene Bentley	Nationalist	0	13,969

Election of 1900	Party	Electoral	Popular
William McKinley	Republican	292	7,207,923
William Jennings Bryan	Democrat	155	6,358,133
John Granville Woolley	Prohibition	0	208,914
Eugene Victor Debs	Social Democrat	0	87,814
Wharton Barker	People's (Populist)	0	50,373
Joseph Francis Maloney	Socialist-Labor	0	39,739
Seth Hockett Ellis	Union Reform	0	5,698
Jonah Fitz Randolph Leonard	United Christian	0	5,500
Job Harriman	Social Democrats of USA	0	n/r

n/r - vote not recorded

Election of 1904	Party	Electoral	Popular
Theodore Roosevelt	Republican	336	7,623,486
Alton B. Parker	Democrat	140	5,077,911
Eugene Victor Debs	Socialist	0	402,283
Silas Comfort Swallow	Prohibition	0	258,536
Thomas Edward Watson	People's (Populist)	0	117,183
Charles Hunter Corregan	Socialist-Labor	0	31,249
Austin Holcomb	Continental	0	1,000
George Edwin Taylor	National Liberty	0	n/r

Election of 1908	Party	Electoral	Popular
William Howard Taft	Republican	321	7,677,908
William Jennings Bryan	Democrat	162	6,409,104
Eugene Victor Debs	Socialist	0	420,793
Eugene Wilder Chafin	Prohibition	0	253,840
Thomas Lewis Hisgen	Independence	0	82,872
Thomas Edward Watson	People's (Populist)	0	29,100
August Gillhaus	Socialist-Labor	0	14,021
Daniel Braxton Turney	United Christian	0	500

Election of 1912	Party	Electoral	Popular
(Thomas) Woodrow Wilson	Democrat	435	6,293,454
Theodore Roosevelt	Progressive (Bull Moose)	88	4,119,538
William Howard Taft	Republican	8	3,484,980
Eugene Victor Debs	Socialist	0	900,672
Eugene Wilder Chafin	Prohibition	0	206,275
Arthur Elmer Reiner	Socialist-Labor	0	28,750

Election of 1916	Party	Electoral	Popular
(Thomas) Woodrow Wilson	Democrat	277	9,129,606
Charles Evans Hughes	Republican	254	8,538,221
Allen Louis Benson	Socialist	0	585,113
James Franklin Hanly	Prohibition	0	220,506
Theodore Roosevelt	Progressive	0	35,034
Arthur Elmer Reimer	Socialist-Labor	0	13,403
William Sulzer	American	0	n/r

n/r - vote not recorded

Election of 1920	Party	Electoral	Popular
Warren G. Harding	Republican	404	16,152,200
James M. Cox	Democrat	127	9,147,353
Eugene Victor Debs	Socialist	0	919,799
Parley Parker Christensen	Farmer-Labor	0	265,411
Aaron Sherman Watkins	Prohibition	0	189,408
James Edward Ferguson	American	0	48,000
W(illiam) W(esley) Cox	Socialist-Labor	0	31,715
Robert Colvin MacCauley	Single Tax	0	5,837

Election of 1924	Party	Electoral	Popular
(John) Calvin Coolidge	Republican	382	15,725,016
John W. Davis	Democrat	136	8,386,503
Robert M. LaFollette	Progressive	13	4,822,856
Herman Preston Faris	Prohibition	0	57,520
Frank T. Johns	Socialist-Labor	0	36,428
William Z. Foster	Worker's (Communist)	0	36,386
Gilbert Owen Nations	American	0	23,967
William J. Wallace	Commonwealth Land	0	1,532
John Zahnd	National Independent (Greenback)	0	n/r
Jacob Sechler Coxey	Farmer-Labor	0	n/r

Election of 1928	Party	Electoral	Popular
Herbert Hoover	Republican	444	21,391,381
Alfred E. Smith	Democrat	87	15,016,443
Norman Thomas	Socialist	0	267,835
William Z. Foster	Worker's (Communist)	0	48,770
Verne L. Reynolds	Socialist-Labor	0	21,603
William Frederick Varney	Prohibition	0	20,106
Frank Elbridge Webb	Farmer-Labor	0	6,390
John Zahnd	National Independent (Greenback)	0	6,390

Election of 1932	Party	Electoral	Popular
Franklin Delano Roosevelt	Democrat	472	22,821,857
Herbert Hoover	Republican	59	15,761,841
Norman Thomas	Socialist	0	881,951
William Z. Foster	Worker's (Communist)	0	102,785
William David Upshaw	Prohibition	0	81,869
William Hope Harvey	Liberty	0	53,425
Verne L. Reynolds	Socialist-Labor	0	33,276
Jacob Sechler Coxey	Farmer-Labor	0	7,309
John Zahnd	National Independent (Greenback)	0	1,645
James R. Cox	Jobless	0	740

n/r - vote not recorded

Election of 1936	**Party**	**Electoral**	**Popular**
Franklin Delano Roosevelt	Democrat	523	27,751,597
Alfred M. Landon	Republican	8	16,679,583
William Lemke	National Union	0	882,479
Norman Thomas	Socialist	0	187,720
Earl Russell Browder	Communist	0	80,159
David Leigh Colvin	Prohibition/National Prohibition/ Commonwealth	0	37,847
John W. Aiken	Socialist-Labor	0	12,728
William Dudley Pelley	Christian	0	1,598
John Zahnd	National Independent (Greenback)	0	n/r

Election of 1940	**Party**	**Electoral**	**Popular**
Franklin Delano Roosevelt	Democrat	449	27,244,160
Wendell Willkie	Republican	82	22,305,198
Norman Thomas	Socialist	0	99,557
Roger Ward Babson	Prohibition	0	57,812
Earl Russell Browdor	Communist	0	46,251
John W. Aiken	Socialist-Labor	0	14,883
Alfred Knutson	Independent	0	545
John Zahnd	National Independent (Greenback)	0	n/r
Anna Milburn	National Greenback	0	n/r

Election of 1944	**Party**	**Electoral**	**Popular**
Franklin Delano Roosevelt	Democrat	432	25,602,504
Thomas E. Dewey	Republican	99	22,006,285
Norman Thomas	Socialist	0	80,518
Claude A. Watson	Prohibition	0	74,758
Edward A. Teichert	Socialist-Labor	0	45,336
Harry F. Byrd	Southern Democrats	0	7,799
Gerald L. K. Smith	America First	0	1,780
Unpledged Texas Regulars			135,439

n/r - vote not recorded

Election of 1948	Party	Electoral	Popular
Harry S. Truman	Democrat	304	24,105,695
Thomas E. Dewey	Republican	189	21,969,170
J. Strom Thurmond	States' Rights (Dixiecrats)	38	1,169,021
Henry A. Wallace	Progressive/American Labor	0	1,156,103
Norman Thomas	Socialist	0	139,009
Claude A. Watson	Prohibition	0	103,216
Edward A. Teichert	Socialist-Labor	0	29,272
Farrell Dobbs	Socialist Workers/ Militant Workers	0	13,613
Gerald L. K. Smith	Christian Nationalist	0	n/r
John G. Scott	Greenback	0	n/r
John Maxwell	Vegetarian	0	n/r

Election of 1952	Party	Electoral	Popular
Dwight D. Eisenhower	Republican	442	33,824,351
Adlai E. Stevenson	Democrat	89	27,314,987
Vincent William Halliman	Progressive/American Labor	0	132,608
Stuart Hamblen	Prohibition	0	72,768
Eric Hass	Socialist-Labor	0	30,376
Darlington Hoopes	Socialist	0	18,322
Douglas A. MacArthur	America First	0	17,205
Farrell Dobbs	Socialist Workers/ Militant Workers	0	8,956
Henry B. Krajewski	Poor Man's Party	0	4,203
Homer Aubrey Tomlinson	Church of God Bible Party	0	n/r
Frederick C. Proehl	Greenback	0	n/r
Ellen L. Jensen	Washington Peace	0	n/r
Daniel J. Murphy	American Vegetarian	0	n/r

Election of 1956	Party	Electoral	Popular
Dwight D. Eisenhower	Republican	457	35,582,236
Adlai E. Stevenson	Democrat/Liberal	74	26,028,887
Walter B. Jones	——	1	0
T. Coleman Andrews	Independent States' Rights	0	275,915
Harry F. Byrd	Independent	0	134,157
Eric Hass	Socialist-Labor	0	44,368
Enoch Arden Holtwick	Prohibition	0	41,547
William Ezra Jenner	Texas Constitution	0	30,999
Farrell Dobbs	Socialist Workers / Militant Workers	0	7,805
Darlington Hoopes	Socialist	0	2,192
Henry B. Krajewski	American Third Party	0	1,892
Gerald L. K. Smith	Christian National	0	n/r
Homer Aubrey Tomlinson	Theocratic	0	n/r
Herbert M. Shelton	American Vegetarian	0	n/r
Frederick C. Proehl	Greenback	0	n/r
William Langer	Pioneer	0	n/r

n/r - vote not recorded

Election of 1960	Party	Electoral	Popular
John F. Kennedy	Democrat	300	34,227,096
Richard M. Nixon	Republican	223	34,107,646
Harry F. Byrd	Independent	15	0
Orval Faubus	States' Rights	0	214,549
Eric Hass	Socialist-Labor	0	46,478
Rutherford L. Decker	Prohibition	0	42,483
Farrell Dobbs	Socialist Workers	0	39,541
Charles Loten Sullivan	Texas Constitution	0	18,169
Joseph Bracken Lee	Conservative Party of New Jersey	0	8,708
C. Benton Coiner	Conservative Party of Virginia	0	3,647
Lar Daly	Tax Cut	0	1,767
Clennon King	Afro-American	0	1,485
Merritt Barton Curtis	Independent/Constitution	0	1,240
Symon Gould	American Vegetarian	0	n/r
Whitney Hart Slocum	Greenback	0	n/r
Homer Aubrey Tomlinson	Theocratic	0	n/r
Byrd Unpledged Democrats			116,248

Election of 1964	Party	Electoral	Popular
Lyndon B. Johnson	Democrat	486	43,129,484
Barry M. Goldwater	Republican	82	27,178,188
Eric Hass	Socialist-Labor	0	45,219
Clifton DeBerry	Socialist Workers	0	32,720
Earle Harold Munn	Prohibition	0	23,267
John Kaspar	National States' Rights	0	6,953
Joseph B. Lightburn	Constitution	0	5,090
Kirby James Hensley	Universal	0	19
Homer Aubrey Tomlinson	Theocratic	0	n/r
T. Coleman Andrews	Independent States' Rights	0	n/r
Yette Bronstein	Best Party	0	n/r
D. X. B. Schwartz	National Tax Savers	0	n/r
Louis E. Jaeckel	American	0	n/r

n/r - vote not recorded

Election of 1968	Party	Electoral	Popular
Richard M. Nixon	Republican	301	31,783,783
Hubert H. Humphrey	Democrat	191	31,271,839
George C. Wallace	American Independent	46	9,899,557
Henning A. Blomen	Socialist-Labor	0	52,588
Dick Gregory	Various Parties	0	47,133
Fred Halstead	Socialist Workers	0	41,389
Eldridge Cleaver	Peace and Freedom	0	36,385
Eugene J. McCarthy	New Party	0	25,858
Earle Harold Munn	Prohibition	0	15,123
Charlene Mitchell	Communist	0	1,075

Election of 1972	Party	Electoral	Popular
Richard M. Nixon	Republican	520	47,165,234
George McGovern	Democrat	17	29,168,110
John G. Schmitz	American	0	1,107,083
Linda Jenness	Socialist Workers	0	97,256
Benjamin Spock	People's	0	78,889
Louis Fisher	Socialist Labor	0	53,815
Gus Hall	Communist	0	25,621
Harold Munn	Prohibition	0	13,497
John Hospers	Libertarian	1	3,697
John Mahalchik	America First	0	1,743
Edward Wallace	Independent	0	460
Gabriel Green	Universal	0	220

Election of 1976	Party	Electoral	Popular
James E. Carter	Democrat	297	40,828,587
Gerald R. Ford	Republican	241	39,147,613
Eugene J. McCarthy	Independent	0	751,728
Roger MacBride	Libertarian	0	172,750
Lester G. Maddox	American Independent	0	170,780
Thomas Anderson	American	0	160,600
Peter Camejo	Socialist Workers	0	91,226
Gus Hall	Communist	0	59,114
Margaret Wright	People's	0	49,024
Lyndon H. LaRouche	U.S. Labor	0	40,045
Benjamin C. Bubar	Prohibition	0	15,898
Jules Levin	Socialist Labor	0	9,590
Frank P. Zeidler	Socialist	0	6,022

n/r - vote not recorded

Election of 1980	**Party**	**Electoral**	**Popular**
Ronald Reagan	Republican	489	43,899,248
James E. Carter	Democrat	49	35,481,435
John B. Anderson	Independent	0	5,719,437
Ed Clark	Libertarian	0	920,859
Barry Commoner	Citizens	0	230,377
Gus Hall	Communist	0	43,871
John Rarick	American Independent	0	41,172
Clifton DeBerry	Socialist Workers	0	40,105
Ellen McCormack	Respect for Life	0	32,319
Margaret Smith	Peace and Freedom	0	18,117
Dierdre Griswold	Workers World	0	13,211
Benjamin Bubar	National Statesman	0	7,100
David McReynolds	Socialist	0	6,720
Percy Greaves	American	0	6,539
Andrew Pulley	Socialist Workers	0	6,032
Richard Congress	Socialist Workers	0	4,029
Kurt Lynen	Middle Class Candidate	0	3,694
Bill Gahres	Down With Lawyers	0	1,718
Frank Shelton	American	0	1,555
Martin Wendelken	Independent	0	923
Harley McLain	National People's League	0	296
Write-Ins		0	16,921

Election of 1984	**Party**	**Electoral**	**Popular**
Ronald Reagan	Republican	525	54,450,603
Walter Mondale	Democrat	13	37,573,671
David Bergland	Libertarian	0	227,949
Lyndon LaRouche	(Independent)	0	78,773
Sonia Johnson	Citizens	0	72,153
Bob Richards	Populist	0	62,371
Dennis Serrette	Independent Alliance	0	47,109
Gus Hall	Communist	0	35,561
Mel Mason	Socialist Workers	0	24,687
Larry Holmes	Workers World	0	15,220
Delmar Dennis	American	0	13,150
Ed Winn	Workers League	0	10,801
Earl F. Dodge	Prohibition	0	4,242
Gavrielle Holmes	Workers World	0	2,718
John B. Anderson*	National Unity	0	1,479

*Withdrew early from campaign but still on ballot in Kentucky.
n/r - vote not recorded

Election of 1988	Party	Electoral	Popular
George Bush	Republican	426	48,138,478
Michael S. Dukakis	Democrat	111**	41,114,068
Ron Paul	Libertarian	0	431,616
Lenora Fulani	New Alliance	0	217,200
David Duke	Populist	0	46,910
Eugene McCarthy	Consumer	0	30,903
James Griffin	American Independent	0	27,818
Lyndon H. LaRouche	National Economic Recovery	0	25,530
William Marra	Right To Life	0	20,497
Ed Winn	Workers League	0	18,662
James Warren	Socialist Workers	0	15,603
Herbert Lewin	Peace and Freedom	0	10,370
Earl F. Dodge	Prohibition	0	8,000
Larry Holmes	Workers World	0	7,846
Willa Kenoyer	Socialist	0	3,878
Delmar Dennis	American	0	3,476
Jack Herer	Grassroots	0	1,949
Louie Youngkite	Independent	0	372
John Martin	Third World Assembly	0	236
Various Other Candidates		0	6,934
Write-Ins		0	20,368

**One vote from West Virginia for Lloyd Bentsen for President and Michael Dukakis for Vice-President.
n/r - vote not recorded

II. Glossary

Back Paper: a paper sheet placed in the reverse opening of a celluloid button. The paper may carry the manufacturer's name, patent dates, union insignia or an advertising message. The use of back papers died out during the 1950s.

Brummagen: a showy, but inferior and worthless thing. The term used for reproduction and fantasy political items.

Celluloid Button or "Cello": a button made with a thin, clear sheet of celluloid covering the paper sheet printed with the image. Both sheets are backed by a metal disk and the three pieces are held together with a metal ring, known as a collet, pressed into the back opening. As celluloid is flammable, it was eliminated in the 1940s and replaced by an acetate sheet, but such buttons are still called celluloid or cellos.

Coattail: any political item that pictures or names a candidate for a high office in combination with one or more candidates for lower offices. For example, a button showing a presidential candidate along with state candidates for governor and U.S. Senator.

Collector Involvement: a term referring to items made by collectors (or dealers) intended for sale to other collectors, rather than political parties or the general public. This practice was most prevelant in 1968 and 1972. Since then, close monitoring by hobby members has greatly reduced the number of collector-involved pieces.

Collet: the circular metal ring on the back of a celluloid button used to hold the celluloid covering and paper with the image to the metal disk.

Curl: the rounded edge of a button.

Disclaimer: an inscription on a button specifying who authorized or paid for the item, usually printed on the curl.

Fantasy Item: a term coined by Hake's Americana in the 1960s to designate items newly created but depicting some older collectible subject. Such items are unauthorized and never existed during the time period that produced other original collectibles relating to the same subject. The main purpose of these items is to appeal to or, most frequently, defraud collectors.

Ferrotype: a tintype photograph held in a brass frame or disk, sometimes with a cloth covered rim. If photos are placed on both front and back surfaces, the rim is usually holed so a small ribbon can afix the ferrotype to the lapel. If only the front displays a photo, the reverse usually has a short stickpin as a fastener.

Flasher: a plastic sheet, usually made as a button, showing one image that shifts to a second image when tilted or viewed from a different perspective.

Foxing: stain marks, usually brown, on the paper under the celluloid covering of a button. Foxing is caused by water, or even long exposure to high humidity, rusting the metal disk behind the button paper. The term also applies to stains on paper artifacts. Foxing on paper can sometimes be chemically removed, but there is no remedy for "foxed" buttons and staining rapidly decreases a button's potential value.

Jugate: any campaign item picturing two candidates, most often a party's presidential and vice-presidential nominees. With a third candidate pictured, the item is known as a "trigate."

Lithographed Tin Button or "Litho": a button stamped from a sheet of tin which has the image printed on the metal. There is no collet on the reverse and the pin is held in place by the curvature of edges rounded by the stamping process. Litho buttons were commonly used for political campaigns beginning in 1920. With just two or three exceptions, all litho buttons for candidates from 1896 through 1916 are reproductions of buttons originally issued as celluloids.

Mechanical: a small lapel device, usually made of brass, that moves or has a covering that snaps open (normally to reveal an image or slogan) when a spring is activated. The term is also loosely applied to any item with moving parts.

Medal: a coin-like medallic item with a size of 1 3/4" or larger, although the term is commonly applied to items regardless of their size.

Medalet: a coin-like medallic item with a size under 1 3/4", although such items are also commonly referred to as medals or tokens.

Repin: a button consisting of a printed paper design produced for a campaign but not manufactured into a finished button until sometime after the campaign.

Reproduction: an exact or close copy of the original artifact.

Ribbon: a piece of fabric featuring candidates' pictures and/or political slogans meant to be displayed on the lapel and often retained for use as a bookmark.

Ribbon Badge: a ribbon that has a medallic or celluloid piece attached to its surface or suspended below. The reverse top edge normally has a stickpin or bar pin fastener.

Sepia: a reddish-brown or brown color often used instead of black and white to enhance the attractiveness of a photograph or illustration. Widely used for buttons from 1896 through the 1940s.

Shell Badge: a lapel device stamped from a thin brass sheet either bearing the candidate's image or with an opening at the center to serve as a frame for holding tintype or cardboard photos.

Stud: a lapel device, often circular in shape, with a metal shank on the reverse to hold the item in a buttonhole.

Tab: a flat metal piece, usually lithographed tin, with an extended segment on the top edge which is folded back for attachment to clothing.

Token: used correctly, the term means a substitute for money; but, within the political items hobby, the term is loosely applied to any small coin-like medallic item. (See Medal and Medalet.)

Union Bug: refers to the small union label found on many button curls or back papers. The presence or absence of a union bug has no bearing on the question of an item's authenticity.

White Metal: the term for a metal containing mostly lead and tin, sometimes referred to as "pot-metal."

III. Campaign Slogans & Candidates' Nicknames

Slogans and nicknames are a significant part of our political language and have been associated with presidents and candidates since George Washington. However, meanings, so apparent to one generation, can quickly become mysteries to later generations. The following alphabetical list attributes campaign slogans and candidate nicknames that actually appear on campaign items, sometimes with a picture of the candidate, but very often without specifying the candidate's name. Nicknames and many slogans apply to a single candidate, but some slogans, particularly throughout the 19th century, are used for several different candidates in elections spanning many years. To identify by candidate those items with slogans used by multiple candidates, referring to *Hake's Encyclopedia of Political Buttons* is probably the best first step.

A Choice for a Change - Barry Goldwater
A Choice Not an Echo - Barry Goldwater
A Christian in the White House - Herbert Hoover (Anti-Smith)
A Public Office is a Public Trust - Grover Cleveland
A Square Deal - Theodore Roosevelt
A Third Term is Better Than a Third Rater - Franklin Roosevelt (Anti-Willkie)
All 48 In '48 - Harry Truman
America Calls Another Roosevelt - Franklin Roosevelt
Americans Cannot Be Bought - Alf Landon (Anti-Roosevelt)
And That Goes for Eleanor Too! - Wendell Willkie (Anti-Roosevelt)
Ask Amy - Ronald Reagan (Anti-Carter)
Back Our President - Franklin Roosevelt
Better A Part-Time President Than a Full-Time Phoney — Dwight Eisenhower (Anti-Stevenson)
Billy Possum - William H. Taft
Billy's Brother - Jimmy Carter
Boy! Do We Need a Change! - Wendell Willkie (Anti-Roosevelt)
Clear Everything With Sidney - Thomas Dewey (Anti-Roosevelt)
Click With Dick - Richard Nixon
Come Home America - George McGovern
Confucius Say...Man Who Stand Up Twice, No Good Third Time - Wendell Willkie (Anti-Roosevelt)
Confucius Say...One Time-Good/Two Time-Good/Three Time-Damn Good — Franklin Roosevelt (Anti-Willkie)
Coxsure - James Cox
Death to Trusts - William J. Bryan
Deeds Not Deficits - Alf Landon (Anti-Roosevelt)
Deeds-Not Words — Calvin Coolidge
Dee-Lighted — Theodore Roosevelt
De-Thronement Day Nov. 5th — Wendell Willkie (Anti-Roosevelt)
Dictator? Not For Us - Wendell Willkie (Anti-Roosevelt)
Dictators Don't Debate - Wendell Willkie (Anti-Roosevelt)
Don't Be a Jackass, Follow the Eagle - Wendell Willkie (Anti-Roosevelt)
Don't Be a Third Term-ite — Wendell Willkie (Anti-Roosevelt)
Don't Blame Me I'm From Massachusetts - George McGovern
Don't Blame Me I'm From Minnesota - Walter Mondale
Don't Send a Boy - Richard Nixon (Anti-Kennedy)
Don't Swap Horses - Herbert Hoover

Don't Tarry Vote Harry - Harry Truman
Dr. Jekyll of Hyde Park - Wendell Willkie (Anti-Roosevelt)
Draft the General - Dwight Eisenhower
Dump the Hump - Richard Nixon (Anti-Humphrey)
8 Years is Plenty - Wendell Willkie (Anti-Roosevelt)
Eleanor? No Soap! - Wendell Willkie (Anti-Roosevelt)
Empty Dinner Pail - William J. Bryan (Anti-McKinley)
First in War, First in Peace, and First in the Hearts of His Countrymen - George Washington
Fore! We'll All Be in the Same Hole Together! - Adlai Stevenson (Anti-Eisenhower)
4H Club (Help Hurry Harry Home) - Thomas Dewey (Anti-Truman)
Four More Years - Richard Nixon
Free Silver - William J. Bryan
From the Tow Path to the White House - James Garfield
Full Dinner Bucket (or Pail) - William McKinley
Give the Smilin' Man a Chance - Jimmy Carter
Gone With the Wind! - Wendell Willkie (Anti-Roosevelt)
Grand Old Party/Good As Gold - William McKinley
Grass Root Democrat - George McGovern
Grass Rooters for Dick - Richard Nixon
Great Society - Lyndon Johnson
Grits & Fritz - Jimmy Carter
Guard Our Peace - Wendell Willkie
Happiness is a New President - George McGovern (Anti-Nixon)
Happy Days are Here Again - Franklin Roosevelt
Hello Al - Al Smith
Hello Bill - William H. Taft (used later by many fraternal organizations)
Help Us to be What We Can Be - George McGovern
He Proved the Pen Mightier than the Sword - Woodrow Wilson
Here's Your Hat Frank, What's Your Hurry - Wendell Willkie (Anti-Roosevelt)
Hero of New Orleans - Andrew Jackson
Hero of Tippecanoe - William Henry Harrison
Honest Abe - Abraham Lincoln
I am a Right Wing Extremist - Barry Goldwater
I Don't Want Eleanor Either - Wendell Willkie (Anti-Roosevelt)
I Intend to Fight It Out on This Line if it Takes All Summer - Ulysses Grant
I Just Want to be a Lieutenant - Wendell Willkie (Anti-Roosevelt)
I Miss Ike! Hell, I Even Miss Harry - Anti-John Kennedy
I Want to be a Captain, Too - Wendell Willkie (Anti-Roosevelt)
I Will Crow in November - James Cox
I'm a Stand Pat Democrat - Harry Truman
I'm an Extremist/I Love Liberty - Barry Goldwater
I'm Working for Peanuts - Jimmy Carter
In God We Trust for the Other 47 Cents - William McKinley (Anti-Bryan)
In Gold We Trust - William McKinley
In Your Guts You Know He's Nuts - Lyndon Johnson (Anti-Goldwater)
In Your Heart You Know He's Right - Barry Goldwater
Indict the U.S. Government for Genocide - Wendell Willkie (Anti-Roosevelt)
It's an Elephant's Job-No Time for "Donkey-Business"! — Herbert Hoover
It's Not Jack's Money He'd Spend...It's Yours - Richard Nixon (Anti-Kennedy)
J.C. Will Save America - Jimmy Carter
Joe for Willkie - refers to boxer Joe Louis

Joe Smith - Adlai Stevenson (Anti-Eisenhower)
Let Us Continue - Lyndon Johnson
Let Well Enough Alone - Calvin Coolidge
Let's Light Up the White House and Clean Out the Bird House - Barry Goldwater (Anti-Johnson)
Let Us Have Peace - Ulysses Grant
Life Begins in '40 - Wendell Willkie
Little Giant - Stephen Douglas
Little Mack - George McClellan
Little Van - Martin Van Buren
Long Live the President - George Washington
Make America Happen Again - George McGovern
Muriel for First Lady - Muriel Humphrey
My Ambassador - Wendell Willkie (Anti-Roosevelt)
My Friends-Goodbye — Wendell Willkie (Anti-Roosevelt)
My Friends I'm Indispensable - Wendell Willkie (Anti-Roosevelt)
My Hat is in the Ring - Theodore Roosvelt
No Cross of Gold, No Crown of Thorns - William J. Bryan (Anti-McKinley)
No Fourth Term Either - Wendell Willkie (Anti-Roosevelt)
No General - Adlai Stevenson (Anti-Eisenhower)
No General Strangewater for America - Lyndon Johnson (Anti-Goldwater)
No Man is Good Three Times - Wendell Willkie (Anti-Roosevelt)
No More Years - George McGovern (Anti-Nixon)
No Oil on Al - Al Smith
No Royal Family - Wendell Willkie (Anti-Roosevelt)
No Third Term - Wendell Willkie (Anti-Roosevelt)
Now More than Ever - Richard Nixon
Old Hickory - Andrew Jackson
On the Right Track with Jack - John Kennedy
One Good Term Deserves Another - William McKinley
100 Million Buttons Can't Be Wrong - Wendell Willkie
Open Mills Not Mints – William McKinley (Anti-Bryan)
Out at Third - Wendell Willkie (Anti-Roosevelt)
Pat for First Lady - Pat Nixon
Peace and Preparedness - Woodrow Wilson
Peace/Progress/Prosperity - Dwight Eisenhower
Peggy for First Lady - Peggy Goldwater
Plumed Knight - James Blaine
Protection to American Industry - Henry Clay, Benjamin Harrison and others
Protection to Home Industries - Benjamin Harrison and others
Re-Elect the President — Richard Nixon
Remember Oct. 9 - George McGovern (Anti-Nixon)
Right on Mr. President - Richard Nixon
Rough & Ready - Zachary Taylor
Safety First - Woodrow Wilson
Sage of Ashland - Henry Clay
See Dick Run/Run, Dick, Run - Hubert Humphrey (Anti-Nixon)
16 to 1 - William J. Bryan
60 Million Jobs - Harry Truman
Sound Money - William McKinley
Stand Pat - Theodore Roosevelt
Stand Up for America - George Wallace

Sure Mike - Alton B. Parker
Thanksgiving Day Nov. 5 - Wendell Willkie (Anti-Roosevelt)
The Farmer of Ashland - Henry Clay
The Grin Will Win - Jimmy Carter
The Hero of Appomattox - Ulysses Grant
The Man of the Hour - Woodrow Wilson/Franklin Roosevelt/Dwight Eisenhower
The New Deal - Franklin Roosevelt
The New Frontier - John Kennedy
The Pathfinder - John Fremont
The Pen is Mightier than the Sword - Horace Greeley
The People's Choice - William Henry Harrison, Martin Van Buren, and others
The Rail Splitter of the West - Abraham Lincoln
The Right Man in the Right Place - Abraham Lincoln
The Sage of Chappaqua - Horace Greeley
The Same Old Coon - Henry Clay
The Union Must, And Shall Be Preserved - James Buchanan, Abraham Lincoln, and others
The Won't Do Congress, Won't Do - Harry Truman
The World Must be Made Safe for Democracy - Woodrow Wilson
There is No Indispensable Man - Wendell Willkie (Anti-Roosevelt)
Tippecanoe and Tyler Too! - William Henry Harrison
Too Many Jacks from Missouri - Thomas Dewey (Anti-Truman)
Two Good Times Deserve Another - Franklin Roosevelt (Anti-Willkie)
Two Times is Enough for Any Man - Wendell Willkie (Anti-Roosevelt)
United We Stand, Divided We Fall - Henry Clay, William Bryan, and others
U-N-I-T-E-D (United or You and I Ted) — William H. Taft, indicating support of Theodore Roosevelt
Vote the Land Free - 1848 Free-Soil Party/Martin Van Buren
Watchful Waiting Wins - Woodrow Wilson
We Are Going to Win this War and the Peace that Follows - Franklin Roosevelt
We Can't Eat Sunflowers - Franklin Roosevelt (Anti-Landon)
We Don't Want Eleanor Either - Wendell Willkie (Anti-Roosevelt)
What's Wrong Being Right - Barry Goldwater
Why Change? - Dwight Eisenhower
Young Hickory - James Polk

IV. Acronyms and Initialisms

This is an alphabetical list of acronyms, initialisms, and numbers actually used on presidential campaign items with reference to specific candidates, political parties, and organizations.

ABC - Anybody But Carter (1980)
ABJ - Anybody But Johnson (1968) or Austin Burton, Jr. (Hopeful for 1976)
ABK - Anybody But Kennedy (Robert 1968 or Teddy 1980)
ACTWU - Amalgamated Clothing and Textiles Workers Union
ACWA - Amalgamated Clothing Workers of America
ADA - Americans for Democratic Action
AFL-CIO - American Federation of Labor - Congress of Industrial Organizations
AFSCME - American Federation of State, County, & Municipal Employees
AFT - American Federation of Teachers
AIP - American Independent Party
ALP - American Labor Party
AuH2O - Barry Goldwater (chemical symbols for gold and water)
B & L - Blaine & Logan (1884)
BAM - Black Americans for McCarthy (Eugene, 1968)
BGB - Barry Goldwater Backer (Arizona Senate campaign, 1980)
BMG - Barry Morris Goldwater (1964)
C & S - Cleveland and Stevenson (1892)
C & T - Cleveland and Thurman (1888)
CDA - Coalition for a Democratic Alternative (Eugene McCarthy organization)
CDC - California Democratic Council
C5H4N4O3 on AuH2O - Urinate on Goldwater (chemical symbols for urine, gold and water)
CLIRR - Conservative Liberal Independent Regular Republicans (Nixon, 1972)
CLU - Central Labor Union
C/M - Carter-Mondale
COPE - Committee on Political Education (AFL-CIO)
CPUSA - Communist Party of the U.S.A.
CT - Commercial Travelers (1896-1908 era)
CWA - Communications Workers of America
DFR - Defeat Franklin Roosevelt (1940)
DNC - Democratic National Convention
EMK - Edward M. Kennedy
EMc2 - Eugene McCarthy the second time (1972)
ESM - Edmund S. Muskic
FCBNH - For Carter Before New Hampshire (1972)
FDP - Freedom Democratic Party
FDR - Franklin Delano Roosevelt
FEF - Forget Eisenhower Forever (1956)
FKBW - For Kennedy Before Wisconsin (1960)
FMBNH - For McGovern Before New Hampshire (1972)
GMG - George McGovern (1972)
H3 - Hubert Horatio Humphrey (1968)
HG - Hoover and Green (Michigan governor candidate, 1928)
HHH - Hubert Horatio Humphrey
H & M - Benjamin Harrison and Levi Morton (1888)
H & R - Benjamin Harrison and Whitlaw Reid (1892)

HUAC - House Un-American Activities Committee
IAK - I Adore Kennedy (1960)
IAM - International Association of Machinists
IBEW - International Brotherhood of Electrical Workers
IGHAT - I've Got Hatred Against Truman or I'm Going to Hate All Trumans
ILA - International Longshoreman's Association
ILGWU - International Ladies Garment Workers Union
IT - Ike Twice (1956)
IUE - International Union of Electricians
IYHYKHR - In Your Heart You Know He's Right (Goldwater 1964)
JB - Jerry Brown (1980)
JBA - John B. Anderson (1980)
JBC - John B. Connally (1976)
JC - Jimmy Carter
JFK - John Fitzgerald Kennedy
JWB - John W. Bricker (OH local 1970)
K - Robert F. Kennedy or Edward M. Kennedy
K3 - The Third Kennedy (Edward)
K-J - Kennedy-Johnson
KMA - Kiss My Ass (McGovern, 1972)
KNKC - Keep Nebraska Kennedy Conscious or Keep Nebraska Kennedy Country (Edward, 1972)
LBJ - Lyndon Baines Johnson
LNPL - Labor's Non-Partisan League (FDR, 1936)
LOTE - Lesser of Two Evils (Carter, 1980)
N/A - Nixon and Agnew
NADC - National Association of Democratic Clubs (Bryan era)
NASW - National Association of Social Workers
NDC - New Democratic Coalition
NEA - National Education Association
NIT - A slang word for "no" usually used to express opposition to Bryan's proposal for silver and coinage at a ratio of 16 to 1 (1896-1900)
NOW - National Organization For Women
NRL - National Republican League
NSRP - National States' Rights Party
NUSJ - National Union for Social Justice (Father Coughlin 1930's)
OAP - Old Age Pensions (Townsend 1930's)
OARP - Old Age Revolving Pensions (Townsend 1930's)
OK - Old Kinderhook, nickname for Martin Van Buren derived from his home in Kinderhook, NY
OS4MY - Oh S__t, Four More Years (Anti-Nixon, 1972)
PAC - Political Action Committee
PFP - Peace and Freedom Party
R & B - Reagan and Bush (1980)
RCL - Republican College League
RIF - Reduction In Force (Anti-Reagan)
RNC - Republican National Convention
RR - Ronald Reagan
SIN - Stop Inflation Now
SLP - Socialist Labor Party
SOB - Save Our Business/Sons of Business (Anti-John Kennedy)
SWP - Socialist Workers Party

TASK - Teen-agers for Stevenson and Kefauver
TED - Thomas E. Dewey
TIRRC - This Is Ronald Reagan Country
TMK - Too Many Kennedys (Anti-Edward)
TR - Theodore Roosevelt
TTP - Tired Tax Payers (Richard Nixon, 1960)
UAW-CIO - United Auto Workers - Congress of Industrial Organizations
UDFH - United Democrats For Humphrey
UFW - United Farm Workers
URFI - United Republican Fund of Illinois (Nixon, 1960)
USWA - United Steel Workers of America
UYN - United Youth for Nixon (1968)
VFBG - Vote for Barry Goldwater
VIP - Voice in Politics (George Wallace, 1968)
VV - Vietnam Veterans (Eugene McCarthy, 1968)
W & M - Woodrow Wilson & Thomas Marshall
WB - William Bryan
WCTU - Women's Christian Temperance Union
WIN - Whip Inflation Now (Ford)
WOW - Workers of the World
YAF - Young Americans for Freedom
YAFK - Young Americans for Kennedy (John, 1960)
YCERSOYA - You Can't Elect Republicans Sitting on Your Ass (Eisenhower era)
YD - Young Democrats (F.D.R. era)
YPR - Young Professionals For Reagan
YR - Young Republican
YRC - Young Republican Club

V. Clubs and Publications

The American Political Items Collectors (APIC) organization is the one group that brings together everyone interested in campaign items. Other clubs specialize in particular types of items such as banks, posters, or watch fobs, but APIC members are bound together by an interest in an incredibly diverse range of items all intended to promote the election of political candidates. Membership in the APIC makes a vast amount of knowledge easily accessible and opens the doors of communications and opportunity for the collector.

After its formation in 1945 by a few collectors, the APIC grew slowly by word of mouth in the 1950s and 1960s. The 1970s brought increased publicity to collectibles in general, as well as publication of the first price guides on presidential campaign items, *Hake's Encyclopedia of Political Buttons*. Additional publicity in magazines and newspapers helped the APIC to rapidly expand membership throughout the 1970s and 1980s.

The APIC provides members with a quarterly magazine, *The Keynoter,* devoted to articles on candidates and associated campaign items. A monthly newsletter listing APIC regional shows (where items are bought, sold and traded) is published in one of the two newspapers that serve the hobby (see below). On an annual basis, the APIC roster is published with a listing of members along with notes on their special interests. This makes communication between collectors sharing the same interests very easy and dealers in campaign items use the new member lists to send sample sales lists and auction catalogues.

Within the APIC are specialty groups that share the same interests. There are groups specializing in Nixon items, local candidates, and third party items. These, and others, publish newsletters for their own membership.

The APIC holds a national convention every two years and during each year, APIC organizations in many areas of the country sponsor shows where members come to buy, sell, trade, display or just talk about campaign items. For a nominal fee, APIC members can rent table space in the bourse, a large room where the members display the items available for sale. Much activity also occurs at the motel the day before the show in a practice called "room-hopping" based on the maxim "the early bird gets the worm."

Over the years, the APIC has published a number of research projects on particular candidates and the best reference for identifying reproduction campaign items. These projects and back issues of APIC publications are available to new members.

Membership in the APIC is recommended for everyone with an interest in campaign items. To obtain a membership application, send a business size self-addressed, stamped envelope to:

APIC Application
Ted Hake
P.O. Box 1444
York, PA 17405

Two newspaper format publications serve the campaign item collector's hobby. Both feature articles, reports on auction prices realized, and advertisements. *The Political Bandwagon* also publishes the APIC's monthly newsletter. For subscription information, write:

The Political Bandwagon
P.O. Box 348
Leola, PA 17540

The Political Collector
P.O. Box 5171
York, PA 17405

Bibliography

Albert, Alphaeus H. *Record of American Uniform and Historical Buttons/Bicentennial Edition.* Third Printing, Boyertown, Pa.: Boyertown Publishing Co., 1977.

Collins, Herbert Ridgeway. *Threads of History/Americana Recorded on Cloth 1775 to the Present.* Washington, D.C.: Smithsonian Institution, 1979.

DeWitt, J. Doyle. *A Century of Campaign Buttons 1789-1889.* Hartford, Ct.: The Travelers Press, 1959.

Hake, Ted. *Encyclopedia of Political Buttons 1896-1972.* Reprinted Edition of 1974. York, Pa.: Hake's Americana & Collectibles, 1985.

Hake, Ted. *Political Buttons Book II 1920-1976.* York, Pa: Hake's Americana & Collectibles, 1985.

Hake, Ted. *Political Buttons Book III 1789-1916.* York, Pa.: Hake's Americana & Collectibles, 1985.

Hake, Ted. *Hake's Americana & Collectibles Catalogues Nos. 48-116.* York, Pa.: 1974-1991.

Hake, Ted and King, Russ. *Price Guide To Collectible Pin-Back Buttons 1896-1986.* Reprinted Edition of 1986. Radnor, Pa.: Wallace-Homestead Book Co., 1991.

Kahler, James G. *Hail To The Chief/An Illustrated Guide To Political Americana.* Princeton, N.J.: Pyne Press, 1972.

Kittler, Glenn D. *Hail To The Chief! The Inauguration Days of Our Presidents.* Second Printing. Philadelphia, Pa.: Chilton Book Co., 1968.

Lorant, Stefan. *The Presidency/A Pictorial History of Presidential Elections from Washington To Truman.* Fourth Printing. New York: The Macmillan Co., 1953.

Levine, H. Joseph. *Collectors Guide to Presidential Inaugural Medals and Memorabilia.* Danbury, Ct.: Johnson & Jensen, 1981.

Klamkin, Marian. *American Patriotic And Political China.* New York: Charles Scribner's Sons, 1973.

Nash, Howard P., Jr. *Third Parties in American Politics.* Washington, D.C.: Public Affairs Press, 1959.

National Portrait Gallery, Smithsonian Institution. *'If Elected...' Unsuccessful Candidates For The Presidency 1796-1968.* Second Printing. Washington, D.C.: Smithsonian Institution Press, 1973.

Sigoloff, Marc. *Collecting Political Buttons.* Chicago, Ill.: Chicago Review Press, 1988.

Sullivan, Edmund B. and Fischer, Roger A. *American Political Ribbons and Ribbon Badges.* Lincoln, Mass.: Quarterman Publications, 1985.

Sullivan, Edmund B. *Collecting Political Americana.* Hanover, Mass.: Christopher Publishing House, 1991.

Name Index

Presidential candidates' names are listed alphabetically followed by page numbers which have items relating to those candidates. Categories of campaign collectibles are listed alphabetically in the Table of Contents.

OTHER COLLECTIBLES PRICE GUIDES BY TED HAKE

The Button Book
(out of print)

Buttons in Sets
with Marshall N. Levin

Collectible Pin-Back Buttons 1896-1986: An Illustrated Price Guide
with Russ King

The Encyclopedia of Political Buttons 1896-1972; Political Buttons Book II 1920-1976; Political Buttons Book III 1789-1916

The Encyclopedia of Political Buttons: 1991 Revised Prices for Books I, II, and III

Hake's Guide to TV Collectibles: An Illustrated Price Guide

Non-Paper Sports Collectibles: An Illustrated Price Guide
with Roger Steckler

Sixgun Heroes: A Price Guide to Movie Cowboy Collectibles
with Robert Cauler

A Treasury of Advertising Collectibles
(out of print)